CHANGE AND CONTINUITY
IN THE FRENCH EPISCOPATE

CHANGE AND CONTINUITY IN THE FRENCH EPISCOPATE

THE BISHOPS AND THE WARS OF RELIGION

1547 – 1610

Frederic J. Baumgartner

Duke Monographs in Medieval and Renaissance Studies Number 7

DUKE UNIVERSITY PRESS   DURHAM 1986

Library of Congress Cataloging-in-Publication Data
Baumgartner, Frederic J.
Change and continuity in the French episcopate.
(Duke monographs in medieval and Renaissance studies; no. 7)
Bibliography: p.
Includes index.
1. Catholic Church—France—Bishops. 2. France—
History—16th century. 3. France—History—17th
century. 4. France—Church history—16th century.
5. France—Church history—17th century. I. Title.
II. Series.
BX1529.B38   1986   262'.12'0944   86-13495
ISBN 0-8223-0675-1

To Theresa and Michael

CONTENTS

MAPS AND TABLES

PREFACE

The topic of this book came to mind as I was beginning a study of the Politique party in France from 1572 to 1598. As I accumulated information on the Politiques, I was struck by the large number of bishops appearing on my roll of men who recognized the Protestant prince Henri de Navarre as king during the succession dispute of 1589. Intrigued by the idea of prelates of the Catholic Church publicly supporting the Huguenot leader's right of succession, I decided to investigate further the divisions within the French episcopate over Navarre's right to the throne. In pursuing that inquiry I discovered that information on the French episcopate as an institution for the late sixteenth century was very limited, and I decided to turn my attention to this study of the episcopacy from 1547 to 1610. (Michel Peronnet's *Les évêques de l'ancienne France*, 1978, became available to me well after I had begun the research for this project.)

I chose those dates for the parameters of the project for several reasons. Most important, I wished to study the impact of the development of Protestantism and the wars of religion on the episcopate. By starting in 1547, the beginning of Henri II's reign, it is possible to present the French episcopate as it was before the Reformation had much success in the realm; and by concluding the study at the end of Henri IV's reign, I can demonstrate the effect of the religious wars and the restoration of peace on the bishops. Second, the dates largely conform to the convocation of the Council of Trent and the delayed response of the French episcopate to its decrees. Henri II's reign was quite likely the period of the worst abuses in the French hierarchy, and by 1610 the reform of the episcopacy was underway. Third, I decided to arrange my prosopographical analysis of the bishops seated in this era according to the reigns of the kings in order to show what changes in the type of bishop occurred from one reign to the next. However, I decided not to study in depth the appointments of François I, partly to keep the numbers of bishops studied manageable and to avoid making the book too large and partly because of the existence of Marilyn Edelstein's articles and dissertation on that king's bishops. I have incorporated some of her data into chapter III.

Much of the research for the book was done at the Archives Nationales and the Bibliothèque Nationale in Paris and in several departmental archives. After perusing the published inventories of Series G (the secular clergy before 1789) of the departmental archives (some three-fourths of the pertinent archives have published inventories), I settled upon the archives of Cher (for the see of Bourges), Eure-et-Loir (Chartres), Hautes-Alpes (Gap), Haute-Vienne (Limoges), Loire-Atlantique (Nantes), Ille-et-Vilaine (Rennes, Dol, Saint-Malo), Lot-et-Garonne (Agen), Morhiban (Vannes), Seine-Maritime (Rouen), and Tarn-et-Garonne (Montauban) as most promising for episcopal records as well as providing something of a territorial spread.

Based on both my perusal of the inventories and my work in the departmental archives, I have become aware of how far more spotty and incomplete the episcopal records are in comparison with those of the cathedral chapters. This conclusion is supported by the secondary literature. For example, in her book in the clergy of Aix-en-Provence (*Entre tours et clochers*, 1981), Claire Dolan, despite exhaustive research, was not able to determine the total revenues of the archbishop, although the income and expenses of the chapter are presented in precise detail. In his study of the *chambre ardente*, N. Weiss expressed his frustration at his inability to trace the cases of those accused of heresy who had been remanded to the episcopal courts. "Of all the judicial registers of the past centuries, the rarest, the most irretrievable, are those of the episcopal tribunals." (*La chambre ardente*, 1889, p. cxxx.) Professor Joseph Bergin of the University of Manchester has suggested to me that one reason for this situation is that the bishops' records often wound up in their family archives. Certainly there is very little of a personal nature in the episcopal records in the departmental archives. As a consequence of the scarcity of these records, it is impossible to develop a systematic set of archival materials for a study of the sixteenth-century bishops as temporal and spiritual lords of their dioceses. Thus I make no pretense at being truly comprehensive in this book, although I hope to be as detailed as necessary to demonstrate those points that I wish to make.

I have restricted the study to those dioceses that definitely fell under the Concordat of Bologna prior to 1610, and I do not include several bishoprics over which the French monarch claimed sovereignty such as Metz, Toul, and Verdun. The book is concerned only with the episcopal ordinaries and not with titular bishops, coadjutors, or cardinals who never held a French see. Thus several prominent churchmen of the era are mentioned only in passing. Last, the book is concerned with the episcopacy as an institution, providing an analysis of its membership, powers, privileges, finances, and problems, particularly the growth of Protestantism. I use details about the personal lives of the prelates only as they are illustrative of those concerns. All dates are new style; i.e., the year begins on January 1, not at Easter. On the coinage system, see Appendix I, but it should be noted here that I use the letter l for livres.

Anyone who has written a research monograph of this sort knows that there are an enormous number of people upon whose expertise an author has to draw, but there are several people whose aid was especially important. Among them are my colleagues at Virginia Polytechnic Institute and State University—A. Roger Ekirch, Larry Morrison, George G. Shackelford, Joseph L. Wieczynski, and Thomas J. Adriance. Among colleagues at other institutions I must acknowledge the help of Joseph Bergin of the University of Manchester, James Farge of the University of St. Thomas, A. Lynn Martin of the University of Adelaide, and Timothy Tackett of the

Catholic University of America. There are also innumerable librarians and archivists to whom I am indebted, especially those of the Bibliothèque Nationale and the Archives Nationales in Paris, the Newberry Library in Chicago, and the Newman Library at Virginia Tech, but most of all the Interlibrary Loan librarians at the Newman Library. The maps were prepared by the graphic artists of the Virginia Tech Learning Resources Center. Financial aid for the project was provided by the American Philosophical Society, the Newberry Library, and the Virginia Tech Educational Foundation. I certainly need to thank the secretaries of the Virginia Tech Department of History—Lisa Donis, Rennie Givens, Patty Mills, and Debbie Rhea—for the numerous times they typed the manuscript. Thanks are also due to the editorial staff of Duke University Press. Portions of this work have been published as "Henry II's Italian Bishops: A Study in the Use and Abuse of the Concordat of Bologna," *The Sixteenth Century Journal*, XI (1980), 49–58, and "Crisis in the French Episcopacy: The Bishops and the Succession of Henry IV," *Archiv für Reformationsgeschichte*, LXX (1979), 278–301; their editors have graciously given permission to include that material in this work. Finally I must thank my wife Lois whose encouragement and patience were essential for the completion of this work.

CHANGE AND CONTINUITY
IN THE FRENCH EPISCOPATE

CHAPTER I

INTRODUCTION

I n contemporary America the image of the Catholic bishop is largely that of a genial, middle-aged clerical bureaucrat who is efficient in financial and real estate management and skillful in public relations and is a man of quiet piety and sometimes of learning. In the past, however, such an image was far from true for most bishops, and in few times and places was it less true than in sixteenth-century France. In that society a bishop was usually not resident in his diocese to administer it, cared little or nothing about what his flock thought of him, and often did not have a university degree. Many bishops had no real vocation for priestly office.[1] Although standards for canonization to sainthood did become more rigorous after the Council of Trent, it is still noteworthy that not a single French bishop of the century was canonized or, it appears, was even considered.

With leadership of the French Church so seriously deficient in religious zeal and often in moral integrity, it comes as no surprise that in the sixteenth century the Church and its bishops came under the most serious challenge that they faced between the baptism of Clovis and the Revolution of 1789. The appearance of a dynamic Protestant movement in France that rejected the episcopal office threatened to destroy the episcopacy or at the very least reduce substantially its authority, revenues, and privileges. The spirit of reform extended to a good number of Catholics as well, who were eager to see the wealth of the Church and its hierarchy put into other hands, often their own, and the life-style of the

1	Senlis	7	Orange	13	Lavaur
2	Tulle	8	Avignon	14	St. Papoul
3	St. Paul	9	Montauban	15	Carcassone
4	Digne	10	Lombès	16	Mirepoix
5	Senez	11	Lodève	A	The Three Suffragans
6	Sisternon	12	Castres		of Avignon

Note: Valence and Die were administered as one see.

MAP I

DIOCESES OF FRANCE IN 1600

bishops extensively modified. In addition the French monarchy, always in desperate need of new sources of income, was covetous of clerical wealth for its own treasury.

Historians of the Reformation era have been well aware of these threats to the French episcopate; they have been equally aware that the prelacy survived them with little apparent loss of power, prestige, and wealth. But little effort has been made to determine the extent of the dangers or how the prelates reacted to them, or what change, if any, the multiple crises of the late sixteenth century forced upon the episcopate. This study of the bishops should also provide some insight into the question of why France remained Catholic and what role the hierarchy had in preventing a national religious change.

The basic reason these questions have been left unanswered is that little is known about the French episcopate of the sixteenth century. In order to understand how the bishops responded to the problems confronting them and how effective their response was, one must learn a great deal more about the institution of the episcopacy and the men who made it up. Accordingly the first part of this work (chapters II–VI) will provide the background needed to comprehend the activities of the bishops during the wars of religion: the system of appointment, the type of men appointed, episcopal finances, and their temporal and spiritual powers. The work will then turn (chapters VII–VIII) to a more narrative description of the response of the bishops to the presence of Protestantism in France, and the last two chapters will examine the crisis over the succession of Henri IV and his reign.

Certainly crucial to understanding how the bishops responded to the Reformation, the financial crises, and their other problems is a study of the manner in which a man received a bishopric. Jules Thomas has sketched the outlines of the mechanism of episcopal appointments under the Concordat of Bologna of 1516, but he did not study in detail the antagonistic relationship that developed between monarchy and papacy over several of its clauses nor the abuses that quickly appeared after 1516.[2] By the time a half century with the Concordat in effect had passed, the Venetian ambassador could write in 1569 that the French king had hundreds of bishoprics and abbeys to pay his debts, reward his grandees, and dower his daughters. At the French court, he remarked, "they deal in bishoprics and abbeys as elsewhere in pepper and cinnamon."

In the past decade some effort has been made to explore what Robert Aubenas calls "the vast spectrum of bishops that is extremely rich in personalities, reflecting the infinite variety of human types in which the best rub shoulders with the worst."[3] Articles by Marilyn Edelstein and J. Michael Hayden provide information about the bishops seated by François I and those in the era of 1614.[4] But the only work that is concerned with the episcopate for the entire century is Michel Peronnet's.[5] His two volumes, however, cover the entire time of the existence of the Concordat of Bologna from 1516 to 1790, and he has devoted most of the work to the generation in office when the Civil Constitution of the Clergy was promulgated. Nonetheless Peronnet provides useful information on the social origins of the sixteenth-century bishops and their prior careers, patrons, ages at the time of appointment and death, and geographical origins. He is particularly concerned with what he terms the standardization of the type of cleric given bishoprics, and he demonstrates how such factors as age, education, and prior Church positions became far more uniform by 1650 compared with absence of any pattern at all for the sixteenth century. Peronnet is primarily concerned with showing the trend toward regularization and does little to set the prelacy within the context of the political, religious, and financial problems of the sixteenth century.

This study will make use of much the same type of statistical analysis of the social origins and careers of the 377 bishops given episcopal chairs between 1547 and 1610 but will place them much more firmly in the context of the contemporary situation. More significantly this prosopographical analysis of the bishops will provide an insight into the structure of French society of the sixteenth century. Bishops in the *Ancien Régime* were certainly among the elite of the realm. Few positions in the government or the patrimonies of few of the great noble families could offer a man so lofty the prestige and status, so vast the revenues, and so broad the author-

ity as did the bishopric, especially if it were one of the prestigious
sees like Paris, Reims, Rouen, or Chartres. Although certain high-
ranking nobles, if they were the royal favorites, enjoyed greater
influence and power than the great bishops, they and their families
rarely held such status for more than two reigns. The enormous
authority and income of the major bishoprics endured through the
Ancien Régime. Even the bishops of the tiny sees of the Midi, some
of which like Toulon had as few as twenty parishes compared with
the 1,380 of Rouen, held in their own regions a status that matched
that of all but the greatest noble families of their provinces.

A study of the French bishops is, therefore, an examination of a
group of elites. Present-day social historians have a tendency to
ignore the elites of a society in order to study the lower levels of
society, on the grounds that true social change occurs only if it
affects the broadest part of the population. While there is a great
deal of truth to that point of view, it is also true that the influence
of the elites is an important element in creating any change in a
society or preventing it from occurring. To ignore the episcopate is
especially hazardous because religion has been one of the most
pervasive social influences in premodern societies, and one in which
the elites have had a particularly strong impact. The history of
Christianity demonstrates clearly the importance of the elites in
determining religious tradition and practice. No better example
can be cited than the Reformation in Germany and England.

As social history a study of the episcopate confronts the historian with the myth of the Church that its highest offices were open
to men of all ranks and estates. In the social theory of the era, the
hierarchy provided the only opportunity for social mobility. According to this myth, in which the Church did take pride, an intelligent,
capable young cleric from the humblest origins could rise to a
bishopric.[6] This monograph will give an assessment of the truth of
that myth for the French Church. It will show whether the episcopate was reserved almost exclusively for those who were already
elites by birth. If perchance a commoner did attain an episcopal
chair, did he enjoy the full measure of prestige and respect to
which the bishop was entitled? The episcopate thus provides a

good test of the rigidity of class lines in early modern France. A study of the bishops ought to reveal as well the impact of the increasing anarchy after 1559 on the French social structure by showing whether the social status of the bishops changed to any extent in the course of the religious wars.

It is impossible, however, to appreciate the importance of the study of the social origins of the prelates without a knowledge of the powers, privileges, properties, and revenues of the bishoprics that made them so attractive to the well-placed men of the century. The French monarchy, well aware of the range of powers and wealth available to bishops, made a concerted effort in the sixteenth century to turn them to its advantage. Not only did the kings use the right of appointment under the Concordat to buy and reward loyalty and service, but the monarchy also sought to transfer much of the episcopacy's jurisdiction and revenues to itself. Thus the six decades between 1547 and 1610 were marked by the first permanent royal tax on the clergy and the forced sale of Church property for the benefit of the monarchy. The impact of these royal demands and depredations on the episcopacy remains to be determined.

To a large extent, however, the monarchy's financial demands on the prelacy were a result of the existence of the Huguenot party in France and the religious wars that followed. Consequently it was the appearance of Protestantism in France that was at the root of the multifaceted crisis the episcopacy faced, threatening the very existence of the institution and causing severe disruption of the life-styles and revenues of the bishops.

That the range of possible responses to the Reformation was very broad was demonstrated by prelates in other European lands. Numerous German bishops embraced Lutheranism despite Luther's rejection of the episcopal office, but much more attractive to a prelate was the continuation of the episcopacy in a national Church as found in the Scandinavian lands and, more obviously, England. In France the strong Gallican tradition of asserting the independence of the national Church from papal discipline and appointive power made that option an attractive one for many French bishops at mid-century, if the monarchy had been prepared to break with

Rome.[7] Bishops also remained Catholic and loyal to the pope while strongly advocating reform of the Church and the episcopacy and compromise with the Protestants. Furthermore, many bishops across Europe simply ignored the spread of the Reform, passively suffering the loss of office or power and prestige in lands that broke with the Roman Church or doing nothing to check the appearance of Protestantism in lands that ultimately remained Catholic. Last, numerous bishops responded with bitter hostility, using their authority and talents in an effort to destroy the threat. All of these responses were exhibited by French bishops, and examining the relative appeal of each will help assess the effectiveness of the episcopate's response to Protestantism.

France, of course, had its own tradition of ecclesiastical autonomy, Gallicanism, which came close to prefiguring Anglicanism in its demand for an independent national Church.[8] If there was one constant in the French episcopate in the sixteenth century, it was adherence to Gallicanism. The first clear expression of the concept dated to 1407 when Charles VI proclaimed two cornerstone edicts on the relationship between the French Church and the papacy. The king declared that the Gallican Church had traditionally enjoyed certain liberties from papal authority, which the pope of the time was denounced for allegedly violating. These liberties remained ill-defined until the seventeenth century but were regarded as involving especially the freedom of the French Church from papal appointive power. The principle of local control over appointments to the French hierarchy was made explicit in the Pragmatic Sanction of 1438, a document drawn up by a national assembly of the French Church and promulgated by Charles VII. Both in the manner of its creation and in its content, it was the quintessential Gallican document. It reflected the ideas that a general council of the Church was superior to the pope and a French national council could legislate for the Gallican Church. It expounded the view that the king was able to call such assemblies and issue any decrees in this authority as head of the French Church, although the Pragmatic Sanction did attempt to remove the king from the process of ecclesiastical appointment as well as the pope. In that regard it was the key document in what historians refer to as ecclesiastical Gallicanism, in contrast to royal Gallicanism, in which the king was seen as the head of the Church in virtually every respect, including the authority to appoint bishops. The consecration of a new French monarch, while no longer regarded as a sacrament as it had been in the early Middle Ages, resembled that of a bishop, and during the Mass of consecration, the king took Communion in both forms, the only layman to have that privilege. The essential document for royal Gallicanism was the Concordat of Bologna of 1516. The distinction between the two types of Gallicanism is not especially pertinent, however, for the sixteenth century, since only over the Concordat itself was there any substantial conflict over principles of Church authority between clergy and monarchy.[9]

Gallicanism likely made it easier for French prelates to ignore the appearance of Protestantism, since it demanded the same independence of a national Church that appeared as a major element of the program of the early Reformers. But it also likely reduced the appeal of the Reformation to the French episcopate and more importantly the monarchy, since they had already achieved a large portion of the desired independence. A further essential point about Gallicanism was that with few exceptions its adherents remained doctrinally orthodox and in some respects more conservative, especially on points of Church discipline, than the papacy. Nonetheless, perhaps a sense of affinity with some of the early Protestant complaints against papal authority along with a rampant disregard for the duties of their offices made it possible for numerous prelates to remain indifferent to the presence of Protestants in France before 1560. Even after the wars of religion broke out, many bishops continued to ignore the problem. But few could remain indifferent to the prospect of Henri de Navarre, the Huguenot *chef*, wearing the crown of Saint Louis. The succession controversy of 1589–93 was the culminating episode of the religious wars and the most dangerous one for the episcopate. If Henri had been able to take effective power while remaining a Protestant, the position of the Catholic Church and its bishops would have been in serious danger, regardless of his apparently sincere pledges to maintain Catholicism.

With the conversion of Henri IV, however, the Catholicism of the kingdom was again secure and the last opportunity for the Reformation to win the kingdom lost. The reign of Henri saw the sudden flowering of the French Catholic Reformation, and many bishops, if far from all, contributed to it. Was there a notable change in the type of bishop appointed after 1595, or was the episcopate's espousal of reform, admittedly rather limited, a response to the grave dangers that the Church had faced? The answers to these questions can help frame an answer to what is ultimately the most significant question, why France remained Catholic despite the dynamism of the Huguenot party during most of the second half of the sixteenth century. The Catholicism of the French people had a profound impact on the future of the nation; no aspect of French culture and society went unaffected by it. An examination of the episcopate of the sixteenth century and its role in the wars of religion will not in itself answer the question, but it is crucial for such a task to know what in fact the bishops did do to defend their Church, protect their office, and secure the Catholicism of the populace.

CHAPTER II

THE SYSTEM OF
EPISCOPAL APPOINTMENTS

Through the agreement with the papacy in 1516 known as the Concordat of Bologna, the French monarchy had taken effective control of the naming of bishops for the French Church. With the exception of a few special cases that the pope was permitted to decide, the king chose the prelates for the 111 bishoprics and nearly 600 abbeys, which were known as consistorial benefices because the nominations still had to be approved in papal consistory. But the kings were not satisfied with the extent of control they had received; they spent most of the sixteenth century working to reduce the pope's rights under the Concordat. Despite a bitter rear guard effort on the part of Rome, the monarchy was largely successful in eliminating the possibility of a papal appointment to a French bishopric. While the kings were so eagerly seeking to diminish the papal prerogatives, they largely ignored more serious limitations on their freedom of choice in naming bishops — long-standing customs by which incumbent bishops or local magnates were able to place their candidates in French sees. Even as the kings were reducing the possibilities of a papal nomination during the sixteenth century, more and more episcopal choices were made by levels of French society below the king. Thus the system of episcopal placement was in the sixteenth century a far more complicated matter than the clauses of the Concordat would suggest.

The Concordat of Bologna had been drawn up largely because the popes had viewed the Pragmatic Sanction from its implementation in 1438 as a schismatic document, hostile to the papacy and thoroughly conciliarist in nature. Thus Leo X eagerly accepted François I's offer in 1515 to reconsider the way in which consistorial appointments were made for the French Church. By returning the right of election to these offices to the cathedral and monastery chapters, the Pragmatic Sanction had removed the pope from any role in seating French bishops. Its intent had been to place the filling of bishoprics and abbeys beyond the reach of the king as well, but the interminable delays, bitterly disputed elections, and heavy royal pressure in important dioceses had permitted the monarch to have a far greater voice than its framers had envisioned.[1] Despite enjoying a much larger role than intended, the kings were annoyed at the disorderly procedures of the cathedral chapters and the long delays in executing their will. François I was, therefore, sympathetic to the pope's desire to overturn the Pragmatic Sanction.

After lengthy bargaining Leo and François agreed on the Concordat, which clearly recognized the pope as the ultimate authority over the French Church while giving the king effective control over episcopal appointments. It restored the annates to the pope while the Church became a huge font of patronage available to the king.[2] The principal advantage of the Concordat to the monarchy was that office holders beholden to the crown would be more likely to approve of or at least acquiesce in royal exactions on the Church's wealth. This fact was clearly demonstrated by the steadily increasing and usually successful royal demands on Church income during the sixteenth century.

Although the Concordat did remove a real obstacle to the papal claim of universal authority over the Church, its advantage to the papacy was largely symbolic; the real impact of the document was to place the monarchy in control of the French episcopacy. Both sides quickly recognized the true nature of the agreement; the papacy after Leo X worked diligently but ineffectively to dilute the Concordat while the monarchy steadfastly refused to allow any changes that might have reduced its advantage.

Certainly the Concordat promised to require quite rigorous criteria for episcopal nominations. A candidate that the monarchy presented to the pope was to have a master's degree or a licentiate in theology or law from a "famous university," be at least twenty-seven years of age (rather than the thirty years required by canon law), be French by birth or naturalization, be a product of a legitimate marriage, and have demonstrated good moral character. The candidate did not have to be an ordained priest at the time of nomination but was obliged to be ordained before his consecration as bishop. These standards were badly undermined, however, by the clause that permitted the king to nominate members of the royal family or great noble families who did not have the expected degrees.[3] The kings took advantage of this substantial loophole to fill French sees with men who did not conform to the criteria. It was the most blatant source of abuse in the Concordat; at times in the sixteenth century less than one-fifth of the bishops had the required university degree.

The agreement of 1516 required that the king submit a nomination to the papal curia within six months of the vacancy. If the pope refused the nominee as unqualified, the king could submit another name within three months. If he failed to do so or the pope rejected that candidate as well, the pope gained the right to fill the bishopric. There were numerous examples between 1560 and 1600 of the rejection of the first nominee, but the second candidate, it appears, never was denied the bulls of office. The pattern suggests that the kings were often willing on the first nomination to try to slip a blatantly unworthy candidate past the curia. If they were challenged, they were careful to nominate an acceptable churchman so that the popes had no pretext to fill the vacant see.

The monarchy's extreme reluctance to give the papacy any opportunity to fill a French bishopric appears more clearly in the long dispute over another clause of the Concordat. It permitted the papacy to fill the consistorial benefices of a churchman who died at Rome, *Ad Sedem Apostalicam*. Since those most likely to die while at the papal court were the cardinals with their numerous benefices, the popes jealously guarded their right to appoint under that clause while the kings worked diligently to eliminate it and often proceeded to seat bishops in disregard of it. During the reign of

Henri II, the conflict over *Ad Sedem Apostalicam* grew especially bitter, to the point that the king refused for several years to allow French prelates to take up residence in Rome.

As written in 1516, the Concordat allowed a number of cathedral chapters to continue to elect their bishops providing they could prove that they had had a special privilege from Rome that predated the Pragmatic Sanction. The fourteen sees that claimed the right included such major bishoprics as Bourges, Sens, Toulouse, and Orléans. Immediately François I set to work to remove this loophole in his authority. In the next several years such chapters that sought to fill vacancies found their elections challenged in the Parlements or at Rome. Finally in 1531 Clement VII issued a bull that removed the right of election entirely.[4]

Not all of the chapters affected willingly accepted the loss of their privilege; many continued to elect bishops for several decades after 1516. Michel Peronnet has found that eighty-six bishops, or more than a third of his roll of bishops seated from 1516 to 1559, were formally elected by the chapters.[5] Most of the elections took place shortly after the Concordat was proclaimed, and some chapters made an effort to conserve the appearance of their right of election by electing the king's nominee. Others successfully asserted their power of canonical election by choosing a member of a prominent family that the king dared not offend by insisting on his own choice. In 1560 the Estates general, citing the grave problems in the episcopacy, called for a return to the elective principle, and the appeal was repeated at Blois in 1576 and 1588. Throughout the sixteenth century the higher clergy continued to pay lip service to the system of election.[6] During the anarchy after the assassination of Henri III in 1589, several chapters elected bishops and had their candidates confirmed by Rome and later accepted by Henri IV.

The Concordat applied specifically to the kingdom of France that had existed in 1438 with the additions of Dauphiné and the marquisate of Die and Valentinois. It did not apply to territories taken under French sovereignty after 1438 such as Brittany and Provence, the *pays d'obédience*. But already by the end of 1516 a papal indult had brought those provinces under similar jurisdiction.[7]

The monarchy was quick to demand that Rome place under the Concordat any new territory that it gained. The papacy's reluctance to do so created periodic conflicts. The longest dispute of this sort involved the Three Bishoprics of Lorraine: Metz, Toul, and Verdun. As soon as France had taken control of them in 1552, the monarchy demanded that the Concordat be extended to them. The papacy consistently refused; not until the late seventeenth century did Louis XIV achieve that goal.

The Concordat was extended with less contention to the diocese of Belley south of Geneva in 1601 and the two sees of Béarn, Lescar and Oloron, in 1617. Before 1617 the pope had the right of appointment to the Béarnese dioceses, but the ruler of Navarre exercised considerable influence over the choice.[8] Several other bishoprics nominally French did not come under the jurisdiction of the Concordat in the sixteenth century because the king did not exercise sovereignty over them. They included Cambrai and its four Flemish suffragans, Avignon and its three suffragans, and Perpignan, Besançon, and Nice. The most difficult case to determine is the see of Orange. François I took it under the Concordat, but it reverted to the prince of Orange in 1559. Orange appears on some lists of décimes and not on others.[9] Accordingly its bishops will be included in the tables of appointments for François I and Henri II but not for the other kings of that century.[10] Until the reorganization of the Church of the Lowlands in 1559 took Cambrai away from Reims, all of the above dioceses except for Avignon and Besançon were suffragans of French archdioceses, and their bishops were often active in the French Church.

Upon its publication the Parlement of Paris and the French clergy, centered in the University of Paris, put up an unusually determined resistance to the Concordat. The clerics objected to the loss of their right of election of their bishops and abbots. The Parlement, alarmed at what it saw as the reestablishment of papal authority in the French Church, attacked it as an infringement of the liberties of the Gallican Church. The magistrates were especially fearful that the papacy would use its right of rejection of candidates to pass to itself the right of appointment. While that

fear proved to be completely baseless when the Concordat began to
be implemented, the dispute revealed the strong streak of antipapal
Gallicanism in France in the early sixteenth century. The opposition in 1516 was strong enough to delay ratification of the Concordat by the Parlement, as required by the document, much to
François's great anger. It was, of course, ultimately futile, as was
the longer resistance of the University of Paris. Frequently throughout the century, and as late as 1605, attacks on the Concordat
appeared.[11]

The most serious threat in the sixteenth century to the system of
episcopal appointment established by the Concordat was the Ordinance of Orléans, which was issued in early 1561. The Ordinance
was a result of the unanimous call of the three Estates meeting at
Orléans for a new system of election. In order to eliminate the
abuses that had occurred under the Concordat, the Ordinance
called for a creation of electoral commissions to present three
candidates, of at least thirty years of age, to the king. The commission for an archbishop was to be made up of the suffragans of the
province and the archepiscopal chapter; for a bishop it was to
consist of the archbishop and the other suffragans, the cathedral
chapter, twelve nobles elected by the nobility of the diocese, and
twelve elected bourgeois. The king, having made his choice from
the three candidates presented, was to forward the nomination to
Rome for approval; strictly speaking that aspect of the Concordat
would have remained in effect. But the Ordinance also suspended
the paying of the annates to the papacy until a new system could be
worked out with the Holy See. A special representative sent to
Rome failed to reach an agreement, but in 1562 Charles IX
rescinded the prohibition on the annates. It is less clear how the
article on the election of episcopal candidates was eliminated, but
it appears that the monarchy simply disregarded it. At Paris, for
example, a commission as called for by the Ordinance met in 1563
and proposed three names, but Charles IX ignored them and
named his own candidate instead. The papacy, as it did in almost
all such cases of canonical election after 1531, confirmed the royal
candidate. At the Estates of Blois in 1576, the deputies protested

the failure of the monarchy to conform to the Ordinance. Many bishops for their part preferred the arbitrariness of the monarchy to the caprice of the many, since they likely would not have received sees under the proposed system.[12]

Although the French clergy and the Parlements were opposed to the Concordat, the bishops assembled at the Fourth Lateran Council in 1516 had no objections, and the Council quickly approved it. Thus it was permanent until changed or abrogated upon the mutual agreement of both parties. But the indults of 1516 for Brittany and Provence terminated with the death of François I. Paul III, who had opposed the Concordat in 1516, refused to renew the indults for the *pays d'obédience* and began to fill the vacancies in those provinces. The next pope, Julius III, was equally determined to reduce royal control over the French Church and at first refused to issue new bulls, asking for a delay to study the issue. When Henri II pledged to observe the regulations of the Concordat exactly and to suppress abuses in the French Church, Julius drew up the indults in October, 1550. The negotiations over Brittany and Provence were described as drawing up the "ultimate Concordat," but it was certainly not achieved.[13]

The contentiousness over the Concordat was made all the more bitter because relations between the French court and Rome were at their lowest point of the sixteenth century during Julius's reign. When the papal conclave that convened upon Paul III's death had dragged on for more than two months, Henri ordered the twelve French cardinals and the French partisans among the Italians to vote for Cardinal del Monte. The French court had examined him thoroughly and had become convinced that he was malleable to French interests. When the new pope showed signs of supporting Charles V's policy in Italy and planning to reconvene the Council of Trent, Henri responded with rage. He declared his intention of calling a national council for the French Church and ordered his bishops to retire to their sees to prepare for it.

On August 5, 1551, the royal council discussed an explosive proposal: the Cardinal de Bourbon was to be erected provisionally as patriarch of the French Church until the papacy admitted defeat.

Henri summoned several prominent bishops to the court to establish the necessary offices for a patriarchate. The imperial ambassador reported that the patriarch would have been established if it had not been for the opposition of the Parlement and, likely more importantly, the Cardinal de Lorraine. The cardinal, who could reasonably have expected to become the French patriarch in the future, curbed his ambition for the sake of Catholic unity against the Protestants and the Turks. His objections apparently carried weight with Henri, who may well have been speaking so belligerently to terrify the pope into retreating.

The Gallican crisis of 1551 revealed that the episcopacy was prepared to accept whatever the king's decision might have been in regard to relations with Rome. Pierre Du Val of Sées wrote a work hostile to the papacy to complement the much better known one of the Gallican jurist Charles Du Moulin. Several other bishops reportedly expressed their support to the king. Except for the Cardinal de Lorraine's opposition to a break with Rome expressed in the royal council, no bishop appears to have objected, although it is true that the tentative nature of the scheme did not yet call for the stand of a John Fisher. The bishops were thoroughly imbued with Gallicanism at mid-century; not a single French-born prelate of the period can be termed an ultramontane. [14]

This fact demonstrates the success the monarchy had had since 1516 in appointing bishops loyal to it, but it also demonstrates one of the key points concerning religion in the sixteenth century: few men of the era challenged the right of the ruler to decide for his realm the major questions of religion, including the possibility of schism or worse. In France the king as head of the Gallican Church decided most issues involving the corporate body called the Church without reference to Rome, and he forced the pope to negotiate the rest with him.

The threat of schism disappeared almost as quickly as the tempest had arisen, but relations between Julius and Henri remained strained until the pope's death in 1555. Paul IV's efforts to get French military support against the Spanish in Italy required that he not raise difficulties over the Concordat, but upon Henri's sudden demise in 1559, a new dispute arose over the clause of *Ad Sedem Apostalicam*. Cardinal Du Bellay, in residence at the papal court, died there in early 1560. The quarrel over his many benefices was bitter, but it resulted in an agreement more favorable to the monarchy: Pius IV was allowed to fill the benefices, and in return he issued a general waiver of *de non vacando*, which waived the right of the pope to fill the sees of prelates who died at Rome.[15] It was immediately renewed for Charles IX, but the waiver did not stop Pius V from trying to invoke the clause in 1571 when Cardinal de Babou of Auxerre died at Rome. The pope tried to seat his own choice at Auxerre, but Charles objected and was able to get Jacques Amyot, the humanist, confirmed. Despite the antagonism between pope and king on these issues, the two authorities were able to work together on most nominations, and the monarch occasionally accommodated a papal request for a French see for an Italian as in the case of Hannibal Rucellai, given Carcassone in 1569.[16]

When Henri III succeeded to the throne, the general waiver was not renewed; and the last major conflict over *Ad Sedem Apostalicam* erupted ten years later when Paul de Foix, archbishop of Toulouse, died *en curie*. The royal court had forced the papacy to accept him as archbishop, after ten years of papal objection that he was a heretic, and had sent him to Rome as French ambassador without the curia's recognition. Accordingly Gregory XIII had refused to issue a waiver. After de Foix's death and with extensive negotiations, Gregory solved the problem while trying to save as much face as possible by naming the Cardinal d'Armagnac, who already held the right of regression to Toulouse having resigned it earlier to de Foix.[17] The clause *Ad Sedem Apostalicam* was heard of no more in the century as the popes thereafter routinely issued the general waivers of *de non vacando*.

By the end of the century, therefore, the monarchy had achieved the de facto elimination of all the rights held by the papacy to fill French bishoprics. Once Henri IV had firmly taken control of France and made peace with Rome, the likelihood of the pontiff appointing to a French bishopric was quite remote. The monarchy had waged a long, often bitter, but largely successful fight to reduce the opportunities for the papacy to name to French bishoprics, but the pope's prerogatives in the Concordat even if exercised to the fullest were only a small limitation on the king's right to nominate whom he pleased.

A more important check on this freedom of choice was the tradition that certain noble families had proprietary rights to certain sees. This situation occasionally was a result of the king's generosity, but far more often it would have been most difficult for the king to refuse to recommend to Rome the scion or client of these powerful families. The domination of several families over the local bishoprics went back for many generations, sometimes predating the Concordat and even the Pragmatic Sanction.[18] The house of Lorraine held Reims from 1500 to 1589. A client, Nicolas de Pellevé, then had it until 1594, and it was returned to the house of Lorraine in 1605 for two more decades. The family Cossé de Brissac controlled Coutances in Normandy for most of the sixteenth century. The Maréchal de Cossé's uncle, nephew, and bastard son held the see, and between the tenures of the latter two, two relatives of his wife kept the see in the family. Various branches of the house of Arue-Gramont provided six bishops for the diocese of Tarbes after 1460. They and their relatives, the Foixes and the Albrets, provided bishops for most of the diocese of the southwest for three centuries before 1600, although rarely in the way that they completely controlled Aire from 1440 to 1594.[19] The Crequi family provided a bishop for Thérouanne (see transferred to Boulogne in 1567) at various times after 1285 with three holding it in succession in the sixteenth century. The Crequis also placed six family members in the see of Nantes in the period from 1450 to 1550. Four members of the Escoubleau family were bishops of Maillezais near La Rochelle from 1543 to 1629, while the local lords of Apt, the Raimbaud de Simianes, provided three members and two clients to that bishopric in the century. In Rodez the Cardinal d'Armagnac and three relatives held the see from 1529 to 1646. Yet another example was the diocese of Sarlat in Guyenne that was governed by numerous members of the local Salignac family until 1686.

At the time that the Concordat was drawn up, eighty sees were held by seventy-two bishops who succeeded brothers or uncles, and many of these bishoprics had been in those families for several generations. The implementation of the Concordat reduced the number of episcopal dynasties as François and Henri II frequently appointed outsiders to break the hold of powerful local families or the cathedral chapters over the sees (the two local influences often worked together), but the dynasties continued to be a significant feature of the prelacy.[20]

These long-term episcopal dynasties were largely the domain of noble families that dominated a particular region, especially in the southwest. Shorter-term dynasties were possible for families from outside of the region, and one of the best examples was in fact Italian. The bishopric of Béziers in Languedoc was governed from 1547 to 1669 by relatives of the Medici including six named Bonzi. Five Villars, originally from Paris, held the archdiocese of Vienne for 140 years. Far more often, such dynasties of outsider bishops held for two or three generations, taking the usual form of uncle resigning to nephew. The example of Sées in Normandy demonstrates a common difficulty in establishing these dynasties: Pierre Du Val, a tutor to François I's sons, received the bishopric in 1545; accused of Protestant sympathies, he resigned it to his sister's son Louis de Moulinet, who in turn resigned it in 1601 to his nephew Claude de Morennes.

It was also possible for a powerful individual to provide bishoprics for a number of relatives; that situation, however, did not always translate into a real dynasty. The outstanding example of this was Pierre d'Amboise whose family provided nine bishops, including Cardinal Georges I, from among his seventeen children and numerous grandsons. At the turn of the sixteenth century they held at least eleven dioceses. But in 1550, at the death of Cardinal Georges II, there were no close relatives in French sees. Less striking but still illustrative was the fortune of the family of François I's superintendent of finances, Semblançay de Beaune: two of his brothers and two grandsons were raised to the episcopate. The de Beaunes were among the most successful of the "Tourangeaux," the wealthy financiers from Tours who among others included the Briçonnets, the Bohiers, and the Huraults. These families provided some twenty bishops in the sixteenth century. On several occasions even a commoner who made his fortune at the court was able to pass on that good fortune to a relative. An example was Henri Le Meignen, who as preacher to Marguerite de Valois was promoted to the see of Digne in Provence in 1569 and passed the bishopric on to his nephew Claude Coquelet in 1587.

Of the 262 bishops appointed between 1547 and 1589, 64 (24 percent) had close relatives (brother or uncle) already serving in the episcopacy; 43 (16 percent) followed those relatives in their sees. Forty-one bishops (15 percent) passed their sees on to close relatives. Sixteen (6 percent) were both preceded and succeeded in their sees by such relatives, creating fourteen dynasties of at least three generations.[21] Furthermore these figures belie the extent to which a small number of families dominated much of the episcopate, because there were nine cases where there was a hiatus of a generation between family members in the period under study. Often clients of the dominant families, these intervening bishops were likely to appear during the civil wars. Clearly the pool from which prelates were chosen was considerably smaller than the potential openings called for. In many of these cases, perhaps the majority, the king had no real choice but to choose from these families.

Other practices that limited the king's freedom of choice in the appointment of bishops were exchange of sees, resignation *in favorem*, and regression. The king, as well as the pope, did have the authority to reject candidates proposed through these practices. But by established custom that predated the Concordat these were ways for bishops to choose their own successors, and only rarely in the century did king or pope refuse to permit the change of incumbents.

The practice of exchanging bishoprics followed no set pattern. Sometimes it involved dioceses of nearly equal income and prestige; other times the bishoprics were greatly disparate as in 1596 when Jean Du Bec of Nantes exchanged his see with Charles de Bourgneuf of Saint-Malo. In this case the exchange took place because the Du Bec family had been discredited in Nantes for its strong support of

Henri IV. Other reasons included a desire to find a bishopric with less responsiblity, to return near one's home, or to get out of a difficult situation in one's see. Often a bishop taking a bishopric with considerably less income would keep a pension on the income of the wealthier see given up. Sometimes a prelate who had a wealthy benefice but was heavily in debt would exchange it for a poorer one and a sum of money from a cleric with cash readily available. Another occasional form of exchange was to give up a bishopric for an abbey as Martin de Beaune did in 1560, giving Le Puy to Antoine de Sennetaire for his abbey. De Beaune, who had never been ordained, found that becoming an abbot enabled him to be secularized. He took a pension of 2,800 livres on Le Puy. Since this practice usually involved two churchmen already approved as bishops, there was ordinarily no valid reason for king or pope to object. In one case, however, the attempted exchange between Jean Du Tillet of Saint-Brieuc and Louis de Brézé of Meaux in 1564, the pope refused new bulls to Brézé. Du Tillet was installed in Meaux, and a new bishop was appointed for Saint-Brieuc.[22]

Far more common than exchanging bishoprics was the practice of resigning a see in favor of a relative, client, or friend. In the sixteenth century a fifth of the bishops received their offices in that way. The document on which a bishop would submit his resignation to the Holy See would include the name of designated bishop. Normally the king, and the pope in his turn, approved the new bishop, since the resignation *in favorem* usually served the monarchy by maintaining in office some powerful family whose loyalty the king had wanted to assure by the nomination of the incumbent. Yet there were occasional rejections.

One limitation on the practice was the rule that a resignation written less than twenty days before a bishop's death was not accepted, obviously to avoid death-bed resignations. This condition created a major incident in 1553 when Claude de La Guiche of Mirepoix died at Rome less than twenty days after resigning his see to his brother. The pope refused to accept the nomination and named his own nephew to Mirepoix, touching off a two-year dispute with the monarchy. When the apostate archbishop of Aix resigned his bishopric to his vicar general in 1563, the pope refused to accept the act and named Cardinal Lorenzo Strozzi instead.[23] In 1577 the monarchy refused to accept the resignation of the bishop of Lavaur, Pierre Danès, to the noted Hebraist Gilbert Génébrard. Consequently the see was vacant for four years. Perhaps the most interesting of these cases was that of Rieux where the incumbent, François Du Bourg, submitted a resignation *in favorem* in 1564. The king refused to accept Du Bourg's designee and named another whom the pope rejected because he had agreed to Du Bourg's nominee. Du Bourg remained bishop until his death in 1568.[24] With so many resignations *in favorem* it is not surprising that king or pope balked at some of them.

The practice had its abuses. It may well have been the most serious cause of corruption in the episcopacy in the era, since it was an open invitation to simony. Until 1550 bishops would often send their resignations to Rome leaving the name of the designated successor blank and later filling in the person who offered the most for the bishopric.[25] This practice was prohibited by a royal decree of 1550, but the opportunities for simony remained ripe. Bishops could still demand substantial sums for a resignation. The principal way to gain them was through taking a pension on the bishop's income, usually one or two thousand livres but occasionally half or more of the bishopric's income. In addition to a pension, a resigning bishop would sometimes keep control over a seigneurie, the episcopal palace, or a title. For example, the Cardinal de Bourbon kept the title of peer of France that went with the bishopric of Laon when he resigned it to Jean Doc in 1552. The retention of the collation of benefices within the diocese was also a common and lucrative practice.

The practice of "confidence" was yet another way that a bishop who was giving up a bishopric could continue to receive an income from it.[26] After Trent the possession of plural dioceses was prohibited, and, with a few exceptions, a bishop moving on to a wealthier see had to resign his current one first. Only the highest-placed prelate could expect to take a large pension that gave him most of the revenues from his old see. Those of lesser rank, however, could arrange for a successor who agreed to pass most of the revenues on to them. Confidence was, therefore, an arrangement by which someone who was not eligible to hold the bishopric received most of its income. Not only churchmen but also laymen or even women could be *confidentiaires*. Since these arrangements were usually done with the complicity of the crown, the curia would not be informed of the arrangement and would confirm the court's nominee —that is, unless the nuncio was alert and informed Rome. Confidence, which Trent condemned as simony as did Pius IV in 1565, differed from the practice of holding monasteries *in commendam* (in trust) in that the latter pertained only to monasteries of men and was accepted, indeed promoted, by the Holy See.

How confidence worked is clearly demonstrated in a document detailing an agreement between the Duc de Joyeuse and Raymond Cavalesi concerning the bishopric of Nîmes in 1573.[27] Cavalesi, after noting that the king had given the see to Joyeuse (his lieutenant general in Languedoc) for his services to the court, agreed to give Joyeuse all the revenues of the bishop except for 1,200 livres for his own livelihood. He was also to allow Joyeuse to collate the benefices of the diocese, and to accept Joyeuse's candidate for vicar and several other offices of the diocese. Joyeuse was to pay the cost of procuring the bulls in Rome. The agreement was to be effective between Cavalesi and Joyeuse or his heir as long as the bishop remained in office. Further proof of how completely Cavalesi was a minion of the Joyeuse family appeared in 1590 when the duke's son, the archbishop of Narbonne, resigned that see to Cavalesi so that he could become archbishop of Toulouse.

Besides the financial chicanery that *resignatio in favorem* promoted, it usually produced bishops who were very young, often not yet twenty-seven years old, and who had little or no standing outside of their relationship to the incumbent bishop. The majority of underage bishops seated from 1547 to 1589 received their sees through resignation. The practice also produced episcopal dynasties. There were two kinds of such dynasties—the one involved the passing of a bishopric within a powerful family that had preeminence in the region or perhaps the entire realm (resignation was occasionally used but probably was not necessary), and the other created through resignations *in favorem*. The latter device could create dynasties that controlled bishoprics far from the family's center of influence or dynasties that arose from families of relative insignificance or even of foreign origin. Thus the Ragueneaus from Tours were bishops of Marseille from 1557 to 1603, the five Villars, originally from Paris, controlled Vienne for 140 years, and the Bonzis, a Florentine family, held Béziers from 1576 to 1669.

The third of the practices that by custom limited the royal prerogative was regression, which was a particular type of resignation *in favorem*. One of the conditions the new bishop, and the king and the pope as well, often had to accept was the return of the resigning prelate if he were still alive upon the resignation or death of the incoming bishop or often if his pension was not being paid by the new incumbent. It was a practice principally of the great churchmen who demanded it along with a healthy pension.[28]

Such was the case of the Cardinal Charles de Bourbon in his see of Carcassone. In 1550 he resigned it on a pension of two-thirds of the see's revenues and the right of regression. In 1565 his successor died, and the cardinal reclaimed the bishopric. The chapter refused to recognize his right of regression, so the king addressed a sharp order to the canons to accept Bourbon as bishop.[29] The arch practitioner of regression was Cardinal d'Armagnac who, having accumulated four bishoprics, was forced to give up three by the edict of Paul III against pluralism. He kept the right of regression for all three. A nephew, Jacques de Corneillan, received Rodez; after his death in 1582 Armagnac returned briefly to his bishopric and resigned it to another Corneillan nephew while keeping all the revenues except 1,000 livres for the new bishop. His principal see was Toulouse, which he resigned to Paul de Foix in 1574 for a large pension and regression. Upon de Foix's death in 1584, d'Armagnac returned as archbishop until his own death in 1585.

The practice of regression caused considerable trouble for a number of dioceses; none was as badly affected as Narbonne where near anarchy flourished for a decade. In 1563 Narbonne had four archbishops. The incumbent Cardinal Pisani died, passing the see to Ippolyto d'Este who claimed it on a right of regression dating back to 1551. He quickly resigned it on a pension and a new right of regression to Cardinal de Tournon who also had a right of regression from 1551 (a year when Narbone had three archbishops). Tournon proceeded to resign in less than two months on his own pension and right of regression. Thus d'Este returned for a third time as archbishop. All of this happened in less than a year's time largely because the two cardinals were in Rome and the transactions were carried on there and quickly approved by the curia. Tournon returned for a brief third term himself after d'Este died in 1572. He then resigned the see to Paul de Foix, touching off a controversy of a different sort.[30]

There were several other ways in which the complete freedom of the king to have whom he wished as bishop of a particular see was limited. The practice of providing coadjutors to bishops was in the sixteenth century not as common a practice or as certain a route to a bishopric as it would be in the eighteenth century, but an occasional coadjutor would be given the right of succession. The king had to approve the coadjutors; but since the king might have died before the episcopal succession took place, the next king was obliged to accept the coadjutor. There was also an isolated example of a royal nominee failing to gain the papal bulls of office because he could not pay the fees required.[31]

Occasionally churchmen refused nominations to bishoprics. A Dominican would not accept the promotion to bishop of Fréjus in 1579 because of his religious zeal, and Pierre de Donnaud, already bishop of Mirepoix in 1587, refused the archdiocese of Bordeaux because it would take him away from the monastery of which he was also abbot. On the other hand Nicholas de Pellevé rejected the pope's offer of Narbonne in 1572 because it was too remote a place in the realm. The pope gave him a pension of 1,000 écus on Narbonne anyway.[32] And on one occasion, the king changed his mind and tried to rescind the letters of nomination for Aymar Hennequin to Rennes in 1573. The papal bulls were already being drawn up, and the appointment proceeded.[33]

The Concordat made no mention of how the royal nomination

was to be forwarded to Rome or what sort of information was to accompany it. By a stroke of good fortune the dossiers that were compiled for the first seven of François I's episcopal appointments under the Concordat as well as for some twenty abbots remained in France instead of being kept in the Vatican archives, whence most of the dossiers for the sixteenth century have disappeared. They were discovered in the late nineteenth century in a private archive and give an idea of the type of information and style used for the nominations.[34] They consisted of a letter from the king to the pope recommending his nominee, similar letters from the king to the papal secretary of state and to the cardinal protector of French affairs at the curia, an inquest into the candidate's moral character and doctrine, and one or more, sometimes many more, letters from prominent French churchmen attesting to the fitness of the candidate for episcopal office.

The Council of Trent in 1563 and Pius IV in 1564 both called for improvements in the way information was passed to Rome but with apparently no immediate success.[35] In 1591 Gregory XIV issued a bull that required a more elaborate procedure. The papal nuncio to France was responsible for procuring a testament of sound doctrine and morals whether through his own efforts or by naming a bishop to obtain it. The nuncio was to send on to Rome three copies of the testament as well as a profession of faith from the candidate. At the first consistory after the materials arrived in Rome, the cardinal-protector of French affairs stated his intention to nominate the royal candidate to the vacant see; at the next consistory he formally proposed the nominee and praised his virtues. The pope, after asking the advice of the cardinals, expedited nine bulls of office that were sent to the king, the candidate, the metropolitan, the cathedral chapter, other men of note, and the people of the diocese. After receiving the bulls of office the new bishop was consecrated by three fellow bishops and, in order to take control of the finances and jurisdiction in his see, swore an oath of fealty to the king.[36] Most of the above steps were in effect before 1591, but inconsistencies from one papal reign to the next and from one king to another as well as the disappearance of many of the documents make it impossible to postulate a standard procedure for the sixteenth century.[37]

Except for about fourteen bishops named directly by the popes during the course of the sixteenth century, the king had ultimate responsibility for the French episcopate. Despite the many ways that the king's freedom to choose episcopal candidates could be circumscribed, he had the authority and the obligation under the Concordat to see that worthy clerics were given bishoprics. Had he tried to refuse sees to the provincial nobles or to those designated in the resignation *in favorem*, he would have touched off a storm of protest. But if the monarchs of the first half-century of the Concordat's existence had been more conscientious in the appointment of bishops, France might have been able to avoid the far more serious troubles of the religious wars.

CHAPTER III

THE KINGS AND THEIR BISHOPS

The criteria of the Concordat of Bologna, if precisely met, would have created a competent, well-educated if not necessarily devout episcopate. Yet the bishops of the sixteenth century as a group fell far short of that caliber, and many were a disgrace to the Church. In order to understand why the Concordat did not result in a better class of bishops and what the nearly disastrous consequences of that failure were for the Church, one must first see how the kings did choose bishops, the extent to which they were responsible for the appointments, and the type of men they favored.

In the sixteenth century there was no *feuille des bénéfices* as appeared in the seventeenth to systematize the dispensing of consistorial benefices.[1] Each king of the century had a somewhat different style of collating ecclesiastical patronage. François I was the most actively involved of the kings until Henri IV in identifying episcopal nominees. He favored clerics with whom he was personally familiar and was partial to the humanists who adorned his court, even if they were commoners. He did not hesitate to appoint members of the great noble families but was less eager to allow the great nobles to promote their clients. Nor was he willing as later kings were to pass the right of nomination to his favorites, which practice made Henri III in particular little more than a postman. In that respect at least, the Concordat under François worked largely as it was intended in that the king had a direct responsibility for the episcopal appointments: François was the true collator of consistorial benefices. That fact also put a greater responsibility on him for the abuses that quickly appeared.

At the time the Concordat was drawn up, there were 102 bishops in office. Michel Peronnet has analyzed their social origins and found that sixty were nobles of the sword; fourteen were new nobles; sixteen, foreigners; four, commoners; and he could not determine the social status of eight.[2] As Imbart de La Tour has pointed out, some two-thirds of the bishops seated in Louis XII's reign should be considered as royal candidates despite the system of canonical elections under the Pragmatic Sanction.[3] Consequently it is no surprise that the pattern of the social status of the appointments made by François I once he began to use his authority under the Concordat changed rather little. Even before the Parlement of Paris had registered the Concordat as the document explicitly required, François made his first appointments under it, less than a month after the agreement with Leo. From these first appointments the pattern of ignoring one or more of the criteria for bishops set out by the Concordat was established. Three of the first four nominees were near relatives of men close to the king. Only one had a university degree, and one was not a priest. Appointees named in 1520 and 1521 were twenty-three and eighteen years of age.[4]

François's comments in his letters nominating his first bishops are informative. The first of these nominees, Arnaud-Guillaume d'Aydie, appointed to Aire in Gascony in 1516, was described as a "very learned man, filled with good morals, virtues and knowledge." Philippe de Montmorency, given Limoges, was said to be "gifted and endowed with good morals and literary knowledge and from a great and noble house." Virtually verbatim comments in the dossiers of the other five early episcopal candidates suggest that a formula for these dossiers was quickly created. The motivation behind these appointments is revealed as well. François wanted d'Aydie as bishop of Aire, on the Spanish frontier, because it was necessary to have the direction of a devoted and trustworthy subject in such a strategic see. Montmorency was cited for his own good and commendable services to the crown and those of his relatives.

TABLE I

SOCIAL ORIGINS OF IDENTIFIABLE FRENCH BISHOPS
UNDER FRANÇOIS I

Category	Number	Percentage of Identifiables	Percentage of All Bishops
Princes of Blood	9	7	5
Nobility of the Sword	93	72	51
Nobility of the Robe	21	17	12
Men of the People	6	4	3
Total	129	100	71

Another of these early nominees was Thomas Du Prat, the brother of the chancellor Du Prat, whose services to the throne were considered sufficient reason for his brother's promotion to Clermont.[5]

Although such explicit information is not available for most of François's 175 nominations, the pattern established by his first appointments remained largely the same throughout his reign. His bishops were churchmen who usually came from the nobility of the sword whose services, or those of their families, to the monarchy were obvious. While influential members of the court were able to gain the appointment of their clients, this practice was considerably less extensive than it was for the later kings of the century. The proportion of *anoblis* and commoners was also less than for his successors. However, many of the bishops seated in the early years of François's reign were still elected by the chapters who usually chose a member of a powerful local noble family. Marilyn Edelstein, who has analyzed the social origins of the bishops of François's reign, has found that 123 were French nobles. Six were French commoners; thirty-eight were foreigners (almost all of whom were Italian nobles); and fifteen were Frenchmen whose status she could not determine. She has broken down further the status of the identifiable Frenchmen.[6]

With such a predominance of members of the royal family and great noble families, it is small wonder that the requirements of the Concordat of Bologna were often not met. Numerous nominees were under the age of twenty-seven, including Charles de Guise, the future Cardinal de Lorraine, age nine, and more than a quarter (27 percent) had not received a university education. With the patronage of 111 bishoprics and some 600 abbeys, many as lucrative as a bishopric, François I had a powerful means of rewarding faithful service and loyalty and of assuring future service from the important people of the realm. It appears that in this regard he was considerably more successful than were his successors in the century.

Edelstein has demonstrated how the king used episcopal revenues to pay for public services. François appointed his ambassadors to benefices to provide them with income for their duties in order not to deplete the royal treasury. Although churchmen had always served as diplomats, François used them more extensively. He also gave bishoprics to foreign churchmen who came to France as ambassadors. That papal nuncios and legates in particular almost certainly received French sees during or after their tours of duty in France in part explains the dramatic rise in the number of Italians in the French episcopacy after 1516. The need to gain the good will of the papacy in pursuit of his Italian policy also dictated the endowing of papal relatives and clients with French benefices. In all, during François's reign, thirty-one Italians were granted French sees, which constituted 17 percent of his total appointments.[7]

Determined to break the control of the cathedral chapters or the local nobility over many sees, François nominated prominent churchmen of the court, often princes of the blood but also several influential *anoblis*, to fill such bishoprics. He also allowed several great prelates, such as the Cardinal Du Bellay, to accumulate several sees as a means of forcing the transition from canonical elections to royal nomination. Clerics from the circle of the court accounted for 38 percent of the nominees in the first four decades of the Concordat.[8]

While domestic and internal politics were the major concerns for François I in appointing bishops, there was one group of bishops whose appointments were ordinarily not based on political considerations and who met the spirit of the intellectual criterion of the Concordat if not the letter—the humanists. François was strongly attracted to the humanists and was supportive of them because of his attraction to Italian culture. He was eager to have them at his court and rewarded them with benefices and bishoprics. As Arthur Tilly has said, "a knowledge of Greek was a sure road to the king's favor." While many of the humanists named to bishoprics in François's reign were appointed for reasons in addition to their studies, others were clearly nominated because of their humanist interests. Of the twenty-seven humanists given bishoprics, at least nine knew Greek, making the French episcopacy one of the most grecophonic groups in western Europe.[9]

The filling of vacant bishoprics usually involved the personal attention of François I, but under his successor, Henri II, the process became somewhat more systematic and less personal. The provincial governors informed the court of what vacancies in the consistorial benefices had occurred in their jurisdictions and suggested candidates to fill them.[10] Often these nominations went through several levels of influence in order to reach someone close to the king. The patron presented his request for an office for a client to the king through one of the four secretaries of state who read them to the king; he in turn approved or disapproved. At most of the sessions that involved ecclesiastical offices, the Cardinal de Lorraine, Charles de Guise, was present. How much real influence over episcopal nominations his presence gave the cardinal is far from clear, but some contemporaries were convinced that he completely controlled ecclesiastical patronage during Henri's reign. It was said in 1553 that one had to refer to him "for all things of the Church and of religion." Certainly many of the bishops seated in Henri's reign had or gained a reputation as Guisards. Yet the *Connétable* Montmorency and the royal mistress Diane de Poitiers were influential in a number of appointments as well. Three of the latter's nephews received bishoprics from Henri, and at least five other nominations can be attributed to her influence. One well-informed observer believed that ecclesiastical patronage was firmly in her hands.[11]

While the Cardinal de Lorraine may indeed have controlled episcopal patronage, his influence did not result in any improve-

TABLE II
SOCIAL ANALYSIS OF FRENCH BISHOPS
SEATED DURING THE REIGN OF HENRI II, 1547−59
(N = 80)

Noblesse de Race		Anoblis		Commoners		Foreigners		Unknown Social Origins	
44	55%	9	11%	3	4%	22	27%	2	3%

ment in following the criteria of the Concordat. The number of candidates who were under the required age of twenty-seven or who were not priests (the two categories were not entirely mutually inclusive) were both over 5 percent of Henri's eighty nominations.[12] (See appendix III, table I.) If Henri's bishops so rarely met the criteria of the Concordat of Bologna, what sort of men were they?

The percentage of bishops from the French *noblesse de race* (all but one of his twenty-two foreign bishops were noble as well) is the same as that of François I's reign. The social category that reveals a noticeable decline is that of the *anoblis*, which was the lowest for any reign until the eighteenth century. Henri's failure to nominate a larger number of men of the long robe is somewhat surprising since his relationship with the Parlements, the major stronghold of the *anoblis*, was clearly better than was that of his father. Nonetheless Henri was far more interested in hunting and rough sports, the sort of activities that marked the nobility of the sword. Henri's closest companions were members of the highest-ranking noble families, and their relatives often appear in the episcopacy. The system of having the provincial governors recommend names for most episcopal vacancies also helps to explain the predominance of the nobility of the sword, since their prejudices favored their own.

Among the commoners seated in episcopal chairs by Henri was a member of an Italian merchant family of Paris, Pierre Danès (Danesi). Danès, one of Henri's tutors, was a respected humanist who was the first lecturer in Greek in the Collège de France.[13] Three of the French *roturiers* named bishops were humanists as well, and in all, nine of Henri's prelates had established reputations as humanists, a slightly smaller proportion than for his father's bishops. Another factor that may have helped to reduce the humanist appointments was the growing rigidity of Catholic attitude, which virtually equated humanism with heresy. Henri preferred lawyers to humanists or theologians. Only three of his eighty appointees had theology degrees while fifteen had studied law. Together the two categories account for only 23 percent of the bishops despite the requirement of the Concordat.

An even more pronounced trend in nomination from 1547 to 1559 was the seating of Italian churchmen in French sees. Twenty-one of the twenty-two foreigners were Italians; the other was Spanish.[14] Numerous members of the *fuoruscuti* families (the Italian refugees, especially Florentines, who had lost out in the power struggles in the peninsula) received bishoprics. Several were relatives or friends of Queen Catherine de Medici, but the real motivation for their appointments was to reward their families for their services and loans to the crown. The same factor along with the pursuit of control of Italy led to bishoprics for members of important Italian families still in power in Italy, such as the Farnese and the d'Este families. Henri used the episcopal patronage available to him to gain the election of his choice for pope in 1555 by promising bishoprics to Italian cardinals. Yet the impression that Henri was overwhelmingly generous to Italians must be tempered by recognition of the role of the papacy in more than a third of the Italian appointments. The death of François I had given the Holy See the opportunity to assert its rights under the Concordat and to refuse to renew the special bulls for the *pays d'obédience*. The conflicting claims of monarchy and papacy, especially prevalent in the first years of Julius III who was determined to reduce royal control over the French Church, resulted in the papacy naming eight of the Italian bishops seated in Henri's reign. In several cases the monarchy rejected the papal appointments and refused to let them take the episcopal revenues. There was no question of most of these bishops actually taking administrative control of their dioceses, and the controversial Italians usually resigned within several years, taking healthy pensions as compensation.[15]

The Italian bishops, whether named by the king or by the pope, resigned or exchanged their bishoprics at a rapid rate. They were not, however, unique in that respect. Henri's bishops as a group had the highest rate of these practices of the sixteenth century. The strong injunctions of the papacy and the Council of Trent against pluralist bishops had had some effect as the holding of plural sees declined considerably, although the practice was far from eliminated. The prelates, however, compensated by holding a diocese for a short time, then resigning it on a pension and transferring to another see, shortly resigning that one for another pension and perhaps going on to yet a third. In a period of less than ten years, several bishops had each held three sees, resigned them all, and were drawing large pensions on them. An example was Alessandro Farnese, the grandson of Paul III, whom Henri II greatly favored. In 1553 he was named to Tours, which he resigned the next year on a pension of 3,000 livres. He then was given Viviers, which he resigned almost immediately with a pension of all the episcopal revenues as well as the collation of benefices, also quite lucrative. He then received Cahors, which he gave up in 1557 on a pension of 1,000 livres. [16]

As a result of the practice of resigning a bishopric after a short time in office, the bishops of Henri II had the shortest average terms in office of the century. Their episcopal careers averaged 14.4 years. When the changes of dioceses are considered as well, they spent 11.7 years in a bishopric and had an average of 1.25 sees in their careers. One-third of Henri's appointments resigned their bishoprics before their deaths. [17] The disruption in the administration of the dioceses created by these frequent changes in bishops, and the changes in vicars that usually followed, certainly must have been a factor in the inadequate response of the French Church in its struggle with Protestantism. Such early resignation also fostered the image of avarice and irresponsibility that pervaded the episcopacy at the end of Henri's reign.

Certainly no one would maintain that the record of episcopal appointments in the other reigns of the century was free of irregularities and violations of the criteria set by the Concordat, but none of the other kings as consistently appointed bishops who did not meet the standards of Bologna or even the much laxer standards of the French Church as did Henri II. Some accountability also belongs to the papacy, which failed to use its right of rejection of candidates to foster a better class of bishops. Part of the responsibility also must be attributed to the Cardinal de Lorraine, especially if his influence over the seating of bishops during Henri's reign did extend as far as his contemporaries and modern historians have concluded. However, those who have expressed that opinion may have failed to have taken into account the practices of *resignatio in favorem* and regression, which even the cardinal dared not challenge, and the numerous papal appointments.

There is far less question about the domination of the Guises over the brief reign of François II, and one can conclude that Lorraine's control over the appointment of bishops was more sure. While eleven bishops do make a small sample, they did meet the standards of the Concordat of Bologna considerably more closely.[18] If indeed the cardinal was responsible for the improvement, then it is likely that he had less influence than he is usually attributed over the filling of sees under Henri II. Only one of François II's bishops is noted as having a degree in theology or law, but all had reached the age of twenty-seven, and all but one were already priests. Seven came from the *noblesse de race*, and an eighth from the *anoblis*. One of François's bishops was a commoner, and the status of two remains uncertain. Only one moved to a second bishopric; two resigned on pensions; and none came under suspicion of Protestantism. They averaged 15.2 years in office. (The death of one nominee the same year as appointed dropped that average considerably.) Although none of François II's episcopal appointees gained reputations for zeal or piety, as a group they stand above the standards for the century.

With the death of the young king in late 1560, control of the government and the nominations of bishops passed to Catherine de Medici who served as regent for Charles IX for the next three years and exercised great influence throughout his reign. Once in control she set about to reward her Italian friends and relatives, appointing five of them to French sees in her first year as regent and four more in the next two years. The nine Italian appointments in three years were the greatest concentration of foreign nominees in the century, but the number dropped sharply after Charles's majority so that the proportion of Italians among his bishops was 17 percent, considerably less than for Henri II.

In two respects at least, Catherine's regency marked the low point of the French episcopacy during the sixteenth century. One was her protection against the curia of eight bishops whom the Roman inquisition had accused of heresy in 1563. She sent one of them, François de Noailles of Dax, as royal ambassador to Rome to persuade the papacy to drop the charges on the grounds that they were untrue and an infringement of the liberties of the Gallican Church. She and Charles IX steadfastly refused to strip the benefices from the accused prelates who had not already resigned despite the repeated demands of popes.[19] In the long run, however, more damage to the Church likely resulted from her willingness to accede to the more than twenty exchanges of dioceses and transfers that occurred during her regency. Most of the bishops involved were seated in Henri II's reign, largely establishing the record of short terms in office for the king's bishops. At the time when the violence of the religious wars was beginning, near anarchy seems to have flourished in the episcopacy as prelates moved from see to see or resigned at an unprecedented rate. Catherine's Italian friends and relatives in particular took advantage of her power to gain more wealthy sees for themselves as four Strozzi and Medici bishops transferred bishoprics in 1561 and 1562.

Was this rash of changes in incumbent bishops in part a result of the first impact of the sectarian violence that erupted in 1560? The pattern of dioceses involved permits no clear answer since many of them show no incidence of religious violence in the first several years of the wars. Yet there are suggestions that some bishops did resign or change sees because of the onslaught of religious strife.[20]

Catherine as regent was also responsible for the seating of three bishops of illegitimate birth, despite the explicit canon of Church law barring bastards, and three who were underage. On the other hand, her record had some positive aspects. There was a higher incidence of nominations of men with university degrees, again mostly civil lawyers. Despite her support of incumbent bishops accused of heresy, none of the nominees during the regency fell under suspicion of heterodoxy, and several gained reputations for their zealous defense of Catholicism and Church reform.

After Charles IX was declared of age in August, 1563, his mother continued to exercise great influence over the appointment of bishops. Her favorites, secretaries, and *aumôniers* continued to receive the miter at a significant rate. Charles, however, also began to make greater use of a practice that had only occasionally appeared in the previous reigns: giving an important courtier or great noble-man complete say over the filling of a vacant bishopric (as opposed to the system in which the notable merely recommended his candi-date to the king for approval). The king passed on to Rome the nomination without question, or so it often appears. Often the candidates presented to Rome in this manner were blatantly unworthy.

After the election of Pius IV in 1559, the papacy, concerned about the high incidence of heterodoxy in the French hierarchy and eager to implement the decrees of Trent on reforming the episcopacy, had become much more careful about approving the French candidates. Rejections for cause and not as a result of disputes over the Concordat became fairly common under Charles and frequent for Henri III. Virtually all such rejections resulted from the relin-quishment of royal responsibility in the choice of bishops. An example was the refusal of the Holy See to draw up the bulls of office for Pierre de La Rouille to whom Henri de Damville had given Montpellier with royal approval. Although La Rouille held degrees in civil and canon law, his scandalous private life precipi-tated the rejection. La Rouille took the episcopal revenues from Montpellier for four years and then gave up his claim on it for a pen-sion of 1,000 livres.[21] Another case was the nomination of Pierre de Saint-Martin to Vannes in 1572 as a favor to the captain of the Royal Guards. After the Holy See refused to grant his bulls, he received a small pension from the next bishop, Jean de La Haye.[22]

TABLE III

SOCIAL ANALYSIS OF FRENCH BISHOPS

SEATED DURING THE REIGN OF CHARLES IX, 1560−74

(N = 95)

Noblesse de Race		Anoblis		Commoners		Foreigners		Unknown Social Origins	
41	43%	15	16%	12	12%	16	17%	11	12%

With so many of Charles's first choices rejected, the above analysis of the bishops seated in his reign may not reflect accurately his real attitude toward the proper social level of episcopal nominees, since several of the commoner bishops were second candidates.

For the first time since the Concordat and likely for centuries before it, the proportion of the nobles of the sword appointed to the episcopacy slipped below 50 percent. However, because of the large number of appointments in the category of uncertain status, it could well be that some were *noblesse de race*. It is difficult to reach clear-cut conclusions about Charles's appointments. But it is far more likely that these bishops were *anoblis* or commoners, since one reason for the inclusion of several in the category of uncertain status is the lack of precise evidence to indicate whether their families had yet graduated to the status of robe nobility that they would hold in the next century. The notable increase in the number of commoners in the episcopal ranks began a trend that continued in the next two reigns as well and made the late sixteenth century the best period for *roturier* bishops for the duration of the Concordat. Were the swelled ranks of commoners in Charles's reign a result of the influence of Catherine de Medici? As an Italian with bourgeois ancestry, she may well have been less in tune with the social prejudices of the French elite. But her own record of nominations during her regency gives only limited support for that hypothesis, and the continued frequency of *roturier* nominees in the next two reigns reduces the possible impact of her influence. Despite Catherine's early binge of Italian appointments, the percentage of foreigners was down from Henri II's reign.

Lawyers were clearly in Charles's favor with nearly one-third of the prelates holding law degrees. (See appendix III, table II.) With the proportion of theologians increased as well, 40 percent of Charles's bishops had the required university degrees.[23] One abuse of the Concordat that increased was the nomination of unordained men, but the practice of seating underage prelates declined significantly. As a consequence the average age of the bishops at appointment was nearly forty-five years, the highest during the Concordat's existence.[24] Despite the relatively advanced age of the nominees, they remained in office an average of 18.9 years, noticeably longer than the bishops seated by Henri II. One factor was a decline in the practice of resigning with a pension, down to 25 percent of Charles's bishops. Despite Catherine de Medici's largesse during her regency in allowing bishops to transfer sees, which profitted mostly Henri II's appointments, the bishops named in Charles's reign had an average term of 15.5 years in the one diocese and held 1.1 sees during their careers. Partly because so many of Henri II's bishops resigned during Charles's reign, the latter had the opportunity to appoint the largest number of bishops per year (7.3) in the three centuries of the Concordat despite the 15 percent increase in dioceses under it by 1789.[25] The improvement in following the standards of the Concordat for this large number of bishops may well have been more a responsibility of the papacy than of the monarchy. But despite the numbers and the better caliber of nominees, Charles's bishops did not include many notable individuals. The two outstanding appointees of his reign, both of whom were better known for their political activities than for Church leadership, were Pierre de Gondi of Paris and Renaud de Beaune of Mende and later Bourges, both key advisers to Henri III and Henri IV.

Henri III came to the throne in the increasing anarchy of the wars of religion. His own lack of effectiveness contributed to a considerable loss of control over episcopal patronage. How much direct responsibility he had for many of the bishops named from 1575 to 1589 is difficult to determine, but it is clear that he abdicated his responsibility in numerous cases. Under Henri grants of episcopal patronage to his favorites became a serious problem, and in much of France, particularly in the Midi, local authorities appear to have nominated prelates with little regard of the monarchy. For example, he granted the collation of the small see of Luçon to his grand provost, François de Richelieu, a grant Henri IV later reaffirmed. Between terms of service by members of the family who served as its bishop, the see was held for short periods by family clients.

Henri passed such nominations on to Rome with little question; there, many were rejected. In 1580 Henri's *mignon*, the Sieur d'O, had been given the right to fill the vacancy at Avranches. He nominated his fifteen-year-old brother who was not confirmed. Georges Péricard, a civil lawyer, was then nominated and accepted at Rome.[26] The nuncio Dandino reported in 1578 that the Maréchal Damville named a man who was "ignorant and probably a Huguenot" to Agde in Languedoc. He was not confirmed. Nor was the nominee of the captain of the royal archers who received the right to fill Sisteron in 1581. The capable Antoine Couppes was then nominated in 1584 and approved.[27] Another example involves the see of Grenoble that Henri gave to another *mignon*, Sieur Du Gast. He hoped to become bishop himself, for the nuncio reported that he was "ignoble and ignorant." He then traded the bishopric to François de Fléard for two priories and 35,000 livres. The cathedral chapter strongly objected to Fléard's appointment because it had not been consulted, and it refused to allow him to take possession of the see until 1586. Fléard served as bishop of Grenoble until 1606.[28]

The most interesting of these cases arose with the death of Jean Le Henneyer of Lisieux in 1578. Henri III had given the patronage of the bishopric to his brother, Alençon, who passed it on to his *maréchal de camp*. The latter nominated a Jacques de Bonnechose who, Alençon assured the nuncio Dandino, was worthy. Dandino received an anonymous letter from the Sorbonne declaring that Bonnechose was a keeper of dogs for Alençon's favorite, had fought for the Huguenots, and had not been to Mass in seventeen years. Several months later Rome received a copy of a doctorate in theology conferred on Bonnechose. Rome called for a committee of four bishops to examine him, but it was never done. By late 1579 Dandino reported that the *maréchal de camp* had decided to exchange his patronage of Lisieux, whose revenues he had hoped to take in confidence, for several abbeys that did not require Rome's approval. Jean de Vassé, a canon lawyer, was confirmed the next year.[29] The sordid tale was not yet over; Vassé died in 1583, and the maréchal again presented a nominee. The new nuncio Ragazzoni told the curia that it was a clear case of confidence, and despite several letters attesting to the candidate's competence and piety, Rome denied him the bulls of office. The Benedictine monk Anne d'Escars was then confirmed in 1584. The king later stated to Ragazzoni that he was pleased that the nomination had been rejected since he had passed it on to Rome only as a favor to his brother.[30]

These episodes indicate that by the time of Henri's reign, the popes and the nuncios, particularly Dandino, took far more care in approving episcopal nominations than had been true for his predecessors.[31] It is likely that most of the rejected candidates would have been confirmed thirty years earlier. Second, these cases show that the monarchy was always careful to nominate a worthy candidate on the second round who was certain to receive his bulls. The court clearly did not want to risk passing the right to fill a French see to the pope because of its laxity in applying the criteria of the Concordat. Acceptable candidates were easily found and confirmed on the second nomination.

Most of the rejected nominations involved the arrangement of confidence, the practice by which ineligible individuals could receive episcopal revenues. One does not hear much of confidence before 1560, likely because the papacy paid little attention to it before then. The only way that the Holy See could become aware of an arrangement of confidence was through the sharp eyes and ears of its nuncios. It is possible, therefore, that Henri III's reign seems pervaded by the practice because the sharpest eyes and ears of the century's nuncios belonged to Dandino, Castelli, and Ragazzoni, nuncios from 1578 to 1586.[32] For example when Renaud de Beaune tried to resign Mende to Antoine de Premblay in 1578 to move to

Bourges, the nuncio Castelli reported that confidence was involved, and neither man received the bulls of office at that time. They were granted in 1581.[33] But the spirit of reform could not in itself be solely responsible for the enormous increase in reports of the practice and condemnations of it in the reign of Henri III.

In 1579 Arnaud de Pontac, bishop of Bazas in Gascony, made a sharp attack on the practice before the assembled clergy at Melun.[34] He stated that nine French bishoprics were held under confidence and noted Cavalesi of Narbonne as a *pensionnaire* of the Duc de Joyeuse. Damville, the dominant figure in Languedoc, had two sees in confidence as did the powerful Baron de La Baume de Suzé in Dauphiné. Pontac listed two women as receiving episcopal revenues.[35] He also denounced the practice of keeping a bishopric vacant so that its revenues could flow to the king or to a person of his choice. The right of the king to take the revenues of a vacant see and to collate its benefices (the latter power was usually delegated to the cathedral chapter) was called *régale*. A vacant diocese was said to be *en régie par économat*—governed by stewardship. The person permitted by the king to take the revenues, often lay, had the see *en économat*. In one respect a diocese *en économat* was worse off than one held in confidence because the latter did have a bishop in office and, because of the need to slip the arrangement past the curia, often one more zealous than usual for the era. Pontac declared that ten sees, including Bourges, had been vacant for inordinate periods of time, ranging up to seven years, putting some of the responsibility back on Charles IX.[36] Such notables as Cardinal d'Este, Cardinal de Birague, the Duc de Grammont, and Renaud de Beaune were taking their revenues. Pontac also complained about three dioceses where bishops confirmed by Rome had not entered their sees and remained unconsecrated despite the passing of three or four years. Last, Pontac bitterly denounced the laymen, military captains, and women who spoke of "my bishopric" or "my abbey." He asked that all sees held in confidence be declared vacant and those under *économat* be immediately filled by election according to proper canon law.

This demand to abrogate the Concordat of Bologna fell, of

TABLE IV
SOCIAL ANALYSIS OF FRENCH BISHOPS
SEATED DURING THE REIGN OF HENRI III, 1574−89
(N = 76)

Noblesse de Race		Anoblis		Commoners		Foreigners		Unknown Social Origins	
40	53%	11	15%	11	15%	5	7%	9	11%

course, on the deaf ears of the king, since it was precisely by these sorts of arrangements that he could reward his favorites and men of influence or buy them off. Henri III had the greatest need of any of the kings of the century to use whatever means possible to gain support because of the deteriorating political situation during his reign. The virtual loss of royal control over much of France, especially the Midi, raises the question of the extent to which Henri controlled the episcopacy of those regions. Did Damville's control over the south extend to naming his own bishops with only perfunctory acknowledgment of the king's authority? The appearance of several unaccredited bishops in dioceses of the Midi suggests that he or other local magnates did try to appoint their own bishops with some success. Peronnet suggests the possibility that with the relaxing of royal authority, several cathedral chapters took advantage of the opportunity to return to election. He notes that several new bishops had been canons of the episcopal cities, suggesting that the chapters had chosen one of their own.[37]

Regardless whether these bishops were seated in virtual disregard of the monarchy, it is true that Henri III through personal inclination and lack of political strength had less control over the nomination of bishops than his predecessors had. The responsibility for the pattern of appointments is less clearly his than the responsibility for the bishops of his reign had been Henri II's.

The typical bishop seated under Henri III was only slightly different from that appointed by his brother. Nobles of the sword returned to over half the appointments, and there was rather little change in the other social categories. The significant change was in the smaller proportion of bishops of uncertain status. Peronnet, who apparently has placed a number of those classified here as commoners into his category of *indéterminés*, argues that commoners or men of unknown status were found largely in the dioceses of the Midi.[38] Often controlled for decades by Huguenots or the objects of bitter fighting, these sees had become less desirable to their traditional clientele. Their revenues were disrupted for years at end, and life for a bishop, should he choose to be conscientious, was often highly dangerous. "These lost sees that nobody wanted" were given to bishops of lower status than usual because the nobility were not interested in bishoprics where the opportunity to exercise authority and to collect revenues was slight.[39] Peronnet's thesis gains credence through a letter in which Henri III discussed his forthcoming nomination of Renaud de Beaune to the see of Bourges in 1577. The king stated that he intended to allow de Beaune to keep his current bishopric of Mende because "it has been so ruined by war, there is no use to appoint anyone else to it." Therefore, Henri suggested that the prelate keep it for three years after receiving Bourges.[40]

Nonetheless, Peronnet's argument has several weaknesses. One is that in several of the examples he has given, Nîmes, Montpellier, and Montauban, the bishops in question were appointed in the 1560's or early 1570's, far too early to speak of these dioceses as lost. Second, in none of the episcopal cities was the control of the Huguenots completely unchallenged throughout the wars of religion. In the sees in question the Catholic nobility would have wanted their scions in place for the time when Catholicism recaptured control of the areas. Third, in most of the dioceses where Protestants and Catholics vied for control, at least part of the revenue was still available to the bishop, and in several cases the monarchy compensated a bishop for income lost to the Huguenots with other benefices.[41]

Peronnet presents a second explanation for the increase in men of lower status that appears more valid. According to this hypothesis a significant part of the nobility of the sword, especially from the outlying provinces like Languedoc, had become Protestant, thus removing these families from consideration for bishoprics. Support for this proposal comes from studying the bishops who apostatized. In at least six cases their families also were Protestant. Three of these families had until then controlled bishoprics in the Midi. Peronnet continues by noting that the wars of religion occupied the attention and manpower of the Catholic nobility. The younger sons of these families, who in the past or again after the wars were intended for the episcopacy, were called on to serve as captains for the Catholic forces.[42]

Beyond Peronnet's explanations, one more reason for the increase in the number of bishops who were commoners appears plausible. The late sixteenth century was a period of great social flux, perhaps the greatest in the five centuries before 1789. The increased importance of bankers and financiers, the enlarged royal bureaucracy, and the new provincial Parlements created a large class of men who were highly valuable to the monarchy, and many were likely more familiar to the king than was much of the provincial nobility. Using their new wealth to buy up estates and titles, many claimed noble status but without complete success. The Paulette of 1604 and the passage of time clearly ensconced many of these families in the nobility, and the bishops chosen from them would be then categorized in the nobility of the robe. But in the late sixteenth century, while their value to the monarchy made them candidates for bishoprics, some were still legally commoners; and the status of others is so uncertain that one must place them in the category of uncertain social origin.

Other characteristics of the bishops seated under Henri III include a substantial drop in the number of lawyer-bishops as compared with the number under Charles IX, causing a net decline in the percentage of bishops with the required university degree. (See appendix III, table III.) The proportion of candidates who were not yet ordained priests was up considerably while underage appointees increased as well. Despite the turmoil of the religious wars, Henri's bishops remained in office until their deaths at a rate far higher than those appointed by his predecessors. His prelates resigned with pensions at only one-third the rate that those of his father did. Consequently they also had much longer episcopal careers, 18.7 years, and longer terms in one diocese, 17.7 years. Since most of those who did resign usually did not go on to another see, the average number of dioceses per bishop is down to 1.05. All these figures are substantial improvements over the statistics for Henri II's bishops, yet one has to ask how much of the improvement was due to the greater vigilance of the papacy. If those nominees whom the Holy See rejected had been confirmed, it is likely that the improvement would have been far less.

Henri III's bishops also showed some increase in zeal for Church reform, although several of the reform-minded did not show their hand until after the wars of religion. Others did demonstrate from the first their dedication to reform. One of Henri's first appointments, Alessandro Canignani of Aix, arrived in his see imbued with Tridentine reform as it was practiced in Milan under Carlo Borromeo; and one of his last, Nicolas Villars of Agen, proved to be one of the most zealous reformers of the era. Villars made extensive visitations and deposed seven curés and thirty-six vicars for ignorance and malfeasance and disciplined forty-eight more priests. Villars also founded a seminary. Others among Henri's bishops who had something of a reputation as reformers from their first years include Christophe de L'Estang of Lodève and Antoine Sorbin of Nevers. However, the active involvement of the latter two in the Catholic League reduced their attention to implementing the decisions of Trent.[43]

In forty-two years the last four Valois kings appointed 262 bishops, a rate of 6.2 a year, clearly above the average of 5.2 a year that Peronnet has calculated for the entire Concordatory era. To use Peronnet's concept of episcopal generations, the length of time to effect what statistically would have been a complete turnover in the episcopate was eighteen years compared with thirty for the eighteenth century.[44]

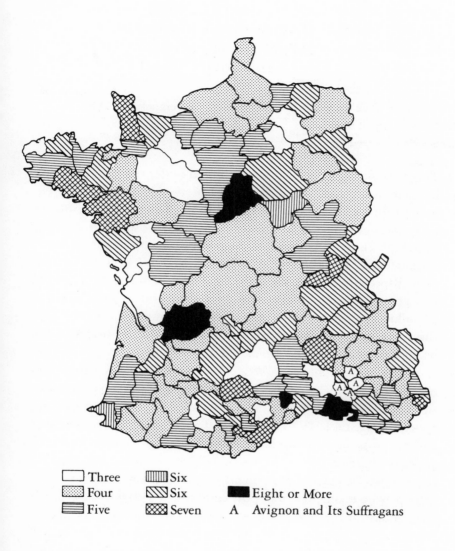

Three ▢   Six ▥
Four ▦   Six ▧   Eight or More ■
Five ▤   Seven ▨   A   Avignon and Its Suffragans

MAP II

NUMBER OF BISHOPS BY DIOCESE, 1547–1610

TABLE V
SOCIAL ANALYSIS OF FRENCH BISHOPS
SEATED DURING THE PERIOD 1547–89
(N = 262)

Noblesse de Race		Anoblis		Commoners		Foreigners		Unknown Social Origins	
132	50%	35	14%	28	10%	47	18%	20	8%

This analysis of all the bishops appointed under the last four Valois kings indicates that one of every two was a noble of the sword. The best families of the realm continued to provide their scions to the episcopacy in numbers far greater than any other social group. The next highest category was foreigners, also mostly noble, at about 18 percent. The other three categories were all near 10 percent each. Especially noteworthy is the small number of *anoblis* seated in this period. Their numbers were brought down in part by Henri II's reluctance to appoint them, but their proportion in the next three reigns was not substantially higher. Of course a percentage of bishops of undetermined status likely were *anoblis*.

While being from the *noblesse de race* clearly conferred an advantage in the competition for a bishopric, certain careers and positions were also likely to lead to an appointment as well. (See appendix III, table IV.) Fifteen members of the royal council and five *maître des requêtes* appear on the rolls as do twenty-five magistrates of the Parlements. What is striking about the statistics on the magistrates of the Parlements is the small number of *anobli* bishops who had held seats in the courts. The Parlements were the strongholds of the new nobility; and the small number of magistrates of that status raised to the episcopate is surprising, even if one assumes that all of the bishops of unknown status who had been magistrates were really *anoblis*. A more certain path to episcopal preferment for new nobles was the position of one's father. The families of *anobli* chancellors, secretaries of state, bankers, and royal physicians provided more than half of the prelates of that category. The financial community, both French and Italian, gave seventeen bishops to the French Church in the period.[45] Some secular careers were less productive of episcopal nominations: provincial administration yielded only seven bishops, and military command, only four.[46]

Certain Church positions were also conducive to episcopal nominations. Ten vicars general and seven coadjutors succeeded their former superiors. Some thirty-seven chapter canons, especially from the chapters of Paris and Chartres, were promoted to bishoprics; nearly half were not placed in the see of their canonicates. There were several more bishops who had held cathedral choir chairs, but they had other positions as well that better explain their promotions. Twenty-eight members of religious orders were raised from their houses to episcopal palaces, but the odds of receiving a bishopric were best for clerics serving the royal court. Twenty-five royal confessors, *aumôniers*, tutors, and preachers were promoted to the episcopacy. Last, three papal nuncios were rewarded with French sees for their services.

The Concordat of Bologna had made no comment on the proper type of career training for an episcopal candidate except that he should have had university training in law or theology. In that respect the bishops seated between 1547 and 1589 were sorely deficient with only a third (eighty-two) holding the prerequisite degree.

The available evidence indicates further that only another 8 percent (thirty bishops) matriculated at a university without obtaining a degree. A number of bishops did hold positions prior to their appointments to the episcopacy for which a higher education was expected, but the paucity of biographical information precludes adding them to the roll of university-educated prelates. For example, François de Noailles, a noted diplomat and prelate, was trained in "Bellelettres" and in the "disciplines proper to an ecclesiastical career," but there is no indication of where he gained that education.[47] Others clearly had gained a good education outside of the universities. François de Foix of Aire, for example, was called the French Archimedes because of his skill in geometry and was regarded as the best alchemist of his era despite his lack of formal education. Nonetheless it is also clear that a substantial number of prelates did not have higher education of any sort. The vast majority of those that did had training in law, not theology. The small number of prelates with theology degrees was clearly not a result of too small a pool of theology graduates from which to choose. There were 836 theology degrees granted (licenses and masters) from 1500 to 1560 by the Sorbonne alone. But while there was a huge potential pool of theologians from which to make episcopal appointments, in practice it was much smaller since few of them were nobles.[48] Already in the Middle Ages there had been a debate over which degree was more appropriate for an episcopal career. The enormous amount of legal work in which a bishop was involved might well have made a training in law more useful even if it did cut against the grain of the ideal of the episcopal office. Since the fourteenth century, perhaps as a result of the lawyer-pope John XXII, there had been a trend toward the appointment of lawyers.[49] Furthermore there is no evidence that bishops with degrees in theology were any more zealous than those with law backgrounds, or for that matter, that university education produced a more capable bishop.

The very small percentage of theology degree holders given bishoprics points out forcefully that gaining a bishop's chair in the sixteenth century, as throughout the *Ancien Régime*, was a matter of privilege. Privilege of blood was somewhat less important in that century than it became later, since an unusually high percentage of the bishops were commoners; but the commoners of this era were clearly privileged in wealth even if not in blood. A commoner like the humanist Jacques Amyot, said to be from a background *très modeste*, was not only a man truly privileged in talent but a member of a prosperous merchant family as well. Only Raymond Cavalesi of Nîmes and Antoine Erlault of Chalon-sur-Saône among the commoner bishops apparently came from truly humble backgrounds.

A bishop, even of the poorest sees, was a man of great prestige and authority. But the episcopal status was in itself hardly enough to make a man of lowly origins accepted and respected by the nobles. Contemporary society found it most difficult to conceive of placing a low-born person in such a position of prestige and influence; a commoner bishop had to have standing of some sort that allowed the upper classes to tolerate him. For most of the commoner prelates it was their humanist reputations. A good knowledge of classical learning was highly prized in the sixteenth century, most of all by François I but also by all of his successors. An education in Latin helped to confer status on those of common birth that at least partly compensated for their origins.[50] But the nobles occasionally failed to disguise their resentment at the low social origins of some bishops. At Angers Bishop Guillaume Ruzé, an *anobli* with strong ties to the Parlement of Paris and himself a member of the *Conseil d'état* under Henri II, hosted a dinner for the Duc d'Anjou. The nobles of Anjou's retinue, feeling insulted at having a parvenu as host, staged a fake quarrel in which dishes, furniture, and windows were broken. Their motive was that "it was unsuitable for a bishop, who was a man of low condition, to have the audacity to wish to give a dinner to a duke of Anjou."[51] At least Anjou condescended to dine with the bishop, even if his retinue acted like spoiled brats. At Evreux Marguerite de Valois apparently refused to accept the hospitality of Claude de Saintes at all because of his *roturier* origins.

With this attitude prevalent, it is surprising that so many commoners were in fact in the episcopate in the sixteenth century. Several of these bishops were the clients of the dominant nobles in the provinces who often supported commoner clerics of high reputation, perhaps in the hope that they could be more easily confirmed. Another reason was the monarchy's desperate need for money that led to the appointment of members of banking families in return for large loans. Many of the French families in the banking community in the sixteenth century were still legally commoners.

These problems were consequences of both the characters of Charles IX and Henri III and the political instability of the era of religious wars. Henri in particular looked upon his control of the royal treasury and patronage including episcopal patronage as a font from which to give large gifts to his favorites and men who served him well. Whether he conceded the right of episcopal appointment to certain powerful nobles as a way to secure their loyalty or they used the ineffectiveness of the royal government to usurp royal authority is difficult to determine. But there is no evidence of any royal protest of the usurpation of its prerogatives in this regard. The monarchy appears to have accepted passively this diminution of its control of patronage. A further consequence of this situation was that since these powerful nobles were often ardent Catholics, their prelates tended to be more zealous than the average bishop of the time. Less beholden to the king as well, they were far more likely to be active in the Catholic League after 1588. The loss of control over a number of bishoprics with their revenues and vast local authority accelerated the monarchy's problems in governing the provinces. That fact demonstrates François I's shrewdness in negotiating the Concordat of Bologna, even if his immediate successors failed to make effective use of it.

CHAPTER IV

EPISCOPAL REVENUES, EXPENSES, AND TAXES

Once a bishop had been nominated and confirmed, he could expect to begin collecting the substantial revenues that were associated with most sees. For most people of the early modern period, wealth and the ostentation that wealth permitted were necessary aspects of high office and authority. As much as for any secular office holder, poverty disgraced the cleric, unless he was a member of a mendicant order. Wealth created prestige and produced authority. Thus one justification for pluralism among prelates was that their high offices required a much greater income than could be gained from one benefice.[1]

The range in revenue and property among French bishoprics was enormous, however, and it was extended further by the impact of the religious wars and royal taxation. A few bishops were virtual paupers, unless they had other sources of income, while others could amass fortunes. To a cleric interested only in revenue, becoming the abbot of a wealthy monastery was certainly more attractive than taking on the duties of a poor bishopric. The income of a vast number of abbeys surpassed that of the poorest sees, and often the cathedral chapter of a diocese had greater revenues than its bishop. The wealthiest 10 percent of French bishoprics were, on the other hand, among the most attractive offices in the entire realm; very few secular offices could compare to them.

While most of the very poor sees were tiny dioceses of the Midi, large size and prestige did not necessarily create great revenues.

Albi, which was well below the median in size, gave its bishop an income that placed it among the wealthiest five, while Bourges, one of the largest dioceses in territory, had episcopal revenues below more than a third of all sees. Several of the archbishoprics like Embrun and Aix fell below many of the ordinary bishoprics in income. A bishop's revenues did not always match the prestige and influence that holding an episcopal chair conferred on him.

The episcopal revenues were essentially of two types: those coming directly from the functions of the Church, referred to as spiritual revenues, and those from the bishop's position as seigneur and landlord, called temporal revenues. A major source of spiritual revenue was the *dîme* or tithe. Made mandatory by the Council of Mâcon in 585, reaffirmed by Trent, and protected in civil law by Charlemagne's edict of 779, the dîme was a universal tax on the fruits of the land and on livestock. Because it was imposed originally on a purely agrarian society, the dîme put special emphasis on grains and wine. Despite its name, it was rarely a tenth of production but varied from place to place and from product to product, often being as low as a twentieth or even less.[2]

Although the purpose of the dîme was to provide a living for the churchmen who had the care of souls, especially the curate of the local parish, through the centuries numerous clerics and institutions had gained shares of it. The cathedral chapter, a local monastery, a lay person, could receive a portion or all of a parish's dîme.[3] Since the curé was expected to live off of his share of the dîme, those who took most of the tithe were obliged by a law of 1567 to leave him a basic living (*portion congrue*) of 120 livres, raised to 300 l in 1629.

The bishop was to receive a portion of the dîme of every parish, but he did not always do so. The proportion of the dîme of the diocese that the bishop collected varied from see to see but the most common amount was a fifth. In Languedoc it was frequently a third.[4] In addition to the dîme the bishop received other revenues including a small tax on the curés of the dioceses; fees to help pay for diocesan synods that were often collected regardless of whether a synod was held; a fourth of the income of the cathedral from offerings, indulgences, and Masses for the dead; a one-time fee to help the bishop pay for his bulls of office and entry ceremony; and procuration, which was lodging and hospitality when he visited a church in the diocese.[5] Also he received the income of vacant benefices, a fee for filling a benefice, and various fees for the use of the episcopal chancellery. From the administration of the ecclesiastical courts he received fines and fees for the reconciliation of excommunicates and desecrated churches.[6] In all the bishop's income was usually between 30 and 40 percent of the total spiritual revenues of a diocese.

Usually substantially higher than the income from the spiritual functions of a bishop were the revenues from the land and properties that he controlled. In 1549 the bishop of Gap received 1,050 écus (2,625 livres) in spiritual revenues while from his lands he gained 1,712 écus (4,280 livres) and 1,080 saumées of wheat and a quantity of other grains, worth about 11,000 livres.[7] The Church had accumulated enormous amounts of land and financial rights since the early Middle Ages. Fiefs granted by the king or great nobles; land or houses given in penance, in wills, or as a pious act; and property seized from convicted heretics all combined to give bishops a large proportion of French property. In Languedoc the seizure of property of the Cathari helped to give a number of bishoprics in that region revenues far beyond those of their equally small neighbors. These property revenues help explain why bishoprics like Albi, Cahors, Rodez, and Toulouse had incomes well above average.

On the other hand sees that because of size or prestige might be thought to have had vast revenues had smaller incomes because of the presence of powerful and long-established monasteries that had received much of the land given to the Church and were true rivals to the bishop in prestige and wealth. In Paris Saint-Germain-des-Prés and Saint-Denis both had incomes well above that of the bishop, and at Reims the presence of Saint-Remi clearly reduced the episcopal revenues although the archbishop was usually its abbot as well. In numerous sees the cathedral chapters also had more property than the bishop; at Bordeaux, for example, the chapter was the largest landholder of the region. Those bishoprics that had major feudal titles attached were more likely to have high incomes since the titles indicated control of extensive lands and fiefs. Another source of episcopal income were the fines collected in the seigneurial courts that the bishop controlled as temporal lord of the cathedral city and estates in the diocese. As lords of the episcopal cities, such bishops also had chancelleries that provided notary services for fees. In 1550 the bishop of Lodève made a contract for the farming of fees for notarizing at 300 livres a year.[8] Those bishop-seigneurs likely also had the right to collect tolls on commerce and sales taxes on goods sold in the city. The archbishop of Lyon, for example, collected the *ban d'aoust* on wine sold in the city. Yet another source of income was the bishop's control over the right to fish in the rivers, which, for example, gave the bishop of Rennes 850 l in 1586.[9]

In the early sixteenth century the bishops depended on their *receveurs* to collect their revenues and to sell what was paid in kind. By mid-century, however, they turned more to farming out their temporal revenues for a set sum contracted for several years, ensuring a more stable income. Thus in 1604 the bishop of Nantes, Charles de Bourgneuf, farmed his temporal revenues for 8,500 l annually during a three-year contract.[10]

Three factors, however, badly complicate the effort to determine the total revenues of the French bishops and to make comparisons among them. The first is simply the lack of complete records for most of the bishoprics; especially scarce are accounts of spiritual revenues. The records of temporal revenues from fiefs and properties are considerably more common. The second problem is the way in which extant records usually indicate income both in silver and in kind. The accounts in silver are in various coins such as the florin of Provence, and the produce in numerous differing systems of measurements.[11] The third difficulty is that the accounts of revenues are usually for a single year or a short series of years, making it difficult to assess the change in revenue over the sixteenth century. The years covered in the sources vary greatly from see to see; thus comparisons among the sees are not truly valid because of the price rise of the era.

For these reasons one must look to the rolls of taxes assessed by both the papacy and the monarchy to get a sense of the range of revenues across the French episcopate. It was on the sum of all these episcopal revenues that the papacy imposed a tax paid at the time of the confirmation of a bishop called the *common services* and the monarchy collected the *décime*. The former were calculated as a third of the annual revenues of a bishop as found in a book of assessments kept by the curia. These assessments were more than two centuries old by 1550. They ranged from 100 florins (a papal florin was roughly the equivalent of a livre) for sees like Bayonne and Vence to 10,000 for Auch and 12,000 for Rouen.[12] The décime was a royal tax, or as the clergy preferred to put it, a gift, of one-tenth of the income of every benefice in the realm. The décime (which will be discussed at greater length below) dated back to the twelfth century, but François I, determined to make it a permanent and regular tax, created a department of benefices in 1516.[13] Its purpose was to determine the revenues of every benefice and impose the tax. The revenues of benefices were calculated at less than their true value, perhaps as low as half, and each diocese was assessed a specific sum, after which a diocesan assembly met to determine the share for each benefice holder. The burden of the décime fell more heavily on the lesser clergy while the greater benefice holders such as the bishop and the chapter escaped with a lesser proportion of their income.[14] Cardinals were exempt from the décime.

It is clear that neither the curia's roll of taxes nor the king's *département* of 1516 is an accurate account, when multiplied by the proper factor, of the revenues of the French bishops. Somewhat more accurate was the roll of décimes of 1563. In theory it was simply a fourfold assessment of the sums levied in 1516, but it is evident that considerable adjustments were made that made it a better indicator of the relative wealth of the bishops.[15] Thus, for example, in 1549 the treasurer of the archbishop of Rouen placed his revenues at 31,277 l; his décime in 1563 was 3,180 l. The revenues of the bishop of Gap were in 1563 about 18,000 l; his

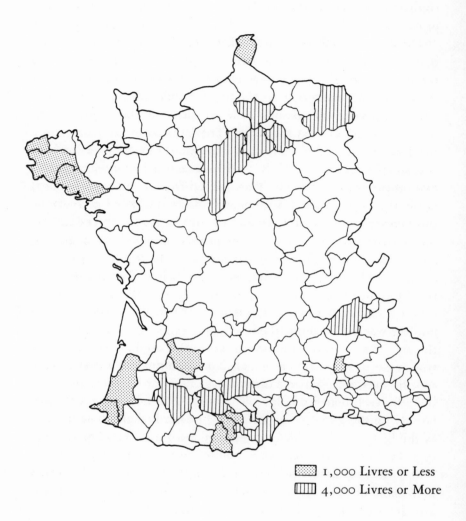

1,000 Livres or Less
4,000 Livres or More

MAP III

BISHOPRICS WITH THE HIGHEST AND

LOWEST DECIMES, 1563

décime was 1,908 l. The revenues of the bishopric of Dax were put at 4,000 l; its décime was 380 l. On the other hand the income of the bishop of Agen was reported to be 7,951 l already in 1521; yet his décime in 1563 was only 318 l.[16] Clearly the roll of 1563 was not a completely accurate assessment of episcopal revenues.

Although the proportion of a diocese's total décime that a number of bishops paid was well under 10 percent, the average of the 106 sees listed in 1563 was 18 percent.[17] There is no clear pattern to determine whether a bishop's share would be high or low, but several bishops of the Midi paid over a third of their diocese's assessment. In general the lower a diocese's total décime, the more likely the bishop paid a large proportion of it. The sample of 106 dioceses is large enough that one can take as generally accurate the figure that the bishops paid 18 percent of the total décimes. One has to add several percentage points to that to account for the tendency of the bishops to underpay in order to determine their true proportion of the total diocesan revenues. But it is probable that the episcopacy received about one-fifth of the total income available to the French Church.

The bishop of Chartres, at 12,720 l, had the highest décime in the episcopate at a time when a skilled laborer earned from 150 to 200 livres a year.[18] The archbishop of Reims paid the same sum, but his assessment included the abbey of Saint-Remi, which contributed almost half of his revenues. Other bishoprics with high décimes included Toulouse at 9,540 l and Paris, Albi, Narbonne, and Auch, all between 6,000 and 7,000 l. The sees with the lowest décimes were Boulogne at 254 l, Agen at 318 l, and Mirepoix at 343 l. The average episcopal décime in 1563 was 3,034 l, but the median was considerably lower at 2,088 l.

The décime of many bishoprics was higher than the annual salary of the first president of the Parlement of Rouen, which in 1570 was 3,000 l, although he did have other sources of revenue associated with the office. A conseiller of the Parlement of Paris drew only 600 l. In 1557 the average salary of the governors of the major provinces received from the *Epargne* was 18,750 l. In 1560 Anne de Montmorency took 32,000 l as *gages* for his several major offices. And in 1582 Henri III set the rate of annual revenues necessary for the creation of a duchy-peerage at 24,000 l.[19] Even if one cannot simply multiply a bishopric's décime of 1563 by ten to get its true income, it is clear that at least a third of the bishoprics had revenues above 24,000 l. Ironically one of those that did not was the episcopal peerage of Laon.

Comparison with the revenues of the English episcopate is also instructive. The "Valor Ecclesiasticus" of 1535, before the English Church lost much of its property, placed the average episcopal income at £1,335 and the median at £1,050. The greatest revenues were those of the bishopric of Winchester at £3,885 and the least, Bangor at £132. Both the inflation of the era and the changing exchange rate complicate any comparison between the revenues of English bishops in 1535 and the role of décimes of 1563; nonetheless, using the exchange rate of 9.2 livres to the pound sterling in 1535, it appears that the French episcopate had greater revenues. This is supported by the curia's assessments for both kingdoms in which the French bishops were assessed an average of 10 percent higher than their English counterparts, although it is true that those assessments were two centuries old. On the other hand the much smaller average Italian see had a curial assessment of less than 10 percent of the average French bishopric.[20]

Despite their often substantial incomes, the French bishops did not have the highest taxed benefices in many dioceses. The cathedral chapter was often assessed at an equal (thirty dioceses) or higher rate (twenty-five dioceses), although one must bear in mind that the chapter was a collection of benefices. At Chartres the chapter's décime was 19,060 l, the highest assessment in the French Church. At Auxerre the dean of the chapter was assessed at the same rate as the bishop. Numerous monasteries were taxed more heavily than their bishops. Saint-Denis in Paris was assessed a tax 4,000 l higher than the bishop's; the tax of Saint-Martin of Tours at 4,422 l was nearly double the bishop's at 2,544 l. In the see of Béziers the priory of Cassan paid a décime greater than either the bishop or the chapter.

Very often, however, bishops were the abbots of such monasteries so that their incomes were enhanced substantially, although the abbott's share of the abbey's income was usually on the order of a third. The practice of allowing bishops to serve as abbots and priors *in commendam*, unlike holding plural sees, was never seriously challenged in the sixteenth century. The term was used to refer to secular clerics or lay persons holding benefices that a regular cleric was supposed to fill. Although numerous regular benefices could be held *in commendam*, the term usually referred to a secular cleric holding the most lucrative position, that of abbot. As has been noted above, 30 percent of the bishops appointed in the period from 1547 to 1589 continued to hold abbeys in trust after their confirmation as prelates. Many others gained such benefices while in office.[21] At least 41 percent of the bishops in office in 1559 held commendatory monasteries.

The great churchmen always had many such benefices; the cardinals and other prelates favored by the crown or the papacy were likely to have five or more monasteries. The Cardinal de Tournon was abbot of twenty-four abbeys at one time and twenty-seven during his career.[22] Odet de Châtillon held sixteen monasteries at once. The revenues of the Cardinal de Lorraine, Charles de Guise, have been estimated at 300,000 l a year for 1550. His see of Reims netted him less than a third of that; his eleven monasteries including Saint-Remi of Reims, Cluny, and Saint-Denis of Paris made up the remainder. Less well-placed bishops also increased their incomes substantially from commendatory benefices. Renaud de Beaune of Mende had revenues in 1578 of 20,000 l from four abbeys he held as well as an annual average of 3,700 l from his position as chancellor for the Duc d'Alençon.[23] The better-placed a bishop was, the more likely he held both a wealthy bishopric and several lucrative monasteries. The bishops of the poorer sees who probably needed the extra income were less likely to have additional benefices.

Computation of a bishop's income from a knowledge of the revenues of his bishopric and commendatory monasteries is, however, badly complicated by the practice of pension taking that could substantially increase the income of a bishop or, as was more likely, greatly reduce it. There were two types of pensions: those "with cause" were created by the churchmen who held the benefice; those "without cause" were created by the king or a lay patron. The reasons for providing the former type included settling a dispute over a benefice by giving one of the claimants a pension on its revenues while the other filled it. An example of this occurred at Marseille in 1550. Julius III had named his nephew, Christoforo del Monte, while Henri II had nominated François Balaguier. The latter eventually was given a pension of 1,000 l on Marseille to settle the dispute. An identical situation occurred in 1570 over the abbey of Jard after the death of the Cardinal de Babou at Rome. The pope gave the benefice to Hannibal Ruccelai, bishop of Carcassone, and the king to Giovanni Alamani of Mâcon. Alamani eventually was installed in the abbey and Ruccelai took a 1,400 l pension on it.[24]

The usual reason for a pension *cum causa* was the resignation of the benefice holder who in his notice of resignation asked the collator of the benefice for approval of a pension. The collator, who for the episcopacy was the king, had the right to refuse a pension, but it appears that he rarely did. The fiction that the collator granted the pension freely as a favor to the resignee, that he was under no obligation to do so, was used to counter accusations of simony in the arrangement. Once the collator approved of a pension, the new incumbent of the benefice did have a legal obligation to pay it.

A pension could be imposed whether the resignation was simple or *in favorem*. The latter could involve an exchange of benefices in which the revenues of one benefice were not as great as the other's. When Martin de Beaune gave up Le Puy to Antoine de Sennetaire in 1561 for an abbey, he kept a pension of 2,500 l on the bishopric. The most common type of pension was the result of a resignation *in favorem* in which the new bishop, with the approval of the king and the pope, agreed to give part of the see's revenues to his benefactor. Resignations with pensions were especially prevalent during the middle decades of the sixteenth century. The French cardinals, forced to concede their multiple sees, took large pensions on their surrendered bishoprics. Jean Du Bellay, for example, in giving up four sees took some 43,000 l a year in pensions.

Canon law dictated that only one-third of a benefice's revenues could be given out as a pension; another third was to go to the incumbent; and the last third was for upkeep of the buildings. This rule was blatantly ignored. Pensions of one-half or two-thirds of the revenues, of all but 1,000 l, or even all the revenues (*cum reservatione omnium fructuum*) were not uncommon. Even if the resigning bishop took only a small part of the revenues, the rapid turnover of bishops in some sees, each taking a pension, caused the sum of the pensions to mount. At Narbonne the pensions of Ippolyto d'Este at 1,000 écus and of François de Tournon at one-half of the revenues amounted to 60 percent of the bishop's revenues in 1552. The pensions for past bishops could continue for decades and through the terms of several bishops. The Cardinal d'Armagnac collected all but 1,000 l of the revenues of Rodez well into the term of the third bishop to succeed him. Louis I de Guise held on to his pension of 10,000 l on Albi through three successors despite an effort in 1578 by Giulio de Medici to have the pope end it.[25]

The pension *sine causa* was given to a third person by the lay collator of the benefice, which in the case of a bishopric was the king. The Gallican liberties had effectively quashed the right of the papacy to create pensions on French benefices, although a few granted by Rome do appear. The pope did, however, have veto power over pensions in consistorial benefices and occasionally denied them. One such denial involved a proposed pension of 2,000 l on the revenues of Arles for a military captain.[26] The right of the king to assign pensions even to laymen was one of the most useful ways that he had to reward or buy service and loyalty since these pensions required nothing of the grantee except accepting the money. While the monarchy was responsible for most of the pensions given to individuals who had no direct connection with the bishoprics involved, some were created by the churchmen themselves with royal approval.

One of the more frank descriptions of how the king used pensions and episcopal appointments came from Henri IV when he heard of the death of the Cardinal Charles II de Bourbon in 1594:

Many people have asked for his remains [his benefices]. I told everyone that they are already disposed of. Will you see if you can persuade the abbé of Tiron to swap for the archbishopric of Rouen, which is worth 30,000 livres a year at least? He could take care of the chevalier d'Oyse by paying him an annual pension of 4,000 écus from the archbishopric's income. As for the abbey of Saint-Ouen, I will reward one of my servants with it, but whoever gets the abbey will have to pay a pension of 10,000 livres annually to you [his finance minister].[27]

The great churchmen and cardinals, especially the Italians, benefited the most from pensions *sine causa*. It was a way of gaining their support without imposing the burden of a bishopric on them or facing the popular disapproval for placing yet another Italian in a French see. Thus Cardinal Giovanni Salviati had pensions of 4,000 l on Albi and 1,000 écus on Auch (of which he had never been bishop) as well as 1,000 écus from Saint-Papoul which he resigned in 1549. Carlo Strozzi was given a 2,000 l pension on Albi without serving as its prelate. Cardinal Simonetta, for a short time bishop of Quimper, which he resigned for a pension of 800 écus in 1560, also received 3,000 l from the see of Lisieux. French cardinals could do as well. Louis de Guise took pensions of 10,000 l from Albi, 6,000 l from Condom, and one-half the revenues of Sens. He had served as bishop only of Albi. The revenues of Narbonne were burdened not only with the pensions of its several former bishops but also of 1,000 écus apiece to three churchmen who had never served there. Even the poet Joachim Du Bellay had a pension of 2,000 l on Le Mans in 1559.

Royal pensions given to laymen became a problem during the reign of Henri II. According to Robert Tattegrain, the king would leave the name of the pensioners blank when submitting consistorial nominations to the Holy See to avoid the possibility of the papacy vetoing them. Henri used such pensions to repay Italian bankers such as Piero del Bene who received 500 l from Lodève after his son was named its bishop. Charles IX and Henri III were more likely to give pensions to military captains. The assembly of clergy protested sharply to the king in 1598, 1608, and again in 1610 about the pensions given to laymen. In 1610 Henri IV

agreed to end the practice.[28] Earlier complaints against lay pensioners had been voiced by Guillaume Ruzé of Angers in 1576 and
Arnaud de Pontac of Béziers in 1579.[29]

As a result of the innumerable pensions, some created by the
incumbent bishops, others imposed on them, the income from
about one-half of the French bishoprics was at a given time reduced
considerably. The wealthier sees of the Midi were the most likely to
be burdened by multiple pensions.

In conjunction with the ravages of the religious wars, the pensions created serious difficulties for a number of bishops who were
obliged to pay the pensions first from what revenues they received.
In 1584 Bertrand de Barrau of Pamiers requested of the king that
the burden of pensions on his revenues be discharged or reduced
because the religious strife had reduced his income to less than the
pensions the bishopric was obliged to pay.[30] In 1572 Jean de Fay,
newly appointed to Poitiers, asked Rome to give him his bulls of
office free of the usual fees because war and a 10,000 l pension for
his predecessor had so severely reduced the episcopal income.[31]

In the see of Lodève Claude Briçonnet resigned in 1566 in favor
of his nephew Pierre de Barrault, reserving half of the revenues,
the titles of seigneur of Lodève and count of Montbrun, and the
use of the episcopal palace. After Barrault died in 1569, the new
bishop, Alfonso Vercelli, found himself in a difficult situation with
most of the bishop's revenues and power as well as his palace still in
Briçonnet's hands. Vercelli took the matter to the Parlement of
Toulouse. It is not clear if he gained any satisfaction, but Briçonnet
continued to serve as seigneur of the city until the Huguenots
drove him out in 1573. Jean de Barbanzon, having publicly converted to Protestantism, resigned Pamiers in 1557 to Robert de
Pellevé for a pension of 1,000 l. It was not paid, and Barbanzon
sent his procurer to Pamiers to secure it. When that failed, he
appealed successfully to the Parlement of Toulouse.[32] Becoming a
Huguenot was not a strong enough reason for denying a former
benefice holder his pension.

This point was made more clear by a protracted dispute in the
Parlements of Grenoble and Paris over the payment of a pension of

2,000 l taken by Gabriel de Clermont of Gap when he resigned his see in 1567 after his conversion to Calvinism. The new bishop, Pierre de Paparin, refused to pay the pension because Clermont was a heretic and the revenues of the bishopric had been depeleted by religious strife. The judicial bodies ordered Paparin to pay the pension in 1577, but he still refused. The royal council sought to settle the issue by reducing the sum owed to Clermont proportional to Paparin's loss of revenues. Clermont agreed to accept 10,000 l on a debt that by 1581 totalled 28,000 l.[33] Clermont's Protestantism was not a sufficient reason to deny him his pension. Clearly pensions were an unavoidable expense that often substantially reduced the real income of a bishop.

Another unavoidable expense of office, which even the most irresponsible prelate had to pay, was the fee for the bulls of office. This fee, often called the *annates*, was more properly known as the common services. France, however, had been given a reduction to one-sixth of the annual revenues instead of the usual one-third.[34] The common services were divided between the pope and the cardinals.

In addition there were a number of other fees. One was called the *petty services*, equal to one-eighth of the common services, which were divided among the papal chancery and other offices of the papal court. Other fees amounted to about one-tenth of the common services. The new bishop was also expected to give a gratuity worth 15 percent of the common services to the cardinal protector who presented his candidacy in consistory and small gratuities to various other prelates and clerics who were involved in expediting the episcopal bulls. Most but not all of the fees for French bishops were reduced by half as were the common services. The dioceses of the *pays d'obédience* did not have that privilege and paid the full services.[35]

Since the king had been taking the revenues of a vacant see *en économat*, a new bishop occasionally had great difficulty in paying the services. Excommunication was the penalty for failing to pay. An episcopal candidate often had to go to bankers for loans, and such debts burdened these bishops for years to come. One episcopal nominee, to Tarbes in 1575, did not procure the money for the bulls and lost the see.[36] In numerous cases after 1560, however, the papacy did grant a reduction or even the elimination of the services to a number of bishops. Their entries in the "Acta Consistorialia" include such phrases as "to whom one-half [or one-third] of the rights of the Sacred College are given gratis" or "to whom the bulls are expedited gratis." Some 8 percent of the bishops appointed between 1560 and 1589 were granted a reduction of the annates, and another 7 percent received their bulls gratis. In one case, involving the appointee to Autun in 1588, the curia agreed not to require the annates because the see had been vacated twice in a year. In several other cases the nuncios asked for reduced fees or none at all for episcopal nominees.[37]

New archbishops had the additional burden of the fees for receiving the pallium, the symbol of their office. The archbishop was expected to go to Rome to receive it, and the provisions and ceremony cost about 1,000 florins. If he did go to Rome, he also had to pay a visitation tax to the pope that varied in amount. For Bourges it was 300 florins. If the newly-seated archbishop remained in his see, the pallium had to be sent to him. Some of the fees were the same as if he had received it in Rome, but the bishop who brought it to him received 1,000 l.[38]

Newly consecrated prelates also had to pay a fee to the king for registering the letter ending régale, the royal governance of a vacant diocese. The rates for the sixteenth century are not available, but in 1673 they ranged from 200 l to 1,200 l.[39] The formal entry of a new bishop into his cathedral city was also expensive. Although much of the expense was met by the local notables, the new bishop had to give gifts to them and alms to the poor. Last, he had to pay feudal dues to the king to assume his rights as fief holder. The bishop of Dax in Gascony paid 1,000 l for fiefs held in low justice in 1556.[40] Obviously these dues for the bishoprics with extensive titles and jurisdiction were much higher. Although many a new bishop went deeply into debt in order to take his episcopal chair, a bishop usually did not have to make major expenditures from the episcopal income from year to year. The net of his income, if not

too heavily burdened by pensions, enabled him to pay off the loans
for his bulls and to begin to accumulate a small fortune, at least if
he were in a wealthier bishopric. The annual expenses in 1544 of
the archbishop of Rouen, Georges d'Amboise, were 9,374 l when
his revenues reached 31,277 l. Among the expenses were 3,588 l
to repair the tower of the cathedral (an unusually high expense),
5,000 l to his vicars and secretaries, 300 l for alms, 72 l for gold
leaf, and 24 l for copies of the papal bull convoking the Council of
Trent. The sums for charity varied considerably from year to year;
that of 1544 was unusually low. In 1523 the archbishop donated
1,000 l in alms; in 1526, 1,016 because of the poor harvest; in
1550, 500 l, a common amount.[41] One must ask, however, whether
giving less than 2 percent to charity was being generous.

Part of the justification for the substantial episcopal revenues
was that the bishop's almoners were responsible for poor relief,
drawing income for charity from the bishops. In some dioceses the
income from specific episcopal properties was set aside for charity
as, for example, at Limoges where four tenancies funded the poor
relief.[42] Beyond that certain bishops had reputations for their generosity to the poor. The most noted example was Cardinal Jean de
Lorraine who, according to an often repeated story, had such a
reputation in Rome for his generosity that when he gave a great
handful of gold coins to a blind beggar, the man exclaimed: "you
must be Jesus Christ himself or surely the Cardinal de Lorraine."
Guillaume Du Blanc of Vence established the custom of providing
the dowry for a needy girl on the feast of the city's patron. He was
said to have "come to Vence wealthy and left poor" because of his
charity. At Apt François de Simiane was reported to have turned
the episcopal properties into a patrimony for the poor, and at
Cahors Jean de La Rochefoucauld was known as "the father of the
poor."[43]

More commonly the bishops followed the medieval practice of
being most generous at the time of death, providing for the poor in
their wills. Three of the sixteenth-century bishops of Châlons
included the poor in their wills, ranging from 1,100 livres provided for the education of poor children by Jérôme de Bourges to

20,000 l set apart by Côme Clause for a foundation for the poor.[44] At Aire, François de Foix's will provided 1,000 écus for the poor as well as any money forthcoming from payment of debts owed him. Another bishop of Gascony, François de Noailles, provided money in his final testament of 1585 for the Churches of Noailles and Dax, and 250 écus in rentes for the poor. His brother Giles, who succeeded François as bishop of Dax, also left money to the same churches but failed to mention the poor. Bishop Antoine Vialiart of Bourges left all of his fortune to the poor except for 1,000 l for the cathedral. He also willed his library to the University of Bourges. While not mentioning the poor, Charles de Bourgneuf of Nantes left his private library to the Pères de l'Oratoire; it became the basis of the public library of Nantes.[45]

On the other hand some bishops desisted from charity even at death. The testament of César de Bourguignon of Limoges made no charitable bequest of any kind. But the most notorious example of episcopal hard-heartedness involved Silvio de Santa Croce of Arles, who refused to aid the victims of the great 1580 flood of the Rhone until the Parlement of Aix compelled him to do so.[46]

Perhaps it was in part because of such a lack of generosity in charity that a number of bishops appear to have accumulated fortunes while in office. Some bishops brought lands and seigneuries and added them to the episcopal patrimony, as did Jean-Baptiste Raimbaud de Simiane of Apt.[47] The Cardinal de Lorraine brought the duchy of Chevreuse from the Duchesse d'Étampes in 1552 along with the Château of Meudon that passed into the patrimony of the archbishop of Reims.[48] Another piece of evidence of accumulated episcopal fortunes was the loan making of Guillaume Pellicier of Montpellier whose family was unlikely to have provided him with the money for such activity. Until his death in 1567 he had several large loans out, including one of 7,000 l to the cathedral chapter at 8.33 percent interest. His successor collected the debt after his death. On the other hand Melun d'Ihiers of Luçon bought a château in 1549 for 8,000 l without deeding it to the bishopric. After his death his lay heirs received a part of it as did his successor and nephew, René de Daillon Du Lude. After several years of conflict over the château, Daillon paid 2,400 l to gain control of their share.[49]

A benefice holder had complete control over his revenues; he answered to no one about how they were used. Bishops far too often spent them in unedifying ways and failed to expend them for more worthy causes such as repairing the cathedrals, which failure was the source of numerous suits filed in the Parlements by the chapters. As the spirit of reform and secularism spread in France, the great revenues of the bishops and their often irresponsible use led to demands that the Church provide financial support for the government.

Legally exempt from civil taxes, the clergy could agree to provide financial aid to the monarchy if the common good required it. The décimes began with the Crusades, and the first formal clerical tenth in 1188 was called the *saladin* because of its use for the Third Crusade. Numerous décimes were collected in the next three centuries but always by consent of the clergy or at least the bishops. In 1516, however, Leo X granted François I a décime for a crusade against the Turks without the consent of the French clergy. François, determined to make the tax permanent, created a *département général des décimes* and appointed royal commissioners from among the clerics in the Parlement of Paris to determine the assessments and collect them. This clerical tenth brought in 379,651 l, although the king paid for the expenses of collecting it. The clergy paid the expenses of collecting future décimes.[50]

With Church income estimated at about six million livres, the décime of 1516 was closer to being a twentieth, and as has been noted above, the bishops' share of the contribution was clearly less than that. The high clergy were not heavily burdened by the décimes and agreed relatively easily to new levies on a regular basis. By 1532 the décime was being imposed virtually every year. Intermixed among the years of one décime were years that the king demanded two or more at one time. In 1521 François I asked for three décimes; in 1527, four. Four décimes became the standard levy from 1542 to 1558 except for the years that Henri II levied two (1550) and eight (1557).[51] For a majority of bishops four décimes were close to being a true tenth of their incomes; for some the eight of 1557 did not go much beyond a tenth. The lower clergy was much harder hit but was in no position to refuse to pay.

The mechanism for gaining approval of the royal request for "a gift of a tenth" varied from year to year until 1561. After 1516 the papacy was no longer directly involved, although as late as 1533 the clergy asked Rome for permission to grant the royal request, often after it had already been collected. On occasion approval was given by the general assembly of French clergy, more often by assemblies of bishops, but most often by provincial and diocesan assemblies. Letters were sent to the dioceses explaining the need for the money, usually war, and declaring the number of décimes the clergy had to raise. Resistance was rare. In 1516 the Norman clergy objected, citing the tax immunity of the clergy, but paid anyway. The archbishop of Rouen, Georges d'Amboise, refused to pay the décime demanded in 1521 on the grounds that the money was meant for the clerics and the poor. The king drew up an *arrêt* for his imprisonment but was dissuaded by d'Amboise's friends. François eventually required the canons and the archbishop's vicars to collect the décime. In 1535 François was forced to draw up letters patent to order the seizure of Church property after a number of refusals to grant the three décimes demanded in the previous year. The threat was sufficient to persuade the clergy to pay.[52]

Even the numerous décimes that totalled about 40,000,000 l up to 1559 did not satisfy the king's need to raise money from the clergy. In 1552 Henri II called a meeting of five cardinals and about thirty bishops to raise funds for the war against Charles V. They agreed to a new levy of 1,400,000 l to be raised through a tax of 20 livres on every church steeple. At that rate, in order to raise that large a sum, there had to be 70,000 church steeples in France. The diocese of Rouen had 1,433 steeples producing a sum of 31,269 l, including the cost of collecting the levy.[53]

When Henri II died in 1559 and the Guises took control of the government, the financial crisis became public knowledge. The Estates-general met at Orléans in 1560 to help solve it. The monarchy announced that it was in debt in the amount of

43,500,000 l, nearly half of which needed to be repaid immediately. The monarchy and the Second and Third Estates looked to the clergy to provide most of the funds needed. One plan proposed by the deputies of the Third Estate was essentially a progressive income tax on the clerics.[54] Those clerics with incomes of less than 400 l a year were not to be taxed. Churchmen with incomes above that were to be taxed on a scale from 25 to 75 percent. In addition, maximum incomes were to be set at 6,000 l for bishops, 8,000 l for archbishops, and 12,000 l for cardinals with the seizure of all revenue above those figures. A second, more drastic plan called for an inventory and sale of all Church property except for the buildings used for worship and one house for each benefice holder. The value of Church property that was to be sold under that scheme was estimated at 120,000,000 l.[55]

These schemes, the most drastic to be considered until 1789 when a plan similar to the second was adopted, terrified the clergy. Certainly the clerics were more willing to contribute when the estates met again in 1561, the clergy at Poissy and the other two estates at Pontoise. The churchmen at Poissy included some fifty bishops and one hundred abbots and theologians gathered to discuss the state of religion in France. It was essentially the national council that a number of Catholics as well as the Reformers had been demanding for some time. The assembly is best known for the Colloquy of Poissy, the debate between Catholic leaders and several Calvinists led by Theodore Beza. But after the theological dialogue broke up in failure, the Catholic clergy stayed on to work out the details of the Contract of Poissy, signed on October 21, 1561.[56] In it the clergy agreed to provide 1,600,000 l a year for six years to enable the king to buy back sources of royal income that had been alienated. After the first six years of the contract, the clergy agreed to provide 1,300,000 l a year for ten years largely to redeem the rentes (a form of annuity) created in the Hôtel de ville of Paris.[57] Interest on these rentes came from various royal taxes collected in Paris that had been alienated to the Hôtel de ville. It was anticipated that the second part of the contract would enable the king to buy back all of the rentes of Paris.

The Contract of Poissy pledged the Church to produce 22,000,000 l over sixteen years for the royal treasury. In return the king promised not to ask for any further subsidies from the Church during the duration of the contract. The churchmen were to supervise the collection of the funds and bear the expense. Thus they avoided the detailed assessment of the Church property and revenues that the other estates had demanded and the clergy greatly feared. Disputes over clerical obligations were to be settled in Church courts. In the long run the most significant of the concessions from the monarchy that the clergy gained from the contract was its recognition that the subsidies were *dons gratuits*, not taxes. This device enabled the clergy to maintain greater control over its payments to the government. It gave the clergy a legitimate pretense for calling general assemblies to agree to new gifts to the monarchy. Thus a general assembly met in 1567 at the beginning of the second part of the Contract of Poissy and met again in 1573, 1579, and 1585. Through this fiction the general assembly of the clergy continued to be called throughout the *Ancien Régime*, long after the Estates-general had become moribund. The pope's assent to the contract of 1563 was procured on the promise to end any thought of a French national council.

The assembled clergy in 1561 created the office of receiver general of the décimes who supervised their collection across the realm. Chosen from the great financiers of Paris because he had to advance great sums to the king, he was paid 12,000 l a year and interest on his advances. He sent out his agents to gather the décimes from the diocesan receiver appointed by the local clergy. The diocesan receiver had the right to call upon the royal sergeants for seizure of the property of recalcitrant clerics. In 1564 the king gave the clergy permission to have its own syndics at court to handle cases arising from the Contract of Poissy. For the most part, therefore, the churchmen had their own agents handling the décimes and any litigation involving them.[58]

Writing in 1581, Nicolas Froumenteau estimated the clergy's annual revenues—what it was entitled to, not necessarily what it actually collected—at 18,200,000 l.[59] Given the price rise of the era, the 1,600,000 l of the contract was, therefore, close to a true tenth in 1561. The annual sum was referred to as four décimes. Since the clergy had been paying an average of four décimes a year since 1545, the contract was no more burdensome. The smallest sum owed by the bishops was 318 l, by the prelates of Mirepoix and Agen. The latter likely was a true tenth; the former certainly was not but still an improvement over the 50 l that the bishop had paid under the *département* of 1516. The bishops paid a total of 318,576 l according to the roll of 1563 or 21 percent of the 1,600,000 l. That latter sum constituted about 9 percent of the monarchy's estimated income in that era of 18,000,000 l.[60]

Much to the clergy's distress, the monarchy quickly found that the money provided in the Contract of Poissy came nowhere near filling its need for funds. The regent, Catherine de Medici, urgently seeking new revenues to pay for the first war with the Huguenots, resorted principally to the forced alienation of Church property, putting into practice on a small scale what the *Tiers* had advocated earlier. An edict of May, 1563, ordered the clergy to sell enough property to create rentes worth 100,000 écus yearly at the standard interest of 8.33 percent. This meant that benefice holders had to sell revenue-producing holdings worth 1,200,000 écus or 3,600,000 l.[61] The *département* of 1516 largely determined the amount for each *bénéficier*. The clerics could sell fiefs, land, buildings, seigneurial rights, or rents. If a churchman had enough cash on hand to meet his assessment, he did not have to sell any property. Places of worship and charity and the lands used to support the parish curés were exempted. Only Catholics could buy the alienated Church properties, but in the Midi this requirement was far from enforced.[62]

Both the clergy and the Parlement of Paris strongly opposed the edict. The latter was not only strongly Catholic, it was also opposed to any breach of property rights. The king had to appear in person in the Parlement to gain the edict's registration. Both groups, however, did recognize the need to fund an army to battle the Huguenots. The religious war made necessary what shortly before would have been unthinkable. The religious strife affected most seriously the poor dioceses of the south that were most adversely affected by the new tax as well. Some of the northern dioceses had to sell little or no property.[63] The bishops of the Midi tried to mobilize their influence against the alienations at a provincial assembly of Narbonne in July, 1563. They vowed to take legal action against the royal commissioners who were to supervise the sale of Church property and to write remonstrances to the court, the pope, and the bishops at Trent.[64]

Nonetheless the sale of clerical property proceeded, and many bishops were forced to sell much of theirs. Guillaume Pellicier, the bishop of Montpellier, sold the barony of Sauve for 12,500 l. In Mende Nicolas Dangu had to give up a seigneurie for 3,200 l and local rents worth 850 l.[65] At Vannes, the sale of the bishop's *métairie* of Brillac brought in 8,004 l, by far the largest of the seven sales of his property that totalled 8,615 l. The bishop of Bourges sold eight parcels for 20,292 l, including a seigneurie for 10,400 l. The father of Guillaume de Saluste bought an estate called Le Bartas from the bishop of Lombès, thus enabling his poet-son to call himself Sieur Du Bartas.[66]

Bishops alienated rights to administer justice and collect tolls as the bishops of Lyon and Gap did. Others sold their abbacies to raise the sum demanded by the monarchy as did François de Bohier of Saint-Malo, selling a priory in Poitiers that had a net annual income of 2,600 l.[67] On the other hand some clerics such as Antoine Erlault of Chalon-sur-Saône and the cathedral chapter at Rouen took advantage of the alienations to buy property themselves. One who did so more blatantly, only a year before he was stripped of his benefices for heresy, was the Cardinal de Châtillon.[68]

The alienation of Church property had been ordered without permission of the papacy. Permission was, however, sought, and Pius IV, told that the money was needed for a war against the heretics, readily consented. He did require that the clerics be given the opportunity to repurchase what they had sold. Faced as well by a loud chorus of protest from the French clergy, the court agreed in January, 1564, to allow repurchasing for a year's time. The royal commissioners, in their zeal to accomplish their task, had often sold the best properties that the benefice holders had.

Thus it was to the clergy's advantage to buy them back. The churchmen began selling some of their less valuable properties to raise the money for repurchase. The alienated property was to be sold back at the original price, but many of the purchasers refused to give it up, often having made very good bargains. Litigation over some property lasted well past the year allowed for repurchase. Eventually a final date of May, 1567, was set.

At Montpellier Pellicier sold a small farm (a *métairie*) that was not a fief in order to repurchase more valuable land. By 1567 he had enough money to repurchase his lost barony, but the purchaser refused to give it up and cut down timber in the meantime. The local presidial judge decided in the prelate's favor, and Pellicier retook possession of it in early 1568, shortly before his death.[69]

Because the bishops were underassessed in the *département* of 1516, they had to sell less property to meet their tax than did most benefice holders. Unless they were faced by overly-zealous commissioners who sold more than was necessary (in some dioceses, they oversold three- or fourfold), the bishops as a group had to sell rather little. A large number had enough cash at hand to avoid selling anything at all.

In 1567 the first part of the Contract of Poissy was completed. Charles IX, still facing enormous financial problems, tried to force the clergy to continue to pay 1,600,000 l of the first part as well to contribute the 1,300,000 l a year of the second part. The clergy dissuaded him by offering a lump sum of 700,000 l in addition to the 1,300,000 l for 1568.[70] The loss of 300,000 l annually when other royal revenues were falling and expenses rising because of the religious strife had to be made good. Charles IX resorted to a second forced alienation of clerical property. The papacy was consulted in advance and gave its approval. But Pius V insisted that the clerics be allowed to select the property to be sold and that a commission of prominent churchmen oversee the collection of money to prevent overselling and the sale of property to Huguenots. This commission had the authority to reduce the assessments for dioceses seriously affected by the religious strife.[71] An edict of 1568 called for the alienation of property sufficient to raise 150,000 livres in rentes. This edict required the sale of 1,800,000 l in property. The king shortly after demanded another alienation to create a further 50,000 écus in rentes. This second edict of 1568 placed the interest rate at 4.17 percent, which doubled the amount demanded from the clergy, 3,180,000 l.[72]

The religious war in the Midi made the sale of ecclesiastical property difficult, since the Huguenots had already seized much of it. The clergy was far less willing to pay or perhaps could not, and this alienation of Church property went on to 1573. In the see of Montpellier René de Rouille, forced to contribute 2,226 l, sold a seigneurie to raise the sum. The assessment of the entire diocese was 9,031 l of which 35 percent was raised by sale of property. The bishop of Lodève, Alfonso Vercelli, also sold a seigneurie; at Saint-Pons, Jacques de Clermont sold a grain mill and land for 2,550 l; and Alessandro di Bardi of Saint-Papoul sold a *métairie* for 4,800 l, three times his assessment. Charles IX did provide a reduction for a number of both individual benefice holders and dioceses. The latter were concentrated in the Midi; they included Vabres and Castres with a reduction of one-half, and Cahors, Périgueux, and Rodez at one-third. As of February, 1572, the first two dioceses had not paid any of their reduced assessment, and Tarbes, Comminges, and Alet still owed over half of theirs. Virtually all of the sees of Midi had not yet met their quota. Clearly that region was having difficulty in meeting the monarchy's demands.[73]

The alienation of 1568 was carried out with no right of repurchase, although the king promised to compensate the clergy with property seized from the Huguenots. The peace of 1570, however, made that impossible. Also in 1568 a second tax on steeples was collected at the rate of 31 l per steeple. Despite the increased rate, this tax brought in far less than the first had. A third steeple tax in 1574 was expected to produce 374,000 l, barely a fifth of the sum it had raised in 1552.[74]

In addition to the décimes of the Contract of 1567 and the alienations of Church property, the monarchy also demanded several extraordinary décimes. The first to be imposed on top of the contract was for 1,400,000 l in 1571.[75] The dioceses ravaged by war and sectarian violence were given a reduced quota. According to Claude Haton, the churchmen were told that they had to sell their chalices and other sacred vessels if they could not raise the money in any other manner.[76] In the diocese of Bordeaux the bishop was among those who had yet to pay the regular décime of 1571, still owing 1,602 l at the end of the year. The bishop of Castres had not paid any of his levy of 1,908 l as of July 1572, nor had the chapter rendered any of the 2,544 l it owed. But the most extreme case was that of Etienne d'Estienne of Gap who was imprisoned in 1569 for failing to pay over 6,400 l in décimes, about a three-year assessment. He was shortly released, but his moveable possessions and the income from a prebend were confiscated.[77] The final three years of Charles IX's reign saw an average subsidy of two extraordinary décimes (800,000 l) imposed on the clergy; most of the money raised in 1573 went to the campaign for Henri d'Anjou's election as king of Poland. None of the money raised in Charles's reign went to buying back the alienated royal taxes and lands.

The succession of Henri III only exacerbated the problem. His court expenses and largess to his favorites compounded the financial problems of the monarchy. Within a year after his return from Poland, he levied an extraordinary subsidy of 1,000,000 l and ordered another alienation of Church property in the amount of another 2,500,000 livres. Benefices with annual revenues of less than 100 l were exempted. Another alienation of clerical property was imposed in 1576, to create rentes of 50,000 écus annually. It was pegged at the 4.17 percent rate of interest so that it required the sale of over 3,900,000 l in Church property.[78] The burden of the alienations of 1574 and 1576 began to affect the bishops more directly. Many had already sold their less valuable property and were forced to give up better pieces. The bishop of Béziers, Tommaso di Bonzi, owed 3,198 l as his quota in 1576, which he had not yet paid in 1578. After two dunning letters from Paris, he was forced to sell one of his best seigneuries for 5,400 l. Even the bishops of Paris and Lyon were forced to resort to selling property to cover their assessments. They had been able to meet the earlier alienations by selling revenue-producing rights and dues.[79]

It was with this background that the general assembly of clergy met at Melun in 1579. The clergy declared that it had fulfilled its part of the Contract of Poissy that expired two years earlier and was under no obligation to create a new contract. Henri III quickly quashed that view. The twelve prelates and other deputies were well aware of his need for money and his intention to get it from the clergy, since he had proposed the year before that a second annate be created to go to the monarchy.[80] The churchmen declared that the Church had contributed 54,741,257 l from 1561 to 1574 and in the next two years another 9,370,000, for a total of over 64,000,000. The clerics realized, however, how essential their contribution had come to be for the royal treasury, since it constituted a third of the royal revenue of 15,000,000 livres in 1576,[81] and they agreed to a new contract of six years calling for an annual sum of 1,300,000 or three décimes. Henri agreed to call another assembly in six years if the royal debts had not been paid, which, of course, they were not.

The new contract, as before, far from satisfied the king's need for money. Quickly Henri again resorted to new extraordinary décimes, steeple taxes, and alienations. With the contract of 1580 due to expire at the end of 1585, Henri called another general assembly of the clergy in late 1585. He asked for an alienation of clerical property to create 200,000 écus in rentes, which at denier 12 (8.33 percent) would have required the sale of over 7,000,000 l in property. The clergy balked, and the meeting of 1585 was filled with bitter recriminations over the financial exaction by the monarchy and the ruin of the clergy.[82] The clerics offered 50,000 écus of rentes. The pope, influenced by the bishop of Paris, Pierre de Gondi, whom Henri had sent to Rome, agreed to an alienation worth 100,000 écus in rentes. The clerics, led by the archbishop of Vienne, Pierre de Villars, protested that the alienation of so much property would make the Church so poor that it could not carry on divine services. Sixtus V replied that he had taken the word of Gondi on the needs of the king and the revenues of the clergy. He agreed to allow the churchmen to alienate the dîmes if necessary to meet the new levy, a measure strictly prohibited by previous popes.

Eventually it was agreed that there would be two alienations, one to produce 50,000 écus in rentes immediately and a second to provide another 50,000 if the war against the Huguenots continued. The second was imposed in 1587.[83]

The alienation of 1586 required increased sale of lands, and some 70 percent of the assessment was met by selling lands. Some benefice holders, however, borrowed heavily to avoid the loss of their patrimony, debts that still were being carried after 1600. The bishop of Montpellier, Antoine Subject, was forced to sell his best estate, the castle and seigneurie of Muriel, for 2,000 écus, an event that he had gone deeply into debt to avoid. Even the archbishop of Rouen was forced to sell twelve acres of meadowland to help meet his assessment of 10,000 l. In the same year he had to part with a fief and a forest to pay the décime.[84]

As a sop to the clergy, the king agreed to allow it to repurchase its property up to a total of two-thirds of the amount sold. Shortly after, this right, which had not been in effect since the first alienation, was extended to all property alienated since 1568. Extremely hard-pressed for money in the next years, the clergy could take little advantage of this right until after 1600. The process of repurchase complicated life for clerics and purchasers alike well into the next century. For example the bishop of Béziers was able to regain his county of Sauve only in 1661.[85]

The general assembly of clergy of 1585 agreed to a new ten year contract at 1,300,000 l annually. That amount became known as the décime of the contract or the ordinary décime into the next century. Henri also levied an extraordinary décime of 500,000 écus in 1588 and still another steeple tax in 1587 at 45 l per steeple. The final steeple tax was imposed in 1588, but little of it was collected because of the anarchy of that year.[86]

The impact of the royal levies on the French clergy was extensive. The estimated 128,000,000 l levied from 1561 to 1587 was nearly 25 percent of the clergy's income for the period. Much was not paid for some time after; many of the dioceses owed half or more of the alienation of 1586 in 1599.[87] The clerics of much of France were close to financial ruin as a result of the twin blows of war and

Protestant occupation and the subsequent royal taxes. It is true, however, that the monarchy provided some relief to the most adversely affected dioceses and benefice holders. Giles de Noailles of Dax owed 21,106 l in back taxes in 1576; the sum was reduced to 15,830 l and eventually to 13,000 l.[88]

The negative impact of the heavy taxes on the episcopacy was fairly short-termed; certainly by the end of Henri IV's reign, most of the adverse effects had disappeared. The only remaining problem was the alienated property: some lost forever, some to be repurchased in the next decades. With the décimes at a steady and relatively low level, the flow of wealth into the bishops' coffers returned largely to what it had been before 1559. But in the decade after 1580, the sense of financial crisis, of impending catastrophe, among the churchmen was clearly evident. The seizure of Church property and revenues by the Huguenots and the royal exactions threatened drastically to reduce episcopal wealth. In particular the clergy blamed Henri III for a large part of their financial woes, both because of his fiscal demands and because of his failure or refusal to destroy the Huguenot party. Such blame was a significant factor in the strong support that the episcopate rendered the Catholic League after 1584. On the other hand, the sense of danger created by the Huguenots evoked far less a response from the prelates. Perhaps because the Protestants caused no real financial or property loss to the bishops before 1560, few bishops were active in the Catholic opposition before that date. It was only after such losses began in the first religious war that many bishops found themselves directly involved in the religious conflict.

While the revenues of the bishops were a major factor in maintaining the prestige of the episcopate, they were also a major element in creating the problems that the prelates faced in the sixteenth century. Their wealth not only attracted the rapacious attention of the monarchy and the bitter denunciations of the reform-minded, it also brought into the episcopacy men whose purpose in gaining a bishopric was largely to enjoy the income that came with the office and who had little intention of fulfilling the extensive obligations that also came with it.

CHAPTER V

THE BISHOP IN HIS DIOCESE: POWERS AND PROBLEMS

T he vast revenues that most bishoprics conferred on their incumbents were both a consequence and an enhancement of the vast temporal authority that the bishops enjoyed in their sees. The bishop was an important political leader, the *chef* of the clergy of his see, and a prominent member of the First Estate. Furthermore, as seigneur of a number of fiefs in the diocese and often lord of his cathedral city, he had secular authority over a large number of people and was responsible for justice, protection, and tax collection.

The extent of these powers and privileges varied greatly from bishop to bishop and diocese to diocese. No bishop of the sixteenth century exercised all of them to the fullest; indeed, it would likely have been impossible, so broad were the duties that corresponded to the powers. Usurpation and the sale of rights and powers had diminished episcopal powers in the sees, however, and indifference on the part of most bishops reduced their effective authority as well. The bishop who exercised his spiritual authority and fulfilled his religious duties as completely as possible was truly rare. The prelate who exercised all of his seigneurial rights and powers was also quite uncommon. Only in their roles as members of the First Estate and leaders of the clergy did the bishops consistently fulfill their obligations. In the sixteenth century duties which were a consequence of a bishop's high place in society, in particular service to the monarchy, often took his full time and attention, forcing him to leave his episcopal duties to vicars.

For virtually every power and privilege that a French bishop had, there were corresponding problems as papacy, monarchy, local clergy, and laity sought to turn the authority and revenues of the prelates to their own advantage. Some of the conflicts were a result of infringement on traditional episcopal rights and powers by other institutions, both secular and ecclesiastical, while others were created by the effort to reform the episcopacy and eliminate privileges that the bishops had taken for themselves against the proper spirit of the episcopal office.

When a new bishop had been confirmed and had sworn his oath to the king, he was permitted exercise of the vast powers and authority that most bishops had in temporal matters as well as in the Church. The symbolic act that emphasized the authority that bishops had over the local nobles and the cathedral city and their submission to him was his formal first entry. It was based on the feudal *jocundus adventus* in which a new lord received the homage of his vassals and cities. Because the precise nature of the legal relationship between bishop and the local powers differed for every see, the entries differed in details and often substance as well. In some cases the entry was still largely feudal, obliging the episcopal vassals to receive him and do homage as at Limoges where 160 nobles rendered homage to the new bishop in 1563.[1] In others the bishop clearly had come to take authority in the cathedral city, which as a corporate body had to make a formal act of obedience to the bishop and have its officers reconfirmed, as at Lyon where the city government paid for the entry.[2] In yet another group of bishoprics the first entry was largely designed to emphasize the bishop's position as ordinary of the see and head of the cathedral chapter.[3] Some entries appear to have included an indiscriminate mix of all three purposes.

The entry ceremonies were highly elaborate and expensive. Two of the most elaborate were the virtually identical entries in Amiens and Cahors. In both cases a local baron met the new bishop outside of the city and helped him mount a mule; the Baron de Cessac at Cahors also had to be bareheaded and coatless and with his right foot in a slipper. The baron then led the bishop's mule into the city. In Amiens the baron helped the bishop dismount and received the mule and its harness for his service; in Cahors the baron had to serve the bishop at table before receiving the mule. The new bishops had to provide dinner for a large crowd of dignitaries. At Amiens several nobles received the tableware, tablecloth and napkins, and the gold ring that the bishop wore that day. He gave the principal canons robes and donated to the cathedral an altar cloth worth 100 écus.[4]

At Nantes the new bishop was led into the city on a white horse led by the four principal barons of the region. Their presence was required under penalty of the seizure of their lands. The bishop had four petty nobles for vassals who walked before him with batons in their hands. The four barons divided the spoils of the day such as the horse and table furnishings. The new prelate of Chartres was carried into the city on a sedan chair on the shoulders of the vicomte and three other nobles. The four barons of Mende had the same obligation; but at the moment when they were to pick up the bishop's chair, he was to say that he wanted to go on foot. The most extravagant of the episcopal entries was that of the archbishop of Bordeaux who sailed into the city on a ship called the *maison navale*. All of the major dignitaries of the region were on it as were local poets who recited verses in Latin and French. The *maison navale* of 1730 cost nearly 9,500 livres; the dinner 1,250; and the total of the ceremony came to 15,836.[5]

Many of the local notables involved felt demeaned by their required roles and resented their humiliation before the bishop and the large crowds that were present. Ill will often appeared, as when the Baron de Montaut felt himself insulted by the Cardinal de Tournon during his entry into Auch in 1547. The bad blood that followed is said to have been a reason why Tournon never returned to Auch.[6] The bourgeoisie of the cities in particular objected to its role in the entry ceremonies. At Lyon in 1540, a fight broke out between the clergy and city youths during the entry procession. The city council supported the youths and argued that the only way to prevent a recurrence was by prohibiting the clergy from marching in the processions in the future.[7] As a consequence of these types of disputes, the elaborateness of the entry ceremonies declined considerably during the *Ancien Régime*.[8]

The entry ceremonies reflected the titles and seigneuries that had accrued to the office over the centuries through purchase or gift. Virtually all the bishoprics had them. One of the most poorly endowed dioceses was Rieux in Languedoc; it had been forced to make do with a parish church for its cathedral when the papacy erected the new sees in the Midi in 1317. The other newly created dioceses were able to take over the lands and seigneuries of the wealthy monasteries that they replaced. Perhaps the bishopric of Montpellier held the most titles—two counties, a marquisate, and five baronies.

The title of bishop-peer was the most exalted of the titles that bishoprics conferred upon their incumbents. The peerages were Reims, Laon, Langres, Beauvais, Châlons-sur-Marne, and Noyon. The first three were dukes of their cathedral cities while the others were counts. The archbishop of Reims had the high honor of consecrating the new king, and the other bishop-peers had special tasks at the coronation. For example, the bishop-duke of Laon carried the ampulla of holy chrism.[9] Five of the episcopal peerages were in the province of Reims in northern France, and the sixth, Langres, was a suffragan of Lyon. The location of the peerages reflected their role in the kingdom at a time when the power of the monarchy was confined to the north.

Numerous other bishoprics conferred noble titles. The archbishops of Arles and Embrun and the bishops of Grenoble and Apt were princes of these cities, and the bishops of Sisteron and Viviers were princes of Lure and Donzière respectively. These titles were relics of the ancient kingdom of Burgundy. The archbishop of Narbonne was duke of that city although he shared power with the vicomte of Narbonne. Fourteen sees conferred the title of count of the cathedral city. Four bishops were barons of their cathedral cities, and the bishop of Tulle was a vicomte. Another four bishops were seigneurs of their cities. In all, thirty-six bishoprics, or about a third of the total number, gave their holders prestigious feudal titles directly tied to the bishoprics. Not all such titles were of ancient origins. Martin de Beaune persuaded Henri II to raise the bishop of Le Puy to a count, and the title of bishop-count of Uzès did not appear until 1601.[10]

The extent to which the episcopal pretensions of power reached is made clear in a document from 1570 pertaining to the bishop of Gap who was count and seigneur of the city. He declared that "upon his bishopric depends total jurisdiction in this city of Gap and its territory, on all of its subjects and inhabitants as much in the temporal as the spiritual, and his judges and officers take jurisdiction in the first instance over all cases civil and criminal."[11]

Every bishopric conferred a different set of powers upon its incumbent. The titles of many, however, were far more impressive than the reality. Medieval bishops were truly the lords of their dioceses and had the authority appropriate to their titles, but much of it had accrued to the monarchy over the centuries or to local authorities. In the Middle Ages the bishops had often been forced to grant charters to their cathedral cities that removed them from a significant voice in municipal government. At Lyon the charter entitled the bourgeoisie to exclude the archbishop and cathedral canons from the municipal assemblies; thus they had little input into local government. In 1563 the archbishop lost the right of exercising *haute justice* over the city to the king.[12]

Thus, despite their titles, the French bishops were not the virtually autonomous ecclesiastical princes of the Empire, but they still exercised broad authority. Accordingly they had a number of officials, bailiffs, clerks, and sergeants under their authority to maintain order and to render and carry out decisions in the seigneurial courts. The bishop-seigneurs had the right to maintain a pillory, a scaffold, and a gibbet and the obligation to see that the sentences that their courts imposed were carried out. They controlled the right to hunt or fish, and Dominique Du Gabre of Lodève (1547–58) in particular gained a reputation for his severity toward poachers.[13] The bishops as administrators of justice confiscated the property of condemned persons and took jurisdiction over the estates of those dying intestate. The episcopal seigneurs could control the commerce of their lands and towns, levied tolls, and gave permission to open or close shops, markets, or fairs. And, of course, they collected feudal dues and fees, rents, and fines. [14] In those places where a prelate was both bishop and seigneur, he possessed vast power over the lives and property of the people. Certainly it was less than two centuries earlier, but an activist bishop in such locales was clearly the dominant figure.

The royal courts for some time had been infringing on the powers of the bishops, both in regard to temporal and ecclesiastical authority. The judicial authority of the bishop's court had once been immense. It had had jurisdiction over every tonsured cleric in every matter whether truly spiritual or more properly criminal or civil. The Church tribunal's competency had extended to a great number of cases that involved lay people as well. Disputes over property or contracts in which an ecclesiastic was involved had belonged to the bishop's court as did crimes committed in a church or religious house. Crusaders, widows, orphans, hospitals, and universities were its special concern. The Church's jurisdiction over the administration of the sacraments and all things that touched on them had given the bishop vast authority over betrothals, marriages and illegitimate children, burials, and cemeteries. The bishop also had authority over usury, sorcery, oaths, and perjury and, of course, blasphemy and heresy.

After 1300, however, the secular courts began to reclaim some of these cases. In 1377, for example, the Parlement prohibited the *officialités* from hearing property cases involving a cleric. By the end of the fifteenth century the practice of *appel comme d'abus* had seriously undermined the authority of the Church courts. It was the right to appeal a decision of a bishop's court to the Parlement on the grounds that the Church court had exceeded its jurisdiction in the matter. The civil courts usually overturned decisions of the episcopal tribunal even in cases where the jurisdiction of the Church was clear. [15]

Having steadily reduced the extent of the jurisdiction of the bishops, the monarchy made its most powerful attack on the Church courts in the Edict of Villers-Cotterêts of 1539. Most importantly, it forbad the citing of lay people before the *officialités* except for matters clearly spiritual or pertaining to the sacraments and gave the civil courts jurisdiction over clerics in all criminal cases. (The most serious crimes committed by clerics were already under secular jurisdiction.) It has been said that the Church tribunals lost five-sixths of their cases as a result of the edict.[16]

Few bishops made individual efforts to counter the loss of their jurisdiction; they preferred to work collectively but ineffectively through the Estates general or the assemblies of clergy. One bishop who did carry the fight to the Parlement was Lorenzo Strozzi of Albi (1561–67) who was determined to regain the jurisdiction over wills and adultery that his predecessors had lost. While the Parlement of Toulouse did give him some small satisfaction on wills, it decided most of the dispute in favor of the civil courts, as one would expect of the lay magistrates.[17]

The monarchy also began to make inroads on the bishops' jurisdiction over heresy. Prosecution of heretics had always been confused between the spiritual authorities and the temporal.[18] The Christian Roman emperors had made heresy a secular crime, as did the early Capetians, who dictated the stake for heretics, and Holy Roman Emperor Frederick II, who clearly defined it as *lèse-majesté divin* and therefore high treason against the king. Consequently the monarch had a major role in its repression, and the French kings swore in their coronation oath to expel all heretics from the realm. In a society that so depended on personal oaths, any threat to the force of those oaths had to be viewed as seditious. For how could one be sure of an oath sworn to a false god or on a false bible? Thus the monarch had a major interest in seeing that the heresy laws were enforced to avoid undermining the basic pillars of society and also protect itself against papal censure, still a dangerous possibility.

But in France during the first decades of the Reformation, heresy prosecution was ineffective. The absence of any clear definitions of doctrine, whether Protestant or Catholic, enabled the less reactionary authorities, of whom there were many, to be lenient in their application of the heresy laws. François I's inclination to halt or at least reduce heresy prosecution when he wanted good relations with Protestant states tended to confuse the judicial authorities and increase the hopes of the Protestants that he would join their cause. When investigations of heresy and blasphemy charges did occur, they were judicial rather than theological in nature and were drawn out by legal procedures and appeals. The penalties for heresy convictions were not uniform; they varied according to the nature of the offense, the locale of the trial, and the status of the convicted.[19]

Perhaps the most important factor in reducing the effectiveness of the heresy laws was the conflict between the civil and the ecclesiastical authorities. The civil authorities, especially the Parlements, were intent on pushing their authority even further into ecclesiastical jurisdiction, including heresy cases. The *Parlementaires'* intervention in heresy cases, however, was further motivated by their perception that the bishops had abdicated their responsibility to eradicate heresy in their sees. Indeed from a conservative Catholic point of view the record of the hierarchy in pursuit of heretics was sorely deficient. A Protestant historian has put it another way: "The reformers might be well justified in regarding the negligence of the bishops as a providential arrangement. Many a feeble germ of truth was spared the violence of persecution until they had achieved greater power of endurance."[20] It is also true that a number of humanist bishops and other prelates sympathetic to the Reform appear to have decided not to use the legal machinery that they controlled against the early Protestants.

In large part because of the lack of enthusiasm for prosecuting heresy cases among the high churchmen and the local civil magistrates, François I began to make changes in the judicial system. An edict of 1540 extended to all the Parlements the right first given to the Parlement of Toulouse in 1539 to take the initiative in prosecuting heresy. The edict defined heresy as sedition so that it was now clearly a criminal matter to be tried as such in the *chambre criminelle* of the Parlements. Clerics, however, remained under the jurisdiction of the Church courts.[21]

Henri II's succession in 1547 gave power to one who was even more determined to use the power of the state to crush heresy.

Despite Henri's boasts to pope and emperor that France had no need for a reforming council since it was free of heresy, he and some Church leaders clearly had become concerned about the rapid growth of religious dissent in the realm. Henri's sincere but uncritical committment to the established faith and his determination to maintain religious unity led him without hesitation to use the power and legal violence of the state for that purpose. Almost no one of the sixteenth century disagreed with the operative political theory that religious disunity naturally led to civil strife and even civil war. Thus unity of state dictated unity of religion, and no one of the period believed that dictum more strongly than did Henri. A strong edict against blasphemy of April 5, 1547, reaffirmed the use of judicial torture, public whipping, and the cutting off of the tongue for such an offense.[22] In the next month a new edict prohibited the publication of books on religion that had not been approved by the Sorbonne and the possession of books on the Index of Forbidden Books. But the most significant step had been taken in October, 1547, when Henri created a new chamber in the Parlement of Paris whose purpose was to hear heresy cases exclusively.[23]

Known from early on as the *chambre ardente* because of its zealous pursuit of heresy, the new chamber was created as a second *tournelle* (civil chamber) to relieve the case load on the original *tournelle* that had been hearing appeals in heresy cases as well as criminal cases. The first *tournelle* was to become exclusively a criminal court. The second *tournelle* entirely bypassed the ecclesiastical courts in many cases.[24]

While the new *tournelle* was clearly a more efficient way to deal with heresy cases, it aroused the ire of both churchmen and other magistrates in the Parlement of Paris. The former resented the complete loss of jurisdiction over heresy except for accused clerics; among the latter some opposed the increased authority of their colleagues and the innovations involved, and others objected to the use of capital punishment for heresy. In November, 1549, Henri tried to reduce the contentiousness with an edict that gave Church courts jurisdiction over simple heresy when the accused had not manifested their beliefs in public misbehavior or sedition. In numerous *arrêts* the magistrates of the new *tournelle* ordered bishops to pay the expenses of cases tried before it that had come from their dioceses; but the repetition of the orders indicates that the bishops often refused to pay.

Complaints over disputed jurisdiction continued to annoy the king, and rumors of heterodoxy in the Parlement itself may have reached him. In response still another edict was drawn up in June, 1551. This last, the notorious Edict of Chateaubriand, clearly showed Henri's exasperation with the bickering over jurisdiction and his recognition that the measures taken thus far had failed to eradicate heresy.[25] The edict again made it clear that what was especially feared about heresy was its perceived affinity with sedition and public disorder. The edict was far more explicit about the power of judges to investigate private beliefs in order to prevent sedition, not only punish it. New prohibitions on the printing, sale, and possession of dangerous books strongly suggested that the spread of Protestant books, especially from Geneva, was an effective means of proselytizing. Both the importing of books from Geneva and communications with the city were expressly prohibited.

In the edict Henri attempted to solve the problem of conflicting jurisdiction by closing the new *tournelle* and returning heresy prosecution to the local courts — the civil courts for heresy cases involving sedition, Church courts for simple heresy.[26] But seditious heresy was interpreted so broadly that few cases were left to the episcopal courts. The edict failed to end all of the bickering over heresy jurisdiction, but it remained with only slight tinkering the system of persecuting heretical opinion to the end of Henri's reign. It made the law governing heresy much more explicit and easier to gain convictions, but nonetheless it failed to accomplish the goal of eradicating Protestantism.

The creation of a French Inquisition in 1557 with three Cardinal-inquisitors, Lorraine, Bourbon, and Châtillon, which was in fact still-born, would have done nothing to change the confusion in heresy procedures since members of the Parlements were to serve on special tribunals to hear appeals from the Inquisition. Finally in 1560 still another edict, that of Romorantin, returned all jurisdiction over simple heresy to the Church courts while the secular courts retained cognizance of all disorder or treason that might have arisen out of heresy. The bishops were told to reside in their dioceses so that they could personally take charge of their courts.[27] With some tinkering this remained the system for the rest of the century with the major change that the edicts of toleration took the Huguenots out of the purview of the heresy courts.

At the Estates of Orléans in 1560, the clergy protested vehemently at its loss of jurisdiction caused by the Edict of 1539. The Third Estate, with some support from the nobility, proposed an even greater reduction in the competence of the episcopal tribunals and objected strongly to the use of spiritual penalties, especially excommunication, in what were essentially civil cases. The two estates voted to restrict Church censure to matters of public scandal.[28] Having received no satisfaction from the Estates in 1560, the clergy made a more determined attack on the Edict of 1539 at the Estates of Blois in 1576. Numerous *cahiers* from the First Estate requested the king to restore the authority of the Church courts to what it had been before 1539 and to eliminate the *appel comme d'abus* except in cases of treason. The other estates, for their part, wanted to restrict further ecclesiastical jurisdiction, but the only change was to give both courts concurrent authority over simony.[29]

Twelve years later, at Blois again, the clergy renewed its appeal for the withdrawal of the Edict of Villers-Cotterêts and asked for the restoration of authority over benefices and the use of the royal gendarmes without the consent of a secular court.[30] But the requests gained no results nor did the many similar remonstrances put forth by the several assemblies of the clergy in the last forty years of the century. The Edict of 1539 had achieved what the monarchy, the nobility, and the royal magistrates had sought for several centuries, and they were not about to give it up on the protest of the hierarchy. The bishops, however, did retain half a loaf by keeping jurisdiction over their own in their courts in civil cases.

The right to have civil suits tried in the bishop's court was one of the privileges the French clergy still had in the sixteenth century.

Another valuable privilege was exemption from taxes, royal or local, although the clergy did pay décimes to the king under the pretext that they were a gift to the monarchy and properties privately held by bishops were taxed unless they were seigneurial lands.[31] Still others were that clerics could not be imprisoned for indebtedness and were free from any obligation of military service. But in a society that was acutely conscious of rank and position and the subtle nuances of dress and place, which defined and disputed these matters to the point that the royal council was called on to decide them, perhaps the greatest privilege the clergy had was comprising the first order of the realm.

The bishops as leaders of the clergy were best able to take advantage of the possibilities that being part of the first order offered. The bishop was addressed in the sixteenth century by the title *messire*, which had earlier been restricted to the nobility, or *Reverend père en Dieu*. The title *monseigneur* was not used until the next century. The episcopacy had its own hierarchy. The cardinals were followed by the archbishops, and the bishops were ranked by date of consecration. Among the archbishops there was a great deal of bickering over who had first rank. The archbishop of Lyon claimed first place under his ancient title of primate of all Gaul. Bourges with its title of primate of Aquitaine disputed that claim as did Bordeaux with the same title. So too did Reims as Primate of Gaul-Belgium, and Vienne as primate of primates. The question of first rank among the archbishops became acute with the creation of the national assembly of the clergy in 1561 and the resulting quarrels over the honor of presiding over it. The various primates all claimed the presidency based on their honors while the other bishops argued that the office was elective. The latter view carried the point in the sixteenth century.

Another dispute over rank during this period occurred between the cardinals and the princes of blood. The corps of clergy had precedence in political assemblies except for the princes who, however, had traditionally given way to the cardinals. At the Estates of Orléans in 1560, the cardinals and the princes of blood appealed to the Estates to settle the princes' claim to precede the cardinals.

The Estates gave first place to princes of blood despite the cardinals' objection that they had always been first. Those cardinals who were also princes of blood accepted the decision, but the others steadfastly refused, to no avail. For the duration of the *Ancien Régime* the princes had the first place.[32]

Like the princes the cardinals had the right by virtue of their office to sit in the royal council, and the Cardinals de Lorraine and Tournon were particularly influential members for much of the sixteenth century. Several bishops also served in the council as part of the king's intimate circle of advisers.[33] Prominent examples were Jean de Morvillier of Orléans and Sebastien de L'Aubespine of Limoges for Henri II, Jean de Monluc of Valence for Charles IX, and Pierre de Gondi of Paris and Renaud de Beaune of Bourges for Henri III. It was as members of the royal council that Monluc and Charles de Marillac of Vienne delivered their often-cited speeches at the Assembly of Fontainebleau in 1560 in which they argued for religious toleration and the convocation of the Estates general.

Bishops made up a substantial part of the diplomatic corps of the French monarchy, especially in the reigns of François I and Henri II. Bishops served as ambassadors for at least one term at every court and capital that had a resident French diplomat in the century. Jean de Monluc was one of the most highly travelled ambassadors of the era, having been posted in Constantinople, Edinburgh, London, and Cracow. Prelates also served the monarchy as royal officials in the provinces. Although no bishop served as a governor of a major province in the sixteenth century, they appeared frequently as *lieutenants du roi* and *sénéchaux*, especially in the Midi where the king wanted to have present a powerful official more amenable to his interests than governors from local families.[34] For example the Cardinals Tournon, Armagnac, and Strozzi served as *lieutenants du roi* in Languedoc from 1536 to 1563. Some thirty-five bishops had royal commissions to serve in a significant capacity as royal officers during the period from 1516 to 1589. Many bishops, however, had such short-term appointments that only the most painstaking research would likely determine all such commissions.

The fact that so many ambassadors and royal officials were bishops reflects more the use of episcopal patronage to reward such royal servants and provide them with an income than any attempt to draw on the talents of the episcopal office holders as a group. There was no example in the sixteenth century comparable to the obvious one of Cardinal de Richelieu in the next where a relatively unknown bishop attracted the attention of the royal court through his role as a leader of the clergy.

Richelieu, of course, first gained special attention as a clerical delegate at the Estates of 1614. While there were three meetings of the estates in the sixteenth century, none served as an opportunity for a new face to come to the fore as a national leader. Those prelates who dominated the estates, like Cardinal de Lorraine in 1560 or Renaud de Beaune in 1588, were already well-established political figures. The rolls of bishops present at the three meetings of the estates show that few of them were not already respected leaders in the episcopate. One reason for this situation may well have been that the number of bishops present at the estates was in fact quite small. In the Middle Ages the bishops generally were accepted as deputies if they appeared at the meetings, but in 1484 the deputies decided that a bishop who was not elected by his bailiwick or who sat in the estates by right of peerage had to sit at his own expense. In 1576 Antoine de Subject of Montpellier sought a seat by right of his office but was denied. This decision substantially reduced episcopal representation in the century. In 1560 there were 11 archbishops and bishops among the 127 delegates of the First Estate (8.7 percent); in 1576, 24 among the 110 delegates (21.8 percent); in 1588, 25 out of 134 deputies (19.5 percent). In contrast, in 1614 the episcopate made up well over a third of the clerical deputies, 59 out of 141 (41.8 percent). But a prelate, usually a cardinal, was always elected to serve as president of the First Estate and was also expected in turn to serve as speaker of the combined estates.[35]

The special position of the hierarchy was more pronounced in the provincial estates. Bishops served ex officio as presidents of nearly all the provincial estates still functioning in the sixteenth century: the archbishops of Narbonne for Languedoc and of Aix for

Provence, the bishops of Autun for Burgundy, of Pamiers for Foix, and Lescar for Béarn. All twenty-two bishops of Languedoc sat in its estates as did the two bishops of Béarn for its estates, the nine of Brittany, and the five of Burgundy. Only Provence among the provinces with still-functioning estates did not give its bishops an established right to participate. The Estates of Languedoc expected the bishops to take seriously their right to sit; Guilio de Medici of Béziers was fined 25 livres in 1562 for not attending or sending his vicar.[36]

Several bishops were also ex officio *conseillers* of the Parlements. The archbishop of Bordeaux was a *conseiller* in the Parlement of Guyenne, the bishop of Gap the same in Grenoble, that of Paris in its Parlement, and of Nantes and Rennes in the Parlement of Brittany. In addition the six ecclesiastical peers of the realm had the right to sit as magistrates of the Parlement and could address it standing up—a privilege permitted to a very few.

Within his diocese one of the most important powers bestowed on a bishop was the collation of nonconsistorial benefices in his diocese.[37] These benefices were of two types: those without the care of souls, such as canonicates and prebends, and those with the care of souls, largely the local parishes. The bishop as ordinary collator had in theory the right to fill all nonconsistorial benefices except for the houses of certain regular orders and the mendicants. In most of the sees of France, however, he had over the centuries lost control over the majority of benefices. The cathedral chapter, the local nobility and notables, the officers of the Parlement, the king, and the pope had gained the right to name to vacant benefices.

The chapters of the cathedral and other collegial churches usually had the right of collation over their prebends and chapels. Control by the canons varied from complete to a division between canons and bishop that took the form of filling alternate seats of the choir or in alternate months. The chapters also filled various curates over which they had jurisdiction. Numerous benefices in a diocese were controlled by the patron, either lay or ecclesiastical, who was the donor or descendent of the donor of the benefice. While the bishop did have the right of refusal of such nominations, he could hardly exercise it because the patron had the right to appeal any refusal to another bishop. The magistrates of the Parlement of Paris had received from the papacy the right, once in their terms of office, to appoint to a benefice of less than 600 livres in annual revenue.

The king was not only the collator of the consistorial benefices but also had the right to name a cleric to the first vacant prebend in each cathedral chapter after he became king and when he visited the cathedral for the first time. In most dioceses the king also could fill a prebend when a new bishop took his oath of loyalty. When a bishopric was vacant and *en régale*, the king had the bishop's right of collation, which he usually granted to the chapter. The pope, besides his limited rights of collation of consistorial benefices under the Concordat, had in some of the sees of the *pays d'état* the right of "anticipation" (*prévention*) by which he could fill vacant benefices, except those pertaining to the king or lay patron, before the collator's nomination reached Rome. The collators often went to great lengths to prevent Rome from hearing of the death of a benefice holder until they had sent off a nomination. In the *pays d'obédience* the pope filled vacant benefices six or eight months of the year except for those belonging to the king. Innocent VIII had reduced the number of months in some dioceses to encourage the bishops to reside.

All ecclesiastical collators, but not the king or lay patrons, could be deprived of their right by a resignation *in favorem* or an exchange of benefices. The Parlement usually considered such transactions as obligatory, leaving the collator without recourse. The benefice holder in effect became his own collator. The consistorial benefices, however, required the king's consent for these types of transactions. One further check on the freedom of choice of the collators was the obligation set forth in the Concordat to provide benefices for the holders of university degrees except those in arts. Benefices coming vacant in four specific months of the year had to be given to these *gradués*. In two of these months the collator could choose whom he wished off of the list of *gradués*, in the other months the benefice had to be given to the highest ranked graduate on the list, beginning with the theologians.

As Marcel Marion has put it, "nothing could have been more complicated or productive of disputes and litigation than the system of benefices."[38] They occurred largely because the collation of benefices was a valuable source of influence and revenue. The ability to name one's relatives and clients to ecclesiastical positions that were often sinecures enhanced the political and social standing of the collator. Collation could also be lucrative, for the collator had the right to reserve a pension for himself from the revenues of a benefice; and accepting bribes, while simonical, was an ordinary benefit of the right of collation.

Under the system of collation as it existed in the sixteenth century, the bishop could fill only a small number of the total benefices in his diocese. It was true that in some sees the bishop collated more than half of the benefices, as in Bordeaux, where the archbishop filled 236 parishes out of a total of 390. But most sees were more in the order of Paris where the bishop collated 215 of 469 curates in the diocese; Clermont, 90 of 735; and Sées and Bayeux, 4 percent.[39] The proportion of sinecures over which the bishop had no control must have been even higher than for the parishes.

Despite the range of persons who had the right to fill vacant benefices, the bishop's major competitor in this regard was the cathedral chapter, which had reduced or even eliminated episcopal authority over a broad range of subjects, including the cathedral itself. In the early Middle Ages the relationship between bishop and chapter had not been intended to be an adversary one. The chapter had emerged as a body of clerics who served as the aides and advisers to the bishop. The ideal was that the bishop and the clergy of his cathedral would lead a communal life, and in a number of places, the chapter was organized as a Benedictine community with the bishop as abbot.[40] Canon law dictated that a bishop needed the cooperation of his chapter in conferring benefices, alienating Church property, and judging cases, since the cathedral clergy was regarded as a corporation in which one part could not act without the other.[41] But the simple corporate theory of the early Middle Ages gave way to a far more complicated view that parts of the corporation could have separate rights. As the duties and interests of the bishop took him away from the cathedral, the canons took greater and greater jurisdiction over it and the cathedral city. Since the bishop was so frequently absent, the chapter developed a tradition of acting without him, since canon law gave the body of the corporation the right to exercise the powers of the head in his absence. The canons so aggressively sought to defend and expand their rights that the resultant quarrels with the bishops virtually assured that all but the most determined prelate would stay away from the cathedral.

When the bishops sought to recover their lost authority in the fourteenth century, the conflicts between chapter and prelate were especially fierce. Under the Pragmatic Sanction of 1438 the chapters regained the right to elect the bishops, albeit often with a certain amount of persuasion from the king. One consequence was a decline in conflicts between canons and bishop. But after the Concordat of 1516, with the king appointing bishops who were not familiar with the canons and their traditions and privileges, the disputes reappeared in great number.

The canons, who varied in number from twelve at Agde to ninety-eight at Chartres, were men of considerable standing and wealth. The entire chapter at Lyon, for example, came from the nobility. The canons often had degrees in law or theology. They usually owed their chairs to their fellow canons, since the bishop's right to fill a choir chair was either nonexistent or limited and in some chapters subject to the canons' veto. Thus the canons felt no obligation to be accommodating to the bishop, who was usually an outsider. Occupying the home turf and far more knowledgable of the statutes and precedents that established their powers and privileges, the canons were formidable opponents of any bishop who challenged them. With few duties in the cathedral or diocese, many canons spent their time on the legal questions concerning their rights.[42]

At their solemn entries into the cathedral cities, most French bishops were obliged to swear an oath at the west door of the cathedral that they would respect the privileges of the chapter before they would be admitted into the church. In a number of French sees, the bishop, despite being nominally the head of the chapter, was not allowed to enter the chapter house or to take part in the chapter's deliberations. In other sees where he could attend the meetings if summoned by the dean, he did not preside. In most dioceses the bishop's rights within the cathedral itself were carefully circumscribed, and in some, he was not permitted to enter the church except on specified holidays and occasions.[43]

This lack of control over their chapters was one reason why at least two bishops did not take up residence in their dioceses. The chapter of Apt refused to permit Pierre de Forli to take part in the deliberations of the chapter despite his demand to be allowed to. Forli, who apparently was a fiery man since he had a long dispute with the crown over a fee owed to the king upon his appointment in 1541, returned permanently to his home in Avignon after the Parlement of Toulouse upheld the canons.[44] At virtually the same time Gabriel Bouvey, named to Angers in 1540, refused to make his official entry into the diocese until 1544 because the chapter had asked Paul III for a complete exemption from episcopal authority. Paul had granted it, but the Parlement at Paris annulled it upon the bishop's appeal. The bad blood between bishop and canons lasted for two decades, and Bouvey was rarely in Angers. In 1562 he attended the council and, apparently impressed by the deliberations on reform, took up residence in his see and was a model prelate until his death in 1572.[45] A third bishop, Robert Cenalis, named to Riez in 1530, asked to be moved because of bitter hostilities with the chapter that apparently predated his appointment. He transferred to Avranches two years later.[46]

Perhaps the ultimate attempt at usurpation of episcopal power was made by the chapter at Châlons-sur-Marne. In 1564 the canons moved to eliminate the bishop, Jean de Bourges, from any authority over the cathedral. Was it because de Bourges was likely a commoner? Specifically they wanted to move the episcopal chair away from the high altar, to prohibit him from preaching when he wished, and from having two ushers precede him into the choir. The dispute went to the Parlement, which decided fully in the bishop's favor to the point of giving him the right to preside over chapter meetings. De Bourges on his part pledged to do nothing without the advice of the chapter.[47]

Another example of chapter interference in the affairs of the bishop involved three very similar incidents about episcopal beards. The chapters of Troyes, Orléans, and Le Mans objected to the beards worn by their new bishops Antonio Caracciolo in 1551, Jean de Morvillier in 1552, and Claude d'Angennes in 1559. The prelates were told that local custom prevented a bishop from wearing a beard, which was a symbol of men of the world and especially the court. They all appealed to the king who informed the chapters that the bishops would be involved in important affairs outside of the realm for which they needed their beards. When Caracciolo was forced to resign his office in 1562 under suspicion of heresy, the chapter of Troyes declared that his successor had been improperly nominated and elected its own candidate. The royal court sharply informed the canons that they were mistaken.[48]

Other examples of bishop-chapter conflict came from Nantes, Paris, and Gap. In 1572 Philippe Du Bec had a quarrel with the chapter over his refusal to contribute to the repair of the cathedral. In this case the magistrates of the Parlement sided with the chapter.[49] In Paris the chapter of Nôtre-Dame refused to accept a coadjutor for Pierre de Gondi, arguing that Gondi was too young and vigorous to need one and that the pretext of his being occupied with the affairs of state was not legitimate.[50] An example of the financial disputes between chapter and bishop involved Gap, where in 1575 Pierre de Paparin took the chapter to the Parlement of Toulouse to force it to recognize its annual obligation of twenty-five florins to him.[51]

After 1588 the chapters tended to support the Catholic League more strongly than the episcopacy did, and in several cases they involved themselves in administering dioceses held by Politique bishops and in trying to replace them. One such case was Beauvais where in 1590 the chapter, incensed by Nicolas de Fumée's support for Henri IV, declared that the bishopric was vacant and elected its own candidate. Rome, however, never confirmed him, and after Henri's victory Fumée was accepted back into Beauvais.[52]

One area where several bishops were successful in regard to their canons was the secularizing of the monastic chapters. In at least five instances in the sixteenth century bishops appealed to Rome for permission to remove their chapters from monastic rules. Since a bishop's position as bishop-abbot of a monastic chapter increased his duties and placed an additional obligation to be in residence, the greater burden was likely the reason for seeking the change.[53]

Although conflicts between bishop and chapter were numerous in the early sixteenth century, they declined after 1560. The canons found that they had more serious concerns such as the presence of the Huguenots and the heavy tax demands of the monarchy. Overall, the disputes were fewer than one might have expected, viewing the jurisdictional maelstrom that surrounded the chapters. Many bishops did not take an active enough interest in their sees to concern themselves with the loss of power and privileges to the canons.

Indeed the bishops had lost much of their authority since the golden age of episcopal power, around 1000, but they still wielded a great deal, which coupled with their revenues made a bishopric a highly sought after prize. It made the king's control over episcopal patronage a valuable means for gaining the support of the important families of the realm. The great range of civil powers and jurisdiction that belonged to most bishops was, however, far from a boon for the Church. They involved the bishop in a wide range of affairs and activities with little or nothing to do with religion. The few bishops who were regularly in residence in their sees found that much of their time and energies were consumed by civil matters and politics. Even the rare zealous pastoral prelate found it difficult to devote much of his time to his spiritual and pastoral duties; how much easier it was for the less zealous to ignore them.

CHAPTER VI

THE BISHOP IN HIS DIOCESE: SPIRITUAL AUTHORITY AND REFORM

For all of the wealth and political power of a French bishop, the fact remained that he was a churchman. As the Council of Trent proclaimed, "The bishops, who have succeeded the apostles, . . . have been placed by the Holy Spirit to rule the Church."[1] The Church had imbued the episcopal office with vast spiritual authority over the flock of Christ, but the sixteenth-century bishop who exercised that spiritual authority fully was rare indeed. The enormous amount of time that he had to allot to his temporal duties and finances vastly reduced the amount of time that a bishop could devote to his obligations in overseeing the local Church. Many, perhaps most members of the episcopate were by nature more inclined to attend to their other functions. Truly spiritual men have never been attracted to high Church office because of the burden of nonspiritual concerns; furthermore, the Church has been reluctant to give them high office. Perhaps more than in any other era, the French bishops of the sixteenth century were largely political operatives more concerned with other matters than their own spiritual well-being and that of their flocks. Such concerns as service to the monarchy often took a bishop's full attention and required him to leave his episcopal duties to vicar generals and coadjutors.

The vicar general was the bishop's deputy whose competence often extended to all areas of episcopal authority, both temporal and spiritual, which did not require ordination as a bishop.[2] He often came from the cathedral chapter since the canons were regarded as partners with the bishop in governance, but the position was not a sure stepping-stone to the episcopate. Only ten vicars in the era under study received such a promotion. The appointments ended with the death or resignation of the bishops who had made them; but the king could extend them while the see was vacant, and the new bishops often reappointed the same vicars.

The coadjutor bishop, on the other hand, attended only to those duties that required episcopal orders. He usually had a titular see *in partibus infidelium* and was often a member of a religious order with little hope of a promotion. In a number of cases, however, the coadjutor came from a prominent family and received the right of succession to the bishopric. Occasionally a bishop of a small, poor see served as coadjutor in a much larger one. The coadjutor bishop administered the sacrament of confirmation, ordained priests, consecrated or reconsecrated churches, and did whatever other services that require episcopal orders. Often he would perform these services even if the ordinary was in residence. In the occasional case of a blatantly negligent bishop, the vicar general could commission a temporary coadjutor to perform these services provided the latter had episcopal orders.

The widespread and time-honored practice of leaving most of the affairs of the diocese to the vicars and coadjutors enabled many bishops to ignore their obligations with a clear conscience. It is difficult to say how badly the Church was harmed by the practice. As Margaret Bowker has observed about absentee English bishops in the early sixteenth century, "Some sees . . . were probably suffering from being run by deputies and never enjoying the authority as well as the wisdom of a more experienced and senior man." On the other hand, the use of a vicar put a man in authority who was likely to come from the local region and be more zealous in the performance of his duties. As was said about Robert de Lenoncourt, absentee bishop of Auxerre from 1556 to 1560, "the diocese was not less better served under the governance of the vicar than if the bishop had directed it personally."[3] In many cases this was likely true.

The extensive use of vicars and coadjutors greatly distressed reformers, since it encouraged absenteeism, one of the principal targets of the Council of Trent. The call for reform of the episcopacy was centuries old, and French preachers at the turn of the century had delivered powerful sermons on the subject that identified the same abuses that Trent sought to correct.[4] Prior to 1560, however, the French political and Church authorities had little interest in reforming the episcopate. François I had refused to endorse the council when it was first called in 1544 because he objected to its location in an imperial city, which was presumed to have made the council a tool of Charles V. Furthermore, the French had little desire to help settle the religious problems in Germany that so usefully distracted Charles and reduced his ability to raise German troops and money. In addition, prior to 1560 the French Church in its Gallicanism had a sense of self-sufficiency and lacked a sense of community of interests with foreign Catholics that made it difficult for Frenchmen to concern themselves with what was happening elsewhere. Both king and clergy saw no reason to be placed in a position to be asked to agree to decisions that might reduce their prerogatives and incomes or infringe on Gallican liberties. Ultimately François sent a small number of bishops to Trent, but their presence was more a hindrance than an aid to the work of the council.[5]

Henri II's attitude toward the council was even more negative; he worked to prevent its reconvening and, when that failed, to break it up. His attitude was formed by the belief that the French Church remained "holy and Catholic"; there was no need for the council or its reforms since he had no difficulty in enforcing the Catholic rite in his realm.[6] Developments in Germany had demonstrated further the advantage to France of the religious ferment there. At the reconvening of the council in 1552 the German Lutherans were again in arms against the emperor after several years of uneasy truce following their defeat at Mühlberg in 1547. The French were not about to let Charles off the hook by working for religious peace in the Empire. Thus Henri on several occasions proclaimed his intention of making an alliance with the English and the Swiss to prevent the council from meeting.[7] When the

council did meet in 1552, Henri refused to send any French prelates to Trent, but he did dispatch Jacques Amyot, a future bishop,
to explain his recalcitrance. Amyot scandalized the assembly by
addressing it as a "congregation" rather than as a "council." The
council refused to allow him to read the letter from Henri.[8]

The French hierarchy was far better represented in the third
convocation in 1562. Sixteen bishops attended at least some of the
sessions, and three future bishops were among the French theologians and abbots present, although the Cardinal de Lorraine, the
French leader, took a decidedly Gallican approach to the issues of
Church authority and discipline, which reduced his effectiveness.
For the most part, therefore, French churchmen had little to do
with formulating the decrees of Trent, and that may well have had
much to do with the refusal of the monarchy to publish them in
France. Despite the failure to implement the Tridentine decrees in
the realm, they provide a convenient summary of what an ideal
bishop was expected to be at mid-sixteenth century. Expanding on
the principles of the episcopal office as found in canon law, the
council drew up a thorough statement of what a bishop's duties
and powers were while sharply denouncing corrupt practices that
had crept in during the Middle Ages. Thus the Tridentine decrees
can serve as a focus through which one can describe the malprac-
tices that existed in the French episcopacy in the sixteenth century
both before and after the council.

Since the principal function of the bishop was to be the pastor of
the people of his diocese, Trent declared that "it is enjoined on all
to whom the *cura animarum* is entrusted to know their sheep." In
1547 the council laid down a severe injunction against episcopal
absenteeism. Any prelate who was away from his see for a period of
six months without good reason was to forfeit a fourth of his
revenues; if the absenteeism continued despite chastisement, the
pope was to remove such a bishop from office.

Certainly absenteeism was a common abuse among the French
bishops long before 1547. When the council issued its decrees on
residency, the French episcopacy took them as an open affront.[9]
François I's use of bishoprics as livings for his ambassadors and

high officials and as a tool of foreign policy by appointing nearly forty foreigners meant that at the end of his reign nearly a third of the bishops were certain to be absentees. A number more were residing in Rome on papal business, and many more were absent from their dioceses for less legitimate reasons. Even if they were in their dioceses, some bishops preferred to stay in their manor houses in the countryside rather than in the bishop's palace. Often quarrels with the cathedral canons would make residence too troublesome to be worthwhile.

Henri II issued his own edicts on episcopal residency in 1551 and 1557. In the latter he ordered all clerics with the care of souls to retire to their benefices to preach and see that sound preaching was done. The only exemption permitted was for service to the monarchy, and the penalty for noncompliance was confiscation of revenues. [10] The reason given for the edict was to combat heresy, which was also the justification for the edict of François II in 1560; residency was deemed "the best remedy for the evils that the Church is suffering." [11] The king added that if the bishops did not reside as ordered, he would constrain them in a more forceful manner. In the following year the Ordinance of Orléans obliged prelates to reside in their benefices under the penalty of the seizure of their revenues. Charles IX wrote a similar letter, urging residency as the best way to combat heresy. Eight years later Catherine de Medici, serving as regent while Henri III was returning from Poland, again ordered the prelates to reside in their sees. [12] The repetition of the edicts on residency by the monarchy makes it clear that they were largely ineffective. The bishops, for their part, clearly did not see absenteeism as a problem. The provincial council of Narbonne, meeting in 1551, did not see fit to make any rule about residency. There was good reason since none of the bishops was present in person, and one had not deigned to send his representative. [13]

The inefficacy of the many decrees on residency is made clear in contemporary sources. Again and again the sources denounced the bishops for ignoring the duties of office by living at the court or in Paris or Rome. Claude Haton, the ardent priest from Champagne, was as harsh in denouncing the life-style of the prelates as was any Protestant. "Beginning with the cardinals and archbishops down to the simplest curés . . . they make their residences where they can take their pleasures. . . . The archbishops, bishops and cardinals of France are nearly all at the courts of the king and the princes."[14]

Less bitter but more informative was the statement of the Sieur de Fourquevaux before the Estates of Languedoc in 1574.[15] "It is necessary to note that the bishops and other prelates are not at their posts in their sees and dioceses." He described them as living at places more accommodating to the chase and pleasure. Fourquevaux stated that the see of Narbonne had not had a bishop in residence since 1513. (It would gain one in 1574 in Simon Vigor.) Fourteen bishops from the other eighteen dioceses were absentee. Of the four prelates who were resident, one lived such a scandalous life that his people would likely have been better off with him absent (no clue given to his identity). Only the bishop of Comminges (Urbain de Saint-Gelais) was "in his sheepfold doing the office of a good shepherd."[16] Five years after Fourquevaux's lamentation, Bishop Pontac of Bazas in his oration to the clergy assembled at Melun made a powerful call for the publication of the decrees of Trent, especially those requiring episcopal residency.[17] He declared that thirty-five dioceses of Languedoc, Gascony, and Guyenne were without resident bishops.

By 1579 the civil wars had so badly disrupted the Midi that many of these bishops were likely justified in abandoning their sees. But the situation across the kingdom had been hardly better twenty years earlier, in 1559, after two royal edicts and the first decrees of Trent on residency. Of the 101 incumbent bishops, only nineteen can be considered as residing in their sees regularly; sixty-two were clearly absent; and for twenty there is insufficient evidence to make a judgment. Adding to the absentees the ten vacant sees and those held by pluralists, while giving the benefit of the doubt to the undetermined, one finds that 65 percent of the French dioceses did not have their bishops present on a regular basis. In several cases bishops of small dioceses were serving as administrators for the great churchmen. The onslaught of the religious wars that drove numerous bishops out of their dioceses was balanced by the appointment of a number of more zealous prelates. Thus the proportion of absentee bishops remained in the range of 65 percent until 1588 when the anarchy and strife of the next several years pushed nonresidency well over 80 percent.[18]

Numerous examples of long-term absenteeism could be cited. In her study of Aix, Claire Dolan has taken as evidence that the archbishop was in residence for a given year if she found at least one mention in the records that the prelate had performed one of the ordinary acts of his office such as Confirmation or tonsure. On that basis, which gives the benefit of the doubt to the prelates, Dolan found that they were in residence at most fourteen years out of the forty-two between 1551 and 1593.[19] Two examples of chronic absenteeism among even the ordinary bishops involve the sees of Digne in Provence and Aire in Gascony. Henri Le Meignen, a commoner and Marguerite de Valois's *aumônier*, was bishop of Digne from 1569 to 1587 without setting foot in the diocese. François de Foix apparently never visited the diocese of Aire in the twenty-four years he was its bishop.

The endemic absenteeism was very much a product of a worldview that saw bishops as belonging to the elite of the realm and permeated the minds of prelates and secular leaders alike. That view was a product of the symbiotic relationship prevalent during the era between the Church and the State that regarded service in behalf of one as benefitting the other. The king was the head of the Gallican Church, and as such he could call on its clergy for service to the state, in particular since Church and State both drew from the same limited pool of men with sufficient talent and the proper bloodlines for high office in either institution. Becoming a bishop was regarded as providing a proper level of prestige and revenue to ambassadors and other government officials or to the younger sons of the great nobility. If the diocese was put in the hands of a capable vicar, then certainly the see was no worse off with the bishop elsewhere using his prestige and income for the good of the realm, thereby also serving the Church, or directly serving the papacy. Only a small band of zealous Catholic reformers challenged that view prior to Trent.

The reform-minded churchmen saw pluralism as a particularly blatant cause of absenteeism. The practice of holding several bishoprics and many monasteries at the same time clearly made it difficult for the prelate to take up residence in his benefices. Usually the great churchmen who held multiple bishoprics were in Rome or at the court, leaving all of their benefices neglected. At the end of François I's reign, pluralist cardinals were a serious problem. Cardinals d'Este, d'Armagnac, Lorraine, Tournon, Longwy, Du Bellay, and Louis and Charles de Bourbon all held three or more sees in 1547. In that year Paul III decreed that a cardinal was to possess only one bishopric. Trent followed with a decree against plural benefices and reiterated it in 1562 with a stronger statement requiring the concession of all but one benefice with the care of souls within a year's time.[20]

The French prelates, with the support of the monarchy, did not respond to the decrees of 1547; only upon the determined insistence of Julius III in 1550 did the cardinals begin to give up their multiple bishoprics.[21] The next two years saw a great deal of feverish bargaining and trading as the cardinals sought to get as much as possible for the bishoprics they had to concede. Ippolyto d'Este, one of the great pluralists of the era, was in 1550 the archbishop of Lyon, Arles, and Narbonne and bishop of Autun and Tréguier in France and held as well the sees of Milan and Ferrara in Italy. His fellow cardinal, François de Tournon, was archbishop of Embrun and Auch. At the end of 1550 d'Este gave Narbonne to Tournon for two monasteries, and in the next year the two cardinals traded Auch for Lyon with Tournon including two more monasteries to make up for Auch's considerably smaller revenue.[22] They then resigned all of their other French sees. They kept large pensions, which were in most cases one-third of the bishop's revenues, the collation of benefices, and the right of regression. Thus Tournon and d'Este held to the letter of the papal decree while maintaining substantial revenues and influence in their former dioceses. D'Este would briefly serve again as archbishop of Lyon, Narbonne, and

Arles under the right of regression in 1562 and 1563, and Tournon reappeared as archbishop of Narbonne in 1563 after d'Este had resigned it for a second time.

After the breakup of these episcopal empires of the cardinals, pluralism was far less a problem for the French Church.[23] As was seen in the examples of Tournon and d'Este, the practice of regression would occasionally create a pluralist situation, but it was usually brief as the returned incumbent quickly found someone else to whom to resign the see. Occasionally special circumstances created brief periods of pluralism as in 1562 when the pope allowed Nicolas de Pellevé to keep Amiens for six months after he had transferred to Sens. Another example involved François de Joyeuse who, having been named to Toulouse, had resigned Narbonne to the family client Raymond Cavalesi of Nîmes. Rome refused to accept Cavalesi, and Joyeuse served as archbishop of both sees for several years until a second request was successful. The practice of confidence was one way the French prelates used to diminish the loss of revenues caused by the prohibition against pluralism, but it differed from pluralism in that it could be practiced by bishops far less prominent than the pluralists were. Furthermore, confidence did provide for consecrated bishops for the sees involved, unlike pluralism.

Another problem in the French hierarchy that the Council of Trent addressed was the failure of many episcopal nominees to be consecrated within the required six months. In 1547 and again in 1562 the Council declared that anyone named as bishop would lose his see if he were not consecrated within six months. The French Church paid no attention to either decree. The problem took two forms: some bishops went unconsecrated for an inordinately long time and some were never consecrated at all. Many of the former were appointed bishop at an age too young to be ordained as priests (twenty-four years) and had to delay their consecration as bishops until that time. The longest delay in the century involved Gabriel Le Veneur de Tillières. Given the see of Evreux in 1531 at age sixteen, he was not consecrated until 1549. The confusion of the last years of Henri III's reign created several cases of delayed consecration such as that of Thomas de Lauro, named in 1588 to Vabres but consecrated only in 1594.

The practice of failing to be consecrated at all was more damaging to the Church since such prelates likely had taken the appointment in order to milk the see for all they could or merely to hold a "family" see until another relative was old enough to take it. Two bishops who became Protestant, Jacques Du Broullat of Arles and Jean de Chaumond of Aix, fall into the latter category. The worst example was Guillaume de Joyeuse, who was named to Alet in 1541 and resigned in 1557 without ever functioning as bishop after his older brother, the family heir, had died. His son would later become archbishop of Toulouse. Jean de Fonsec similarly held the title of bishop of Tulle from 1551 to 1560 without ever being consecrated. Pontac of Bazas complained in 1579 that three bishops had held their titles for three or more years without consecration.[24] Despite Pontac's jeremiad, it appears that the problem was becoming less serious by 1579, except for the period of anarchy after 1588.

Equally ignored was the prescription of canon law that preaching the Gospel was the chief duty of bishops. The sight of a bishop preaching was prior to Trent so rare that for a prelate to mount the pulpit created doubts about his orthodoxy. This seems to have been true of Antoine Caracciolo of Troyes. The announcement that he intended to preach shortly after his entry into the city in 1551 brought out a great crowd, for few had seen a bishop "step up into the pulpit."[25] In the same year the humanist Du Chastel also brought out a great crowd curious to hear a bishop preach when he became bishop of Orléans. In the sixteenth century only two kinds of bishops preached—the humanists, several of whom were accused of heresy, and the zealously orthodox, who later in the century saw the pulpit as a means of combating Protestantism, as Trent had proclaimed. Most of the prelates were like de Bourges of Châlons. When a Huguenot demanded to know why he did not preach, he replied that he had delegated the task to those of his clergy better at it than he.[26]

Hubert Jedin has defined three distinguishing marks by which the success of the Tridentine reform can be measured: the convocation of reform synods to institute the Tridentine reform, episcopal visitations according to its norms, and the founding of Tridentine seminaries.[27] This program largely assumed a resident prelate, and for that reason alone the French Church showed little sign of reforming prior to 1600. Information on the pastoral activities of the French bishops of the sixteenth century is, however, very sparse, in part because so few of them fulfilled many of their spiritual duties and in part because of the loss of the source material.

The council reaffirmed the requirement of canon law that bishops were to hold diocesan synods every year and archbishops to call provincial synods every three years. Before 1600 they were rare indeed. The first half of the century saw an average of 3.7 synods a year; this figure dropped to 2.9 for the period from 1550 to 1575 and climbed slightly to 3.1 for the next twenty-five years. A third of the sees had no synods at all during the sixteenth century.[28] Provincial synods were more uncommon. One such synod, of Narbonne in 1551, called because of Henri II's letter to the bishops of that year, had no bishops in attendance. The Cardinal de Lorraine held a provincial synod for Reims in 1564 where an important item of business was a protest against the loss of three former suffragans in Flanders to the new province of Malines.[29] In 1572 Antoine d'Albon of Lyon also called a synod for his province. After 1580, with the slow infiltration of the principles of Trent and the appointment of more zealous archbishops such as Alessandro Canignani of Aix, a disciple of Cardinal Borromeo, provincial synods were more frequent. Between 1580 and 1590 seven such synods met. In 1581 Cardinal Charles de Bourbon convened a provincial synod that demonstrated an interest in instituting tridentine reform in the province of Rouen. A strong statement on residency was issued, which threatened to deprive absentee bishops of their incomes. Rules on proper decorum for the clergy were issued and a list of forbidden books drawn up to be read over the pulpits. The synod also dictated the founding of seminaries in every diocese, although the first in the province did not appear until 1659. In general, despite the good intentions, there is little sign that the synod had much of an impact.[30] Ironically the most successful was that of the worldly politician Renaud de Beaune of Bourges. Its decrees on Church reform were influential in the next century.[31]

A bishop also had the obligation to see that a competent priest was assigned to the parish. The bishop was to choose examiners from among his clerics to test new curates on their learning and morals. In order to insure that there would be competent priests available, Trent obliged the bishops to found seminaries. This requirement was one of the decrees of the council most ignored in France. Only the Cardinal de Lorraine in his see of Reims and the Cardinal de Joyeuse in Toulouse established what can be considered seminaries before 1600, although several bishops have been credited with attempting to found seminaries before then. For example, the pensions that Jérôme de Bourges of Châlons provided for poor students of his diocese have been styled a seminary.[32]

The third episcopal obligation that Trent reaffirmed was the annual visitation of the diocese. The Ordinance of Orléans of 1561 likewise enjoined prelates to make their visitations. This may well have been the most ignored of the duties of a bishop since it was the most burdensome. Unlike a diocesan synod, which could be held in a period of a week or two and called by a normally absentee bishop without too much effort, a diocesan visitation was a far more difficult matter. Except for the very smallest sees, it required a great deal more conscientiousness and zeal on the part of the prelate. Although information on visitations during the sixteenth century is very limited, it appears that very few extensive tours of the parishes of any diocese were made in that period, but Henri II's letter of 1551 ordering visitations did have some results. Evidence has been found that visitations were made in fourteen dioceses, at least three of which covered the entire diocese. In six cases—Autun, Carcassone, Gap, Grenoble, Valence-Die, and Paris —the bishops were the visitors, but the tour of Grenoble by Laurent Allemand appears to have been the only complete visitation made by a bishop. Giovanni Valerio, bishop of Grasse, who served as vicar of Agen, did make what appears to have been a thorough tour of the latter diocese. In the small sees of the south, especially the southeast, visitations were more common than in the large sees of the north where only the Cardinal de Lorraine in his diocese of Reims made an effort to visit more than a token number of parishes.[33]

In the sixteenth century even the most conscientious of bishops who bestirred themselves to make visitations came nowhere close to completing all the expected tasks in the parishes. The clerical visitor was far more interested in the conditions of the buildings, the sacred vessels, and furnishings than in the spiritual life and morals of the priests and people.[34] Certainly it was understandable that Pierre de Paparin of Gap, during his visitation of 1599, emphasized the ruined condition of most of the churches of the diocese. But in fact he was reflecting a spirit clearly in evidence throughout the sixteenth century. When Antoine de Crequi inspected the deanery of Retz in the see of Nantes in 1554, he visited forty-two establishments in twenty days, which clearly was not sufficient time to accomplish all of what was expected of a visitor. He listed the number of priests and monks at each establishment; the condition of the buildings and furnishings; the incidence of concubinage among the clerics; and for the parishes, the condition or existence of registers for baptism, marriages, and burials. The recorded impressions of Giovanni Valerio at Agen in 1551 were less orderly and dealt largely with the living conditions of the clerics and the appearance of buildings and furnishings. Valerio at the conclusion made a self-satisfied comment about the amount of paper required for the record of his visitation. The improvement made after 1600 was clearly demonstrated by a visitation made in the diocese of Vannes in 1633, which went into considerable detail about the morals and religious education of the laity.[35]

The framers of the decrees of Trent clearly believed that a reformed episcopacy was necessary for the well-being of the Church; they also intended that these reformed bishops should have far greater control over the lower clergy. The bishop alone was to be responsible for the examination and ordination of candidates for the priesthood. To avoid the problem of vagabond priests, bishops were not to ordain anyone who could not give proof of having a living. Priests were not to be absent from their parishes without permission of the bishop, and he was to see that they wore clerical garb and to strip them of their benefices if they did not. The council also increased episcopal control over the religious houses and the preaching of the members of religious orders in the diocese. In general the bishop was responsible for the moral behavior of his clergy, to see that the clerics were serious, modest, and devout.[36] Yet one can be certain that at a time when the most obvious of a bishop's obligations such as being in residence were being ignored, the required supervision of the lower clergy was also ignored by all but a very few zealous prelates.

One reforming activity that many bishops did undertake was the promotion of new religious orders in their dioceses. Ironically some of the more worldly prelates were active in this respect. The new order that received the most support was the Society of Jesus. The first French bishop to encourage its foundation in France was Guillaume Du Prat of Clermont, who had met several Jesuits at Trent in 1546 and was deeply impressed. In 1550 he gave them the use of the Collège de Clermont in Paris, but when he tried to give them ownership of the property, he found that the Jesuits had to be naturalized. The legal difficulties of that process required a more powerful patron, who was found in the Cardinal de Lorraine. He would remain a staunch supporter of the order, establishing them in Reims. The request for naturalizing the foreign Jesuits ran into fierce opposition from the Parlement, the Sorbonne, and the bishop of Paris, Eustache Du Bellay, a thorough-going Gallican. Lorraine was able to persuade Henri II to grant the letters of naturalization, but the Parlement registered them only in 1560. Du Bellay's opposition stymied Jesuit activity in Paris until his death in 1563; his successor, Guillaume Viole, was more favorable to the society.[37]

By that time other bishops had moved to form Jesuit colleges in their dioceses. Du Prat supported two in the see of Clermont. Robert de Pellevé invited the Jesuits to Pamiers in 1559, but he failed to provide financial support for the college that was founded.

Cardinal François de Tournon was a strong advocate of the Jesuits. In 1561 he established them in Tournon and helped to gain them entrée into Lyon in 1562. In Languedoc Cardinal Georges d'Armagnac invited the Jesuits to his sees of Toulouse and Rodez, although he was bishop of neither by the time they were established. In 1565 Cardinal Charles de Bourbon encouraged the society to come to Rouen, although the college there was not organized until 1593. The archbishop of Bordeaux, Antoine de Prévost, encountered considerable opposition in his effort to establish a Jesuit college, but he achieved his goal in 1572. Several other prelates invited the Jesuits to their dioceses in this period, but the lack of manpower prevented them from immediately accepting. They were far more likely to respond favorably to the great prelates.

The establishment of other new orders like the Minimes and the Capuchins was less controversial and was done with less fuss wherever it was attempted. Amyar de Rochechouart of Sisteron played an important part in securing royal permission for the Capuchins to come to France. Among the bishops noted as inviting the Capuchins into their sees were the Cardinal de Bourbon of Rouen in 1580, Côme Clausse of Châlons-sur-Marne in 1584 and Hannibal Rucellai at Carcassone in 1592.[38]

Reform of the Church through the introduction of the decrees of Trent and the new orders would have had little effect if the bishops did not reform themselves. At mid-century the episcopate was replete with examples of personal vices and weaknesses. There were numerous examples of sexual incontinence among the bishops. Among the prelates known to have had bastard children while already in office were Claude Dodieu of Rennes, Guillaume Pellicier of Montpellier, and Jacques Spifame of Nevers, all of whom had at least two children. Jean and Charles de Lorraine, Jean de Monluc, Martin de Beaune of Le Puy and the Cardinal de Bourbon, the League's candidate for the throne in 1589, were among prominent prelates who had illegitimate sons as did Giovanni Valerio of Grasse, who, according to Beza, upon sighting a beautiful girl while administering Confirmation, would place the miter on her head and say that she would make a beautiful évêquesse. At Castres

Claude d'Auraisin's seduction of an abbess motivated the hardly puritanical Henri III to seek his removal from office.[39]

In two cases bishops resigned their offices in order to make honest women of their mistresses, although both prelates, Spifame of Nevers and Jean Lettes of Montauban, became Protestant to marry. It is not clear whether the Huguenot woman Rolland de Chauvigné of Saint-Pol married after resigning his see was already his mistress. In recording the death of Aymar de Rochechouart of Sisteron in 1580, the Parisian diarist Pierre de L'Estoile reproduced a piece of doggerel that accused the bishop of the seduction of virgins, adultery, and incest. L'Estoile characterized him as "a true portrait of an Epicurean and one of the worst and filthiest of the flock."[40]

Perhaps the worst reputation in this regard was held by Cardinal Jean de Lorraine. Brantôme, that ever-eager gossip-monger, wrote about the cardinal:

I have heard tell when there arrived at Court some pretty girl or new matron who was beautiful, he would at once accost her, and, while conversing with her, would say that he wished to train her himself. . . . It was said that there was scarcely a married woman or girl resident at the Court, or newly arrived, who had not been debauched or ensnared by her avarice or by the liberality of the said cardinal; and few or none emerged from that Court honest girls or women.[41]

A different vice was noted in Cardinal Louis I de Guise, who was known as "the Cardinal of Bottles," and in Cardinals Louis and Charles de Bourbon.[42] Avarice was a frequent problem also, which usually presented itself in the accumulation of multiple benefices, or in some cases, such as Charles de Lorraine, by acquisitions of artworks and books both ancient and contemporary. Lorraine spent 400,000 écus in 1550 for a library of Greek manuscripts.[43] More serious examples appeared in the persons of the bishop of Coutances, Arthur de Cossé de Brissac, who was accused of plundering his diocese and abbeys, and the archbishop of Arles, Silvio di Santa Croce, whose penuriousness forced the Parlement of Aix to order him to provide alms to the victims of the great flood of the Rhone in 1580.[44] Two bishops were implicated in the treason of Charles de Bourbon in 1525; Jacques Hurault of Autun was eventually pardoned but the fate of the other, Antoine de Chabannes of Le Puy, is unknown.[45] François de Dinteville, bishop of Auxerre, had his first brush with the law when he was accused of executing summary justice on a peasant of one of his fiefs for poaching. He avoided punishment through the protection of his cousin Anne de Montmorency. Five years later a far more serious charge was laid against him, that he had conspired to poison the Dauphin François. Dinteville fled to Rome, and again Montmorency was able to have the charges dropped.[46] Another bishop who fled abroad to escape prosecution was Pierre d'Albret of Comminges who in 1565 was accused of minting coins in his château. Having fled to Spain, his service to Philip II prompted the Parlement of Toulouse to condemn him in absentia for *lèse majesté*.[47]

The reputation that the bishops had for personal immorality as found in the contemporary works is far worse than the number of specific instances of such vices might suggest, and it must be balanced by the many examples of righteous prelates. But the negative image appears far more dominant in the popular·imagination as recorded in contemporary works even if it is not entirely fair. In the era before the religious wars there are far more comments about the vices of the prelates than about saintly and pious bishops in works of Catholics like Pierre de L'Estoile, Pierre de Ronsard,[48] and Claude Haton, to say nothing of the Protestant writers. Perhaps the attitude of a large part of the French population can be best summed up in the story about Philippe Lenoncourt of Auxerre. After his heart had been entombed at the high altar of one of his abbeys, dogs broke in and ate it. The local populace said that its fate was the judgment of God on the bishop's sins.[49]

Clearly when the high officials of the Church fared so badly in the popular imagination, a movement that proposed the elimination of the episcopate was sure to have considerable appeal. It was indeed a sad commentary on the French episcopate that the bishop who most favorably impressed his people was Michel d'Arande of Saint-Paul-Trois-Châteaux, who was openly sympathetic to the Reformation.[50]

CHAPTER VII

THE BISHOPS
AND PROTESTANTISM:
THE SYMPATHIZERS

The sixteenth-century bishop with his vast powers, properties, revenues, and his life-style and indifference to his spiritual office constituted one of the major objections that the Protestants raised against the Catholic Church. They could find no justification in the Scriptures for the authority and wealth of an office that the Church declared the apostles had founded. While the abolition of the office of bishop was not a dominant theme of the Reformation, except among English Puritans, the reformers' objections to the Catholic tradition of the wealthy and powerful bishop were well known and often expressed. In the view of most Reformers, the bishop was to be superintendent of the preachers, not a feudal lord, but the Genevan Confession of Faith of 1536 and the French Confession of 1559 went further to deny the office. The latter stated that "all true pastors, wherever they may be, have the same authority and equal power."[1]

The reaction of the French bishops to this very real threat to their office, power, and revenues was considerably weaker and more disorganized than one might have expected, given the strength of the threat. Few bishops were involved before 1560 in the efforts to counter the Reformation. The lead came largely from the Sorbonne and the Parlements. Even after the religious wars had erupted in 1561, barely a quarter of the bishops in office between 1560 and 1589 can be cited as clearly involved in anti-Protestant activity of any kind. Perhaps as damaging, however, to the effectiveness of the

Catholic response as the uninterested attitude of the majority of bishops was the open sympathy for the Reform exhibited by some thirty bishops during the sixteenth century. Twelve of the prelates publicly joined the Protestant movement and can be termed apostates. The others to varying degrees demonstrated public support for the Reform, although they never fully embraced it themselves.

During the reign of François I the close relationship between humanism and religious reform complicates any examination of episcopal opposition to Protestantism and sympathy for it. A number of bishops who were humanists or patrons of humanism were interested in religious reform or supported those who were. Several patrons of humanism, such as the Cardinals Charles de Lorraine and François de Tournon, had reputations as being staunchly orthodox; yet, they contributed to the Reform movement through their patronage. Lorraine extended patronage to a number of humanists whose thought verged on heresy — Ramus, Rabelais, and several members of the Lyon circle noted for their free and sharp criticism of Catholic practices. Tournon, who in 1536 wanted Rabelais arrested as a Zwinglian, was nonetheless the patron of Nicolas Bourbon and Jean de Boysonné; the latter was arrested for heresy by the Parlement of Toulouse in 1532.[2]

Several other humanist bishops whose own orthodoxy was not under suspicion made a contribution to the spread of Protestantism through patronage of humanists whose beliefs were heterodox if not heretical. As late as 1561 Cardinal Georges d'Armagnac, another of the defenders of Rabelais and Clement Marot, was regarded as "weak" by the more militant Catholics because of his moderate stance on persecution of the Protestants.[3] Guillaume Petit de Parvey of Senlis and Troyes defended Lefèvre in 1519 in the controversy over the three Marys of the Gospel and helped him escape to Strasbourg in 1525; he was also Marguerite de Navarre's principal advisor in her dispute with the Sorbonne over her book, *Mirror of a Sinful Soul*. He was associated with several members of the Circle of Meaux until its breakup in 1525 and provided protection at the court where his stock was very high.[4] Another such bishop was Philippe de Cossé of Coutances who had among his friends and clients Nicolas Bourbon and Theodore Beza. Beza stated in a letter of 1542 that he was in residence at Cossé's house in Paris.[5]

Paris was a relatively safe place for the reformers until 1534, despite the Sorbonne, because its bishops, Etienne Poncher and especially Jean Du Bellay, were very open-minded. Du Bellay and his brother Guillaume were deeply involved in an unsuccessful project to bring Melanchthon to France to work out a religious compromise. He provided protection for Guillaume Bigot to return to France after his flight to the Protestant Swiss cities. Such activities prompted the Sorbonne in late 1530 to accuse Du Bellay, then still the bishop of Bayonne, of Lutheranism. A royal commission charged with hearing the case took testimony from his brother René, later bishop of Le Mans, that Jean had friendships with a number of suspected heretics; but he was acquitted. The charges failed to harm his standing at court, since he was shortly appointed ambassador to England where he strongly supported Henry VIII in his divorce case and was also promoted to the diocese of Paris. René Du Bellay served as administrator of Paris and allowed several evangelicals to preach, most notably Gérard Roussel, who preached at the court in 1533. In the eyes of the Sorbonne they were blatantly heretical, and Roussel and several other preachers were cited for heresy. François I assigned Guillaume Petit to aid René Du Bellay in hearing the case. They merely admonished Roussel and the others to be more careful in the future while Noël Béda, the leader of the Sorbonnists, was expelled from the city for writing a pamphlet on the case that was less than favorable to the king. In a letter of 1534 Etienne Dolet credited both Du Bellays and Guillaume Budé with protecting him from the Sorbonnists.[6]

The case that Gérard Roussel was heterodox can more easily be made. He was Lefèvre's companion as early as 1501 and has been attributed with strong influence in bringing Lefèvre to his liberal opinions on Purgatory and veneration of the saints. In 1525 the Parlement of Paris ordered that Roussel be seized wherever he was found, even if in church. After the flight to Strasbourg with others of the Circle of Meaux, Roussel went on to the Swiss cities. He was able to return under the protection of Marguerite de Navarre to be her confessor and *aumônier*, and in 1536 she used her influence to give him the bishopric of Oloron. In a letter to Calvin in 1540, Farel suggested that Marguerite had exerted considerable pressure on Roussel to take the bishopric. The Catholic author Florimond de Raemond remarked on Roussel's appointment to Oloron: "Thus the lambs were given to the care of the wolf." Nonetheless he admitted that while Roussel's doctrine was corrupted, his life was without reproach. He retained the bishopric until his death in 1555 despite frequent attempts to cite him for heresy. In 1550 the Sorbonne condemned a series of propositions attributed to Roussel that included a call for communion under both species, clerical marriages, the primacy of faith over works, and *sola scriptura*. On the other hand Roussel's and Marguerite's moderate reform brought down on them Calvin's denunciation as Nicodemites. Roussel was charged with refusing to profess Protestantism fully because he wanted to continue to enjoy the fruits of his bishopric. A zealous parishioner of Oloron gave the final opinion of his bishop's religious beliefs: he weakened the legs of the cathedral pulpit so that it collapsed when Roussel stood in it. He died shortly after from his injuries.[7]

Despite the protection that the Du Bellays gave Roussel and the early Reform, perhaps the most extensive from the French bishops, there is no evidence that they were not orthodox in their own beliefs. They were liberal humanists eager for Church reform and compromise with the Protestants. Other humanist bishops afforded protection to heterodox humanists, but their own doctrine came under suspicion as well. Certainly the most famous of these bishops was Guillaume Briçonnet whose Circle of Meaux provided a center of refuge for a number of reformers including the young Guillaume Farel. The most "Lutheran" of the reforms Briçonnet effected at Meaux was the distribution of Lefèvre's French New Testament to the poor, to the point that the diocese "began to smell of heresy." In 1525 he was called before the Parlement on the charge of erroneous instruction of the faithful and of favoring heretics. Although he was acquitted, he took a harder line toward the Protestants, and the Circle of Meaux broke up.[8]

Among its members who fled to Strasbourg was Michel d'Arande. He shortly returned to Paris under the protection of Marguerite de Navarre, and was given the bishopric of Saint-Paul-Trois-Châteaux. There he worked diligently but ineffectively to reform the clergy. Before his death in 1539, d'Arande received a letter from Farel that apparently chastised him bitterly for abandoning his earlier zeal for reform. His reply expressed regret at not having been able to accomplish as thorough a reform in his diocese as he had hoped.[9]

Another of Marguerite's protégés who faced charges of heresy was Guillaume Pellicier of Montpellier. He was a friend and patron of several Protestant humanists, and under his protection the Reform flourished in the medical school of Montpellier. While ambassador to Venice, he had married and had several children. Upon his return to France he was brought before the Parlement of Toulouse in 1551 on charges that he was a heretic, had allowed a heretic to preach, was married, and was despoiling his diocese. In fear of losing his see, he renounced his family and suspect opinions. His funeral provides the best evidence that he was not in good standing in the Church. He was refused episcopal honors and buried without any of the usual pomp.[10] Another noted humanist bishop accused of heresy was Pierre Du Chastel of Mâcon. Royal librarian after Guillaume Budé, he defended Robert Estienne when the Sorbonne began heresy proceedings against him for his text edition of the Bible. Estienne's son later declared that Du Chastel had made a profession of the Gospel during the reign of François I, a point affirmed by Beza who presented him as "a man of gentle spirit who favored the Reformation from the beginning."[11]

The bishop of Angers from 1530 to 1540, Jean Olivier, was never charged with heresy, but the Reformed Church of that city was said to have been organized under his protection. Beza referred to him as a "gentle spirit who favored as far as he could those of the religion."[12] His nephew Antoine Olivier first began to attract attention to his religious opinions in 1552 when he transferred from Digne to Lombès. There his views on the reform of the clergy and preaching the Gospel gave rise to rumors of Protestant sympathies. He was pressured into resigning in 1564.[13]

The brothers Haag, authors of the nineteenth-century *La France protestante*, described Pierre Du Val of Sées as "a patron of the Reform although a timid one." In 1552 he wrote an attack on the papacy as part of Henri II's Gallican offensive against Julius III. When Catherine de Medici came to power, he became a court preacher and was attacked for the doctrine revealed in his sermons. The attacks increased when he served as a Catholic representative at the Conference of Saint-Germain in 1561 immediately after the Colloquy of Poissy, Catherine's last effort to get a religious compromise. The only result of the conference was a vague statement of the Eucharist that the Sorbonne denounced as heretical. Largely because of the attacks Du Val resigned his see in 1564.[14]

Although François I appointed a considerably greater number of humanists than did his successors, three humanist bishops seated after 1547 also fell under the suspicion of heresy. Pierre Danès, the first professor of Greek in the Collège de France, is a good example of a humanist interested in Church reform who was accused of embracing the Reformation without formally being charged with heresy. Noël Béda, the Sorbonnist scourge of the early reformers, objected in 1534 to the courses on the Bible that Danès and three other *lecteurs royaux* of the college were delivering. The Sorbonne enjoined them from delivering any commentaries on Scripture. The *Histoire ecclésiastique* described Danès as one "who had entered into some knowledge of the truth" and classified him among the Nicodemites against whom Calvin had raged. Danès wrote a work condemning the abuses of papal power that apparently is no longer extant. By the time he became bishop in 1557, however, there was little question of his Catholic faith, and the curia made no objection to his nomination.[15]

Among Danès's students at the Collège de France was Jacques Amyot, whose career was quite similar to that of his teacher. From a *roturier* family of Melun, he became noted for his knowledge of Greek and served as tutor to the young Duc d'Anjou. The prince helped to make him bishop of Auxerre in 1570. Amyot was also

deeply interested in Protestantism, but by the time he received his
bishopric he had clearly reverted to Catholic orthodoxy. Amyot
abruptly left Paris for Bourges after the day of the Placards in 1534
and, according to Melchior Wolmar, professor of law at Bourges,
accepted the new religion there. The memoirs of Marguerite de
Valois, the daughter of Catherine de Medici, blamed Amyot for
Protestant influence on his pupil Anjou, who at the time of the
Colloquy of Poissy was very interested in "Huguenoterie," saying
his prayers in French and using Marot's Psalms. [16]

Still another humanist prelate whose orthodoxy was questioned
was Charles de Marillac, archbishop of Vienne. A member of the
royal council and ambassador to Constantinople and England,
Marillac had received the tiny see of Vannes in 1550 and then the
archdiocese of Vienne in 1557 as a reward for his services to the
crown, although he always remained a layman. As early as 1550 he
was suspected of penning an apology for an executed Protestant. [17]
The archbishop confirmed the suspicions of the conservative Catholics by his speech at the Assembly of Notables at Fontainebleau in
1560. In his address Marillac seconded the demand made by the
Admiral de Coligny for a free national council to settle the religious issues. He launched a bitter attack on the large number of
Italians in the French hierarchy who, he said, held a third of the
benefices and "suck our blood like leeches." Reform of the Church
required the residence of the bishops in their diocese and the
elimination of simony, the worst example of "that great Babylonian
beast, avarice." The most Protestant of the opinions he expressed
was the call for preaching the pure Word of God in French. Coming from an archbishop, the speech was very satisfying to the
Huguenots and was reproduced in all their histories from the
period. [18] The English ambassador stated that Marillac "discovered
himself to be a Protestant" at Fontainebleau. His point of view was
more Erasmian than Protestant, and, while it had been common
thirty years earlier, it was already rare by 1560. According to
Jacques de Thou, Marillac died three months later from melan-
choly caused by the mounting turmoil in France. [19]

None of these bishops, despite the accusations against them, appears to have been truly Protestant, although their beliefs and activities, viewed in the more rigid atmosphere of the Council of Trent and the reign of Henri II, were denounced as heterodox. All but two retained their bishoprics until their deaths, and those against whom formal charges of heresy were laid defended themselves strongly and for the most part effectively. Perhaps d'Arande would have made clear commitment to the Reform if he had lived to see the period after 1560 when the sectarian lines were more clearly drawn. Most of the humanist bishops, however, who lived on into the reign of Henri II and beyond it, drew back from the more radical element of the humanist movement. Nonetheless, through their patronage and sympathy in the formative years of French Protestantism and their refusal to use the legal machinery against heresy, they made a contribution of some importance to its growth.

François de Pisseleu, a brother of François I's mistress, named bishop of Amiens in 1546, was more aggressive in his support of those accused of heresy. A correspondent of Calvin's, he was termed the protector of Lutherans in Amiens, likely because of his stand against the *chambre ardente*. He refused to pay the fee of 100 livres that the court demanded for the processing of suspected heretics from his diocese; the court issued an *arrêt* against him. He also wrote to the court demanding the return of suspected heretics from Amiens to his *officialité*. Henri II, just before his death, wanted to have him named legate to Scotland, but the papacy objected because of suspicions about his orthodoxy. Pisseleu shortly after resigned his see, and no further notice about him can be found.[20]

Far more scandalous was the open apostasy of twelve French bishops. Their careers and the reason for their appointments were quite different from the humanist-bishop. Only two of these bishops can be considered humanists, but largely because of their patronage of humanists, not for their own scholarship. Five of the apostate bishops were seated in the reign of François I; Henri II, despite his reputation as a Catholic zealot, appointed six, and the last gained a see under Charles IX. Contrary to the high incidence of commoners among the humanist bishops, the apostate prelates were entirely noble. Ten were members of the *noblesse d'épée*, and two were *anoblis*.

The two humanists among the apostates were Gabriel de Clermont of Gap and Cardinal Odet de Châtillon of Beauvais. Clermont, who was seated at Gap in 1527 by the pope, began his episcopal career by insisting that the city enforce the decrees against Lutheranism. He was converted by Guillaume Farel, a native of Gap, in 1561. He helped Farel preach the Reform, married at about the age of sixty-five, and was deposed by the curia in 1568. He then resigned his see formally, keeping a pension of 2,000 livres on the bishopric.[21]

The Cardinal de Châtillon was far more notorious. The brother of the Admiral de Coligny, he had the highest rank in both the Church and the nobility among the prelates who became Protestant. He was named a cardinal at the age of sixteen and became archbishop of Toulouse in 1534 while holding sixteen abbeys *in commendam*. Despite remaining a deacon, the next year he also received the see of Beauvais. After he resigned Toulouse in 1553, he continued to hold Beauvais because it conveyed the rank of peer of the realm.[22] As early as 1551 the English ambassador reported that Châtillon favored the Protestants, and by 1560 he had clearly joined the Huguenot party. In that year the papal nuncio reported on his heretical statements, and at Easter, 1561, Châtillon was reported to have celebrated the Eucharist "in the mode of Geneva." This act was repeated at the Colloquy of Poissy with two other prelates. In 1562 several Parisians told the nuncio that the pope could not defer any longer from proceeding against the cardinal.[23] Consequently the curia cited him for heresy in November, 1562, and the next March he was excommunicated and deprived of his title as cardinal and his benefices. Although the French court strongly protested what it saw as an infringement of the liberties of the Gallican Church, it persuaded Châtillon to resign Beauvais to his friend François de Noailles, himself shortly cited for heresy. Because of his skills as a diplomat and his family ties, Châtillon remained in the good graces of the court despite his public marriage to a Huguenot woman in 1564. In 1570 the nuncio Frangipani angrily reported that Châtillon intended to reclaim his benefices. He died in 1571 before doing so.[24]

Perhaps the most notorious case of Protestantism in the episcopacy involved Jacques Spifame of Nevers. After taking a law degree
at Orléans, he became a *conseiller* of the Parlement and the chancellor of the University of Paris. He was appointed bishop of Nevers
in 1546 and served as a canon lawyer at Trent in 1547. In 1558
while giving Communion in his cathedral, he said: "Receive the
symbol of the body of Christ." The dean of the chapter seized the
ciborium from him and gave Communion under the proper rubric.
Word of this reached Henri II who ordered an investigation, since
Spifame came from a family that had been making large loans to
the throne. Before a decision was ready, Spifame resigned his
benefices to his nephew and fled to Geneva. The city council
recognized his marriage and granted him citizenship. He returned
to France in 1561 as a Reformed minister and ably served the cause
as a diplomat. In 1564 he became chancellor for Jeanne d'Albret.
But within a year they had a bitter falling out. In 1566 charges
were laid against him of adultery and treason against the city of
Geneva. He was quickly convicted and executed. The impact of
the Spifame case on both sides of the religious split reverberated for
many years.[25]

An earlier example of apostasy in the French episcopate was Jean
Lettes of Montauban. He had served as his uncle's vicar general
until he received the see for himself in 1539. Several authors have
attributed his conversion to Calvinism to the influence of a woman
he married in 1556, although the *La France protestante* has ascribed
the decision to a curé of Montauban who had converted earlier.[26]
He resigned his benefices for a large pension in 1556 and retired to
Bern the same year. He is usually noted as the first French bishop
to convert publicly to Protestantism.

Another apostate bishop whom François had seated was Jean de
Barbanzon, the nephew of his mistress, who was given Pamiers in
1544 when he was only seventeen and a student at Paris. Never a
priest, Barbanzon openly accepted the Reformation and in 1557
resigned his see for a pension and the title of Seigneur de Varesnes.
He was later active as a Huguenot captain.[27]

Another see of the Midi to suffer an apostate bishop was Arles where Jacques Du Broullat, a relative of the *Connétable* Mont-morency, had been named archbishop in 1550. He was never ordained a priest, nor did he ever enter his diocese. In 1552 he asked Rome to allow him to continue receiving the episcopal reve-nues without being consecrated. He joined the Prince de Condé as a chaplain to his army, and the Parlement of Paris deprived him of his benefices in 1560. He retained control of at least one of his monasteries, for he gave it over to the Huguenots in 1563 for use as a stronghold. After Catholic forces retook it, Du Broullat fled to Germany, where he married. He died there in 1576.[28]

By 1560 the incidence of heretical bishops in the French Church had reached the level that Rome began to take serious notice of it. Paul IV, despite his reputation as a zealous foe of Protestantism, had done nothing to purge the French hierarchy of its apostates and those sympathetic to the Reform. The election of Pius IV in 1559 placed in the Holy See someone more aware of the problem and determined to correct it. The sense of uneasiness about the reliabil-ity of the French episcopate reached the point that the papal secretary of state, Cardinal Borromeo, wrote to the nuncio in France in April, 1561, that he should not press the French bishops too hard on going to the reconvened Council of Trent because their doctrine was "little sure."[29] This uneasiness certainly must have increased when reports of the Colloquy of Poissy and its follow-up, the Conference of Saint-Germain, reached Rome later in 1561.

These reports informed the curia that three bishops had cele-brated the Eucharist "in the manner of Geneva." Three other bish-ops had refused to sign an oath affirming the Catholic doctrine of the Eucharist. Yet another bishop had served as a Catholic represen-tative at the Conference of Saint-Germain, the queen mother's attempt to carry on the discussions of the Colloquy of Poissy on a more informal level. It had issued an ambiguous statement on the Eucharist. In 1562 the Roman Inquisition began to investigate the orthodoxy of a number of French prelates. In the next year it issued citations against eight of them and ordered them to come to Rome within six months to answer charges of heresy. The eight were Jean de Chaumond, archbishop of Aix, Antonio Caracciolo, bishop of Troyes, Charles de Guillart of Chartres, Jean de Monluc of Valence, François de Noailles of Dax, Jean de Saint-Gelais of Uzès and the incumbents of the two Béarnese dioceses, Louis d'Albret of Lescar and Claude Regin of Oloron.[30] The inquisition apparently decided to deal only with those prelates who had not already resigned or been deprived of their benefices. It appears that those cited had drawn the tribunal's attention by their conduct at the Colloquy of Poissy or by their service to Jeanne d'Albret; only Chaumond of Aix does not fit in either category. Among the other possibly heterodox bishops of the time only Du Val's activities at Poissy likely had come to the Inquisition's attention; the others were not yet sufficiently notorious. Why Du Val was not included is not known.

The highest-ranked in blood among those charged was Caracciolo of Troyes, the son of the Prince of Melfi who had served François I in the Italian wars.[31] As a youth Antonio spent some time as a Carthusian, but his family ties and the friendship of Marguerite de Navarre quickly brought him a better position as abbot of Saint-Victor de Paris. His *Le mirouer de vraye religion* of 1544 indicated considerable agreement with Protestant belief at that early date, especially the idea that man is justified by grace alone.[32] Despite his notions about Church reform, he ruled his abbey in an autocratic and extravagant way, provoking deep resentment from the canons. Their efforts to remove him led to the appointment as bishop of Troyes in 1551. The pope and the curia questioned his nomination because of reports of his heterodox views. But Cardinal Caraffa, a relative of Caracciolo, strongly defended him and pressured the curia into granting the bulls. In 1563 Pius IV remarked that Caraffa, so severe toward others, had been too beneficent toward his own. Caraffa, as pope, did refuse to give the red hat to Caracciolo despite pressure from Henri II.[33]

Despite his reputation as a supporter of the Reformation, or perhaps because of it, Caracciolo was invited to the Colloquy of Poissy as a Catholic representative. There he decided that the atmosphere was right for a further step and asked the Reformed Church of Troyes if he could serve it as both bishop and minister.

The request went to Calvin through Beza. Calvin's reply must have disappointed Caracciolo, for Calvin stated that he must abandon his title, although apparently he could serve as superintendent of ministers of the Church of Troyes. He could also retain the temporals if he used them for the benefit of the Church. Caracciolo proceeded to attend Protestant services and to preach, declaring himself to be "bishop and minister of the Holy Gospel."[34] After strong objections from the Catholic clergy and the dashing of his hopes that the court would support a moderate reform, Caracciolo resigned his diocese in late 1562 with a pension of 2,000 livres and married. He soon found that his ambiguous position on doctrine rendered him undesirable to the Huguenots as well. At that point the inquisition began to move against him.

From a less substantial family than Caracciolo but far more influential at court was Jean de Monluc of Valence. Brother of the famed captain Blaise de Monluc, member of the *conseil d'état* and trusted diplomat, Monluc was rewarded for his diplomatic missions with the see of Valence. Beza stated that he "made a mélange of the two doctrines." The Sorbonne censored several pamphlets that Monluc published between 1557 and 1561 for their statements on free will, the Eucharist, veneration of the saints, and numerous other points of doctrine. As one of the Catholic participants at the Colloquy of Poissy, he refused to assist at Mass with Cardinal d'Armagnac and celebrated the Lord's Supper "à la mode de Genève." In 1562 his brother Blaise reportedly asked Rome to deprive him of his see and punish him for heresy.[35]

The prelates who celebrated the Protestant service with Monluc were Cardinal de Châtillon and Jean de Saint-Gelais of Uzès. The cardinal was the subject of a separate process; the latter was one of the eight charged in 1563. Saint-Gelais had a licentiate in both civil and canon law and was twenty-six years old when he followed his uncle as bishop of Uzès in eastern Languedoc. According to one tradition, Saint-Gelais abandoned his see in 1543 and married an abbess, but it is most unlikely that the marriage occurred that early, since his election as a representative for the First Estate in 1561 explains his presence at Poissy. Like Monluc he refused to take Communion from the hands of Cardinal d'Armagnac and to swear the profession of faith affirming the real presence in the Eucharist demanded by the assembled clergy. These were the reasons for his indictment by the inquisition, but he added to them in late 1562 when he and Cardinal de Châtillon went to Languedoc to persuade the Comte de Curssol to place himself at the head of the Protestants in the Midi.[36]

Another bishop who alerted the Roman Inquisition by his refusal to sign the confession of faith at Poissy was Charles de Guillart, from a prominent family of the long robe, who succeeded his uncle Louis as bishop at Chartres in 1553 at the age of twenty-four.[37] According to the records of the papal consistory, he also vehemently refused to subscribe to a document promulgated by the Parlement that acknowledged the primacy of the pope. The *Histoire ecclésiastique* reported that Guillart allowed an apostate monk to preach in his cathedral and was himself present. A letter to Beza of 1566 mentions a Reformed catechism that had been recently printed in Chartres with the approval of the bishop.[38]

The highest-ranking churchman on the inquisition's list was Jean de Chaumond, archbishop of Aix, a twenty-seven-year-old canon from Lyon when he was appointed to the see in 1551. According to the inquisition's report on him, very soon after his entry into Aix he allowed apostate priests to preach and was present at Reformed services. De Thou declared that Chaumond publicly professed the new religion and sought to establish it in his diocese, in part by giving benefices to known heretics.[39]

The two Béarnese bishops cited by Rome owed their positions to Jeanne d'Albret; both were appointed in 1555. Louis d'Albret, a civil lawyer, was the great uncle of the queen of Navarre, and Claude Regin of Oloron served as her secretary. Their close relationships with Jeanne likely precipitated the charge against them as there is no obvious evidence of heresy in their beliefs.

If the inquisition's evidence against Regin and d'Albret appears weak, it was even weaker in the case of François de Noailles of Dax, whose diocese lay astride the border of Béarn. From a prominent Gascon family, Noailles became bishop of Dax in 1556. He owed his appointment to the Châtillons and to his position as an *aumônier* for Henri II. He was never in residence because of his diplomatic missions to England and Italy. It has been maintained that the inquisition accused him of heresy partly because of his close relationship to the Châtillons and partly because of his views on religious toleration. Noailles claimed credit for negotiating the terms of the agreement concerning the regency between Catherine de Medici and Antoine de Bourbon after François II's death. The evidence against Noailles appears considerably weaker than that available against several bishops who were not indicted.

Although the citations of the Roman Inquisition against these eight prelates were posted only in Rome, the news quickly reached Paris. Monluc and Noailles immediately protested their loyalty to the Roman Church, while Caracciolo in a letter to the nuncio declared that the news had moved him to tears and compelled him to prove his fidelity to the pope. More importantly Catherine de Medici raised the charge that the citations had violated the liberties of the Gallican Church and asserted that the bishops had to be tried in France. Although Catherine strongly defended the orthodoxy of Monluc and Noailles, whether the bishops were guilty of heresy was quite beside the point. The real issue for her was the papal infringement of the Gallican liberties. Since the Cardinal de Châtillon had already been deprived by Rome of his benefices, he resigned Beauvais to Noailles, and the queen mother gave his brother Giles the see of Dax. She then named Noailles ambassador to Rome to procure the bulls of office for himself and his brother. Not only was this act a demonstration of her faith in him but a deliberate tweaking of the papal beard as well. Pius IV agreed to separate Noailles's case from the other seven prelates as a concession to the French Court, but he refused to accept him as French ambassador.

The Grand Inquisitor offered a compromise by which Monluc, Caracciolo, and d'Albret were to be deprived of their benefices and the other four were to be suspended from their spiritual duties until they gave clear evidence of repentance. Even this plan was unacceptable to the monarchy, and the matter dragged on until the death of Pius IV in 1565. His successor, Pius V, was the Grand

Inquisitor who had begun the process. He was determined to see the matter finished. In December, 1566, the pope, declaring the seven prelates obstinate in their errors, pronounced a final sentence against them, depriving them of their titles and benefices. The French court ignored the sentences, allowed the accused to continue to receive their revenues, and refused to nominate replacements.[40]

In two cases the problem had already been solved since Chaumond and Caracciolo had resigned their bishoprics before 1567. The archbishop of Aix, upon hearing of the charge against him, mounted the cathedral pulpit, delivered a bitter blast against the pope, threw down his miter, and marched off to join the Huguenot army. He tried to sell his office to his vicar general, but the pope refused to recognize the transaction. Cardinal Lorenzo Strozzi was named to fill the see. Chaumond took an active part in several Huguenot expeditions in Languedoc and later married and went to Geneva. Caracciolo had resigned the see of Troyes before he heard of the inquisition's citation. In 1563 he had a long conversation with the papal nuncio in hopes of returning to the good graces of the Catholic Church. A year later, however, he wrote letters to the Reformed Church of Troyes and to Beza asking their forgiveness for the scandal he had caused.[41] He retired to his estate on the Loire and died in 1570.

Two of the prelates, Monluc and Saint-Gelais, appealed to the king to reject the sentences of 1566 as an intolerable infringement of the Gallican liberties. They both also protested that the charges were false and that they were good Catholics. Monluc, however, was quoted as saying that not the pope but the king was the patron of the bishops of France and that he would recognize as his superiors only God and the king.[42] The Parlement of Paris with the approval of the king ordered the chapters of the two dioceses not to accept anyone else as bishop.[43] Throughout his life Monluc continued to hold the ambiguous doctrine that had led to the heresy charge. It enabled him to serve as a negotiator between Catholics and Protestants for the court and to go to Poland to explain away the Saint Bartholomew's massacre before the election of Henri d'Anjou to the Polish throne. He resigned the see of Valence to his nephew shortly before his death in 1579. The papal nuncio Salviati reported that, after a marriage to an abbess and several years as an active leader of the Huguenots in the south, Saint-Gelais formally reaffirmed his Catholicism between the hands of Cardinal d'Armagnac shortly before he resigned his bishopric in 1574. On the other hand Guillart of Chartres retained his reputation as a Protestant longer than his bishopric. During St. Bartholomew's Day a mob pillaged his house in Paris, and it was said that he was fortunate to be elsewhere at the time. He shortly resigned his see to Nicolas de Thou.[44] Both Béarnese prelates remained in office until their deaths.

After the inquisition's charges against the eight churchmen, the incidence of apostasy declined sharply. By serving notice that Rome was now prepared to deal with prelates it deemed heterodox, the inquisition's actions likely caused some bishops to reconsider their opinions. Likely as important, however, was the drastically changed atmosphere in France with the wars of religion now raging and church property being destroyed. Nonetheless two more cases of apostasy in the episcopate did occur. The first involved Jean—Baptiste Raimbaud de Simiane. He had a degree in civil law and was bishop of Vence from 1555 to 1560 and then of Apt from 1560 to 1571. He was one of the bishops who refused to take the oath affirming the Catholic doctrine of the Eucharest, yet the cathedral chapter was apparently taken by surprise when he, his vicar general, and an abbess he later married fled Apt for Germany in 1569. Simiane resigned his bishopric to his brother, a Carthusian, who had to receive a testimonial from his superior to his sound doctrine.[45]

Despite the monarchy's zeal in protecting the bishops charged by the inquisition, it was far more careful to nominate orthodox bishops after 1563. The curia was as well far more careful in examining the doctrine of the nominees. As a result only one appointment slipped through to embarrass the Church by later apostatizing. André d'Auraisin, nominated to Riez in 1570, was another civil lawyer, and had served as a military officer before the appointment. He came to Riez in full armor to take possession of the see and collect his revenues. He continued his military career and helped his brother take Riez for the Huguenots in 1574. By

1577 d'Auraisin had agreed to resign his bishopric for a pension of 800 écus, openly confessed Calvinism, and married.[46]

The last example of a bishop over whom the cloud of suspicion about his orthodoxy hung heavy was Paul de Foix de Carmaing.[47] In de Foix's case the controversy arose because the court, wishing to reward an important adviser, insisted on giving him a bishopric despite the adamant refusal of the papacy. Yet another civil lawyer and a "mécène des savants et des étudiants," de Foix became a conseiller clerc of the Parlement of Paris in 1555. He was one of the five magistrates of that court who were arrested in 1559 for heresy. Unlike Anne de Bourg, who was executed, de Foix was obliged to make a public confession of his belief in the Catholic doctrine of the Eucharist and was suspended from the Parlement for one year. The significant points on which de Foix found himself under suspicion were his belief in Communion under both species and his strong stand on the need for a national council. While several Protestant authors considered de Foix to be sympathetic to their cause, they agreed that he never identified himself directly with Protestantism. But in 1568 the English ambassador in Paris reported that de Foix, who had been French ambassador to London, had been ordered home, "being suspected to be of the Religion."[48]

Within a year of his conviction the Parlement had annulled the entire proceedings against de Foix and accepted his orthodoxy without reservation. The papacy, however, ignored the acquittal; and when de Foix, always a trusted adviser to Catherine de Medici, was nominated to the see of Narbonne in 1572, Gregory XIII refused his bulls. Since the court refused to submit a new candidate, the pope used the clause in the Concordat of Bologna that gave him the rights to fill a see in such circumstance to appoint the theologian Simon Vigor. Both men went to Rome to secure the bishopric, but Gregory refused to see de Foix. Vigor thus became archbishop of Narbonne. A new commission of the Parlement again cleared de Foix of heresy, and Henri III nominated him to Toulouse in 1577. Again the pope balked, and the nuncio's correspondence for the next five years is full of references to the problem. In 1582 Gregory finally granted de Foix's bulls to Toulouse, but he died within a year without taking possession of his see.[49] De Foix's case makes it clear that when the monarchy was determined and persistent, it could secure an episcopal appointment for whom it wished, even one whom Rome considered guilty of heresy.

One can divide the bishops discussed above into two groups: those who, while sympathetic to the Reformation and willing to accept some Protestant doctrine, did not apostatize and those who did. Among the former were two prelates who reportedly abjured their new religion before their deaths but who did live openly as Protestants for a number of years. Nine of the twelve bishops identified as apostates made public marriages, and it appears that for five of them the desire to make honest women of their mistresses was a factor in the decision to become Protestant. Six of the apostates sought refuge in Protestant areas, and all resigned their bishoprics, although Guillart was able to keep his until 1573. All were able to resign their offices for sizable pensions and usually to clerics of their choice, although in several cases the pensions or the papal bulls for their choices as successors were not forthcoming. It is likely that the promise of a continued income from their bishoprics made the decision to resign easier. Ten of these bishops were from the *noblesse de race* (including Caracciolo), while the other two were *anoblis*. If significance can be attributed to such a small sample, it is that the nobles of the sword, who dominated the episcopacy but not to the point of 84 percent, were more willing to give up the status of an episcopal office since they could fall back on the standing and wealth of their families. At least six of the apostate bishops came from families that were heavily Protestant and probably were supportive.

Six of these prelates were under the age of twenty-seven and seven were not priests at the time of appointment; all but one of the latter never were ordained priests during their episcopal careers. Most of the apostate bishops likely had no real vocation for a career in the Church but, as members of the nobility, accepted an episcopal appointment as a duty to the family. When attracted to the Reform, whether for theological or political reasons, they were willing to abandon their sees and confess Protestantism publicly.

The social status of these bishops is pertinent to a point first raised in the *Histoire ecclésiastique*. Followed by other Protestant historians, it argued that while many bishops showed an interest in the Reformation, so few actually joined it because of their unwillingness to give up the status and lucrative benefices of a prelate.[50] Paul Geisendorf has suggested that if Calvin had been more sympathetic to Caracciolo's request to keep his office, more bishops would have become Protestants, "and a kind of French Anglicanism" might have appeared.[51] While this statement ignores the necessary role of the monarchy, the prelates of the lower social categories did reveal a determination to avoid a strong commitment to Protestantism that would have cost them their bishoprics. The bishops from the *noblesse de race*, however, were more willing to give up their offices. There were nineteen nobles of the sword among the thirty-one bishops in question, a number that corresponds closely to the 55 percent of the French episcopacy that was from the *noblesse de race* at mid-century. Ten of the twelve who apostatized were from that social status. These statistics suggest that nobles of the sword were attracted to the Reformation at a rate about equal to their presence in the hierarchy, but a higher proportion were willing to resign their sees and become Protestant publicly. The argument that the desire to hold on to their bishoprics kept bishops in the Roman Church may well have been true for the minority who came from the lower social orders but appears far less true for the *noblesse de race*, the majority of bishops. Beza's argument is also diminished by the fact that even an apostate bishop could resign his see for a healthy pension and other considerations. A benefice was treated as a property right in the sixteenth century, and even the condemnation of the Roman curia could not prevent a recalcitrant bishop from enjoying the temporal fruits of his see as long as he wanted.

There also appears to have been something of a geographical factor involved as well. Twenty-one of the thirty-one bishops held sees in the Midi. Dauphiné had five from among its seven sees and Languedoc five from its twenty-two, but the worst affected was Provence with four bishops in office in 1560 who apostatized. It is true that the Midi had slightly over half of the French dioceses, but the incidence of heterodoxy was far higher, especially compared with areas like Brittany, which had no cases.

In several cases like those of Caracciolo at Troyes and Clermont at Gap the bishops seem to have been influenced by the strength of the Reformation in their cathedral cities; in others like that of Jean Olivier at Angers, the strength of the local Protestant movement depended upon the protection of the bishops. But the larger incidence of apostate prelates from the Midi appears to be in large part a consequence of the fact that, with the exception of Châtillon of Beauvais, those apostate bishops whose families were strongly Protestant were found in the Midi. The greater appeal of the Reformation to the southern nobility was reflected in the southern episcopate as well.

Another factor, more pertinent for the bishops who were sympathetic to the Reform than for the apostates, was the pattern of François I's nominations of humanists who had little standing beyond their scholarly reputations; they received the smallest and the poorest sees, most of which were in the south. It was that sort of humanist bishop who was most liberal in religion yet drew back from personally accepting the Reformation.

The failure of the papacy to remove bishops like Monluc or Guillart from office indicates the enormous difficulty Rome had in dealing with heretical prelates protected by the court. Much of the responsibility for the general toleration of heterodoxy in the episcopacy lay with the monarchy, which often nominated individuals whose views were suspect and did almost nothing to force accused prelates out of office. Perhaps the monarchy might have moved against some of the apostate bishops if they had not quickly resigned; but not a single case in this study reveals a major role for the court in dismissing suspect bishops. In the early years of the Reformation the lead in the opposition to heterodox prelates came from the Sorbonne, but it later came from the chapters. Most of the thirty-one bishops cited above left the administration of their sees to vicar generals, and while there is one example of a vicar general joining his bishop in fleeing to Germany, many were busy directing the prosecution of Protestants while the bishops were elsewhere promoting Reform. The antagonism between bishop and cathedral chapter, endemic in the period, often left the canons taking the lead in denouncing heterodox prelates. Regardless of how the suspect opinions of these bishops came to the attention of the higher authorities, the monarchy protected them against the Sorbonne and the Parlements, or later the inquisition, and placed many in high positions of government. To a large extent this was true for Henri II, despite his reputation for strict orthodoxy, as it was for François I or Catherine de Medici.

Nonetheless the responsibility for failing to purge the hierarchy of its heterodox members was not the monarchy's alone. Inaction on the part of the papacy permitted men with suspect beliefs to gain episcopal office and hold them until 1559, when the election of Pius IV began a more active role for the curia. Before then the action taken against the prelates was done by the Sorbonne and the Parlements, and it was largely ineffective without concurrent action from the curia. There is little evidence that Paul III, Julius III, and Paul IV involved themselves in combating Protestantism in the French episcopate. Bishops who already had a reputation for Protestant sympathies were welcomed to Rome, and Cardinal Caraffa defended his relative Caracciolo against accusations of heresy. The nuncio's reports before 1559 are void of reports or discussions of the heterodox bishops. Yet the problem had certainly become serious before 1559. Paul IV, despite his reputation as fiercely anti-Protestant, took no action against these bishops, except Spifame whose flight to Geneva in early 1559 forced a response.[52] Effective action on the part of the papacy began only with election of Pius IV, whose efforts to purge the episcopacy were frustrated by Catherine de Medici. In the next ten years the most blatant cases were removed, and only two of the bishops involved were appointed after 1559. While Cardinal Borromeo's statement of 1561 was clearly alarmist, it was important because it demonstrated that the papacy had finally become fully aware of the danger to the Roman Church among the French bishops, and, as events showed, had begun to take steps to remedy it. The Counter-Reformation, as far as it concerned the French episcopacy, began in 1559.

CHAPTER VIII

THE BISHOPS
AND PROTESTANTISM:
THE OPPOSITION

T he popes and the kings were not the only authorities who were derelict in their duty to purge the French Church of its openly heretical clerics before 1561; prior to that date the bishops also largely ignored their obligation to use their offices to protect the Church from doctrinal deviation. Protestant antagonism to the episcopal office and zeal to seize the vast properties and revenues held by the prelates placed most bishops in a relationship of confrontation with the reformers, yet a large number of bishops ignored the presence of Protestants in their dioceses. That number was substantially higher before the first religious war had broken out; but even after 1561, with Church property being seized or ruined and a number of bishops physically threatened or forced to flee their dioceses, many bishops, even in some of the most severely disrupted dioceses of the Midi, left no evidence of any activity in opposition to the Protestants. The response of the episcopate was far weaker and less effective than one could have expected from a group whose way of life and prestigious status were so strongly under attack.

The episcopate left the early condemnation of Lutheranism to the Sorbonne and the Parlement of Paris, but an occasional bishop was involved in heresy processes against "Lutherans." For example, Claude de Langwy of Amiens played a significant role in the second arrest and trial of Louis de Berquin in 1526.[1] Berquin was tried a third time in 1529 and executed. At Châlons-sur-Marne, Giles de Luxembourg announced in 1526 his intention of bringing in a

special preacher for Lent because of "the smell of heresy and the
Lutheran sect that are now polluting in certain places."[2] At the
Assembly of Notables of 1527 that François I called to raise the
ransom required to free his two sons, Cardinal Louis de Bourbon,
possessor of three sees, called on the king "to uproot and extirpate
the damnable Lutheran sect that has recently entered the realm in
secret." The king promised to order the French archbishops to call
provincial synods to deal with heresy and to approve of new décimes
levied for the ransom.[3] Thus three synods were held at Sens,
Bourges, and Lyon. At Sens the archbishop, Cardinal Antoine
Du Prat, led the way in drawing up a long series of decrees of
heresy. They included the requirements that the bishops examine
every book on religion printed in the past twenty years and that
they visit each parish in their dioceses and compel three men of
good reputation to denounce those with heretical opinions. The
other two provincial synods came up with similar if not quite as
demanding decrees against the "Lutherans."[4] Since few bishops
were in residence in their sees to attend the synods or to enact these
proposals, enforcing the decrees fell to the zeal of their vicars
general.

Four prelates closely associated with the royal court established
the strongest reputations for opposing Protestantism during François
I's reign, yet they appear to have had little impact on the king.
They were Du Prat of Sens, Cardinal François de Tournon of Bourges,
Robert Cenalis of Riez, and at the end of François's reign, Cardinal
Charles de Lorraine. All four were patrons of humanists, including
some scholars suspected of heresy, but they more than made up for
it by their zeal to stamp out Protestantism. Cenalis, who was a
strong advocate of orthodox reform both at the court and in his see,
wrote several books attacking Calvin and Luther and defending
clerical celibacy and the use of force against heretics. His efforts at
reforming the diocese of Riez drew the implacable opposition of
the cathedral canons, causing him to transfer to Avranches in
1532. Of the four bishops Tournon in particular has been described
as a fanatic. He has been considered, along with the archbishops of
Aix and Arles, Pierre Filhol and Imbert Antonine, as the prime

mover behind the destruction of the Waldensian communities in Dauphiné in 1545.[5]

During François I's reign, however, it is easier to find examples of bishops showing sympathy for the Reformation than those actively opposing it. Even some of the instances of bishops involved in the persecution of Protestants reported in the *Histoire ecclésiastique* may not be accurate since several of these bishops were definitely not in residence. Their vicars general may well have been responsible for the legal acts against heretics attributed to the bishops, perhaps because they were in residence and saw the incursion of the Reformation more clearly.

The connection between the success of the Reformation and the French episcopacy has already been noted in a negative way: absenteeism and indifference kept their bishops from taking action against the Protestants until it was too late.[6] It is also true that a number of humanist bishops and others sympathetic to the Reform appear to have decided not to use the legal machinery that they controlled against the early Protestants. The moral authority of the French bishop was at this time quite low, while his vicar general, often from the local clergy, was more aware of popular currents and was in a better position to respond to the appearance of Protestantism.[7] Nonetheless it is hard to deny that the lack of involvement on the part of most bishops in the early years of the Reformation made the Catholic response considerably less effective.

The reign of Henri II saw some increase in the number of bishops active in the opposition to the Reformation. This increased zeal was in part a consequence of the clearer danger that Calvinism posed to the Church after 1547 and in part a result of the harder line that the new king took toward Protestantism. Several bishops present at the court who were sympathetic to the Reform in the previous reign opposed it in the new one. An example was Pierre Danès of Lavaur who turned from liberal humanist to Catholic zealot. He was involved in the interrogation of several Protestant artisans in front of Henri II who was interested in ascertaining their beliefs. One of them was later executed. The *Histoire ecclésiastique*, which had in an earlier reference noted Danès's sympathy, now referred to him as a "great enemy of those of the Religion." A similar case was that of Pierre Du Chastel, royal librarian after Budé and bishop of Mâcon in 1544. Under Henri II Du Chastel reflected the change in attitude at the court by becoming more hostile to the reformers. His change of heart led Beza to call him "that remarkable apostate."[8] According to Beza, when Du Chastel entered his new see of Orléans in 1551, he mounted the pulpit, and seeing such a crowd gathered out of curiosity to hear a bishop preach, made a forceful sermon against the Protestants. His denunciation of his former friends so distressed him that he became melancholic and died shortly after.

During Henri II's reign several prelates who did not have to live down a reputation as sympathetic to the Reformation established themselves as anti-Protestant controversialists. Two Italians, Lorenzo Strozzi of Béziers and Giovanni Valerio of Agen, must be placed in that category. As much a soldier as a churchman, Strozzi's zeal against the Huguenots began to manifest itself after he took up residence in Béziers in 1556. In 1559 he called for royal forces to suppress the heretics, which, however, he did not receive. In 1561 he was promoted to the see of Albi to replace Louis de Lorraine who was considered not energetic enough to deal with the Protestants. The diocese was "infected with heresy."[9] The *Histoire ecclésiastique* described Valerio of Agen as a "great persecutor of the people of the Religion, who, however, used his power of excommunication indiscriminately against anyone who crossed him."[10]

Native-born bishops active against the Protestants were not much more prominent during Henri's reign. The above-mentioned Tournon, Lorraine, and Cenalis continued their anti-Protestant labors. Another activist was Cardinal Antoine de Crequi of Nantes, a member of the royal council. He was one of the very few bishops of the period who used his *officialité* to try suspected heretics. He held two diocesan synods to formulate a response to the spread of Protestantism and visited a number of parishes. Crequi took an active role in the sectarian fighting in Nantes that broke out in 1561. Sharply criticized for it, he shortly transferred to Amiens. A second bishop who used the *officialité* against the Protestants was

Pierre Bertrand of Cahors. The Huguenots responded by imprison-
ing him in his episcopal palace for a time in 1561. A third bishop
said to have tried Protestants in his tribunal was Charles d'Humières
of Bayeux, but he was rarely in residence. It may well have been his
vicar general who was the zealot.[11]

While the episcopate did show more fervor during the reign of
Henri II in comparison to the preceding period, the record was
still very limited. However, after 1559 the situation changed sharply.
Bishops were active in the principal verbal confrontation between
Catholics and Protestants—the Colloquy of Poissy—although several while there scandalized their colleagues by their open adherence to Reformed ritual. The Cardinal de Lorraine was the star of
the conference for the Catholic side with his oratorical skill and
keen political sense. Cardinal de Tournon was the most blunt and
outspoken of the defenders of Catholic orthodoxy, but most of the
fifty bishops present strongly opposed permitting the Protestant
theologians led by Theodore Beza to present their case. A substantial portion were staunch Gallicans like Etienne Boucher of Quimper,
who had been one of the most outspoken prelates supporting
Henri II in the Gallican crisis of 1551; but they were hostile to the
idea of letting the Protestants present their case before the king
instead of being judged by the bishops themselves. When Beza
made a strong denunciation of the Catholic doctrine of the
Eucharist, the bishops almost as one cried: "He blasphemes!" The
bishops' strong resistance to Beza's doctrinal theses convinced Catherine de Medici, who as regent had arranged the conference, of the
danger of allowing Beza to speak again. Instead she arranged for a
private meeting of theologians at Saint-Germain, which also failed
to gain an agreement. While Catherine truly wished to achieve a
settlement to head off the threatening civil war, she saw the futility
of pursuing a policy against the opposition of the majority of the
hierarchy.[12]

Even before the colloquy the antagonism between Catholics and
Protestants had turned violent. Significantly more bishops begin
to appear in the chronicles as activists, especially in the role of
military commander of forces directed against the Huguenots.

Strozzi, now at Albi, received the title of *lieutenant du roy en Languedoc* in order to deal more effectively with the Huguenots. In 1561 he commanded a force of three hundred men who retook the church of Saint-Pierre in Albi from the Protestants who had barricaded themselves inside of it.[13] The bishop of Rodez, the Cardinal d'Armagnac, summoned his clergy in March, 1561, to take arms to recapture the churches of the nearby city of Villefranche. Some four hundred clerics answered the call, and the prelates distributed arms to those who had none. It was not, however, until Blaise de Monluc entered the city with his army at the cardinal's request in April, 1562, that Catholicism was reestablished. In the following year, in the cardinal's absence, his vicar, François de La Vallette, bishop of Vabres, led a force of forty men to a neighboring village to arrest the local Calvinist preacher.[14] At Lodève, Michel Briçonnet led thirty horsemen to help defeat a Huguenot company near his cathedral city in 1562. In the same year Bishop François de Fauçon was ordered by the Duc de Joyeuse to command a company of troops to dislodge the Huguenots from a nearby village.[15]

Most such events involving bishops in violence occurred in the Midi. They were fewer in the north, but the event that is often cited as touching off the first civil war occurred in Champagne in March, 1562, although extensive violence had already broken out in the south. The Massacre of Vassy involved the bishop of Châlons-sur-Marne, Jérôme de Bourges (or Bourgeois). Considerably more zealous than most of his fellow bishops, he had confronted the Protestant preacher at Vassy in the previous December and felt that he had been insulted. According to Theodore Beza his complaint to the Duc de Guise was one reason why Guise passed through the village in March. At virtually the same time as the Massacre of Vassy, the Huguenots drove Bishop Charles d'Angennes out of Le Mans. Three months later he returned at the head of a company and forced them to evacuate the city.[16]

In the Midi the violence accelerated after Vassy and ensnared several more bishops. The bishop of Lavaur, Pierre Danès, having, as Beza put it, now "shown himself as a great enemy of those of the Religion," gathered his priests in 1562 and secretly armed them.

Then under the pretext of a religious procession, they attacked the Huguenot temple in the city. But the city magistrates restored order without many casualties or much damage.[17] In another southern diocese, Conserans, Bishop Hector d'Aussan had raised a company of harquebusmen to defend the city, and in 1562 he went out at the head of an army of four thousand men to meet a Protestant force. In 1567 and 1569 he commanded smaller Catholic forces with the result that as long as he was bishop, the Huguenots were unable to establish themselves in the diocese. The bishop reportedly said Mass with his helmet on one side of the altar and his armor on the other.[18] Other bishops said to have borne arms during the early years of the religious wars included Aymeri di San Severino of Agde, Pierre de Marcilly of Autun, and René de Daillon Du Lude of Luçon. The latter supposedly resigned his bishopric because of the impropriety of a bishop carrying arms. He reverted to his military career and fought the Huguenots in the vicinity of Poitiers for the next ten years.[19]

In March, 1563, the two cardinals whose sees were in the Midi, Strozzi of Albi and d'Armagnac of Rodez, decided that a stronger and more coordinated response to the Huguenot surge was necessary in light of a religious riot in Toulouse. As lieutenants of the king in the *sénéchausées* of Albi and Toulouse, the two prelates arranged a meeting with several other important Catholic officials to organize an anti-Protestant league. They called for Blaise de Monluc to come to Languedoc to take command of a Catholic army. The articles of this league make it clear that they believed that they were acting in the name of the king to restore order in the face of Protestant rebellion. Yet they apparently did not ever request royal recognition. The Parlement of Toulouse approved of the articles of the league that are quite suggestive of those of the Catholic League of 1576. The members began to collect men and weapons in Languedoc but ceased upon the news of the Edict of Amboise that ended the first civil war. The Languedocian league seems to have broken up quickly afterward.[20]

Only one of these militant bishops suffered a fate more common to their less combative colleagues — being driven out of their sees, or their lives being endangered, or even being captured and held for ransom. The bishops as obvious symbols of Catholicism often found themselves and their property special objects of Huguenot wrath. Several prelates appear to have been caught quite unprepared for the outbreak of religious violence in 1561. In that year three bishops, Pierre Bertrand of Cahors, Antoine Erlault of Chalon-sur-Saône, and Arthur de Cossé de Brissac of Coutances, were captured and held for ransom. Bertrand's ransom was 1,000 écus, which was paid a year later. The sum demanded for Cossé's release is not known, but he escaped on his own, disguised as a miller. Erlault was released in 1563 after the Edict of Pacification of that year.[21] At Bayeux in 1562 Charles d'Humières was taken captive, but the Catholic townspeople quickly freed him.[22] Bishops who were forced to flee from their cathedral cities when they were occupied during the first civil war included Jean de La Brosse of Vienne, Charles d'Angennes of Le Mans, and Antoine de Sennetaire of Le Puy.

Because so few bishops were in residence in that period, the number of bishops who were captured or forced to flee likely was kept down. Even the absentee bishops, however, suffered the destruction or seizure of their cathedrals, palaces, and other properties. Examples of such destruction include Castres, Luçon, and Montpellier where the cathedrals and bishops' palaces were burned. At Montpellier the bishop's lands, especially his forests, were plundered and the fruits seized. Whether the plunderers were Protestants or local peasants eager for their share of the bounty of the earth is not clear. Similar examples in the Midi were common throughout the era of the wars of religion.[23]

After a four-year truce that was not devoid of incidents of violence, open civil war erupted again in 1567. Again bishops appeared in the ranks of the Catholic forces. In September, 1567, Charles IX made an appeal to the clergy "who wish to go to war and carry arms" to defend the Catholic religion. In the next year Pius V sent a bull to Toulouse absolving from any irregularities those clerics who had or would take up weapons and shed blood.[24] Most of the bishops noted as bearing arms in the first civil war appeared again in the second. They were joined by Jérôme de Bourges of Châlons-sur-Marne, Antoine de Sennetaire of Le Puy, Pierre de Paparin of Gap, and Gentian de Bussy d'Amboise of Tarbes. The last two, however, failed to hold their episcopal cities and were forced to flee. The bishop of Vabres, François de La Vallette, complained in a letter to the king that in 1567 he had been taken prisoner along with several other clerics, mistreated badly, and held for an excessive ransom. He added that for the past four years the Huguenots had controlled the diocese and taken the revenues of the benefices. In the same year François de Salignac of Sarlat was captured after a short resistance and was later released for a ransom of 4,000 livres.[25]

With these sorts of problems and passions abounding in the realm, it is hardly surprising that several bishops reacted very favorably, even enthusiastically, to the St. Bartholomew's Massacre. It is true that only Claude de Bauffrement of Troyes was implicated directly in the several urban riots that made up the massacre. He helped to persuade the city council of Troyes that the royal order to protect the city against the Huguenots called for their elimination.[26] But three bishops, Arnaud Sorbin of Nevers, Aymar Hennequin of Rennes, and Pierre de Gondi of Paris, strongly defended the massacre in sermons and pamphlets. Sorbin had for some time been attacking the king for not eradicating Protestantism; he enthusiastically endorsed the event from the pulpit. Sorbin has also been accused of writing a letter to the Catholics of Orléans encouraging them to follow the example of Paris and slaughter the heretics. He and Gondi published pamphlets that justified the massacre as did a future bishop, Claude de Saintes, long an active Catholic controversialist who was named in 1574 to Evreux.[27] The most prominent French churchman, the Cardinal de Lorraine, who had been fired upon in 1568, had been in Rome since May, 1572; he greeted the news from Paris with virtual rapture. Accompanied by Cardinals d'Este and Pellevé he had what for him certainly was the pleasant task of explaining the events in Paris to Gregory XIII. He defended it in terms of Huguenot conspiracy against the monarchy.[28] On the other hand there is the report about the bishop of Lisieux, Jean Le Henneyer, who was said to have offered refuge to Huguenots in the city and to have defied the royal order to execute them.[29]

The massacre precipitated a new round of civil war, but incidents involving bishops were considerably less numerous, perhaps because so many bishops had already fled from their sees. Serious cases of destruction of Church property occurred at Gap and Mende. In Gap the Protestant army of Sieur de Lesdeguières destroyed the episcopal palace and most of the churches in 1577, the cathedral having already been ruined. In 1581 Bishop Pierre de Paparin complained that he had not received his revenues for the previous five years. In 1578 the Huguenot Captain Merle had captured Mende and destroyed the episcopal palace. In 1579 Bishop Renaud de Beaune and the other clerics of the city were forced to raise a sum of 14,000 écus to buy a barony to give to Merle as a ransom for Mende. In 1584 the bishop complained that his revenues since 1578 had amounted to only 1,000 to 1,200 écus or about 20 percent of his expected income. De Beaune was later involved in a law suit to recover his lost revenues.[30] Another bishop involved in a court suit over lost property and income was Bernardin de Saint-François of Bayeux. In 1579 he procured *arrêts* from the Parlement of Paris against those who had made off with the moveable goods of one of his baronies and those peasants who refused to pay their dîmes, claiming that the Protestants had burned the records.[31]

Bishops who took up arms in the civil wars after the massacre were also less numerous. At Lodève the former bishop Michel Briçonnet, who had kept the bishop's feudal titles upon resigning in 1561, had successfully led the Catholic defense of the city until a 400-man Huguenot force took the city in 1573. Both Briçonnet and the incumbent bishop were forced to flee. In addition to the ruin of the cathedral and bishop's palace, the "martyrdom" of St. Fulcian, the patron of Lodève, occurred. The remarkably well-preserved body of the saint was dragged out of its tomb and desecrated. In 1582 a new bishop of Lodève, Christophe de L'Estang, helped the Duc de Joyeuse retake the city, but in 1585 the Huguenots captured it again. In compensation Henri III gave L'Estang the revenues and episcopal palace of Carcassone because its bishop, Hannibal Rucellai, had returned permanently to Italy in 1581. Another bishop who served with Joyeuse in the Catholic army in Languedoc was Tommaso di Bonzi of Béziers. They retook that city in 1586. In the previous year the archbishop of Embrun, Guillaume d'Avançon, fled before an Huguenot attack that destroyed the cathedral.[32]

With so much violence involving bishops or raging around them, it is not surprising that violence directly touched several bishops and that two paid the price of death. Pierre de Paparin of Gap, for example, was wounded in the knee in 1574 by a pistol ball.[33] The first case of the assassination of a bishop occurred at Périgueux in 1575. Bishop Pierre Fournier, who was said to have been a close friend of the *Maréchal* Saint-André, a prominent associate of the Guises, was murdered in his episcopal palace. Although his assailants went unidentified, the fact that the Huguenots captured the city several days later suggests that they were responsible. Fournier was noted to have been very zealous.[34]

The other assassinated prelate, Jacques Lettes de Prés de Montpézat of Montauban, was also noted as one of the most fervent anti-Protestants in the episcopate. In 1576 he raised a military unit and prevented a Protestant attack on the nearby city of Cahors by arranging an ambush for the local Protestant captain. Thirteen years later de Prés fell victim himself to an Huguenot ambush at Caussade, some twenty kilometers to the northeast of Montauban. Of the numerous bishops who in the previous three decades had found themselves in perilous situations, only Fournier and de Prés paid so dearly. They were among only five French bishops to die violent deaths in the sixteenth century.[35]

As befitted a group of men who prided themselves on their family tradition as warriors and who likely had some military training before joining the Church, bishops from the *noblesse d'épée* made up three-fourths of the prelates who carried arms or commanded troops during the religious wars. Italian bishops, a number of whom also had been military captains before joining the episcopate, constituted the second largest group of militant bishops. Numerous *anobli* and *roturier* bishops were victims of the religious violence, but bishops of those categories who bore arms were very few. It is likely, however, that a bishop with such a social status would have found it difficult to lead a regiment both because of his own lack of experience and the reluctance of soldiers to follow someone of lower social status. Such bishops did appear as anti-Protestant polemicists. One fairly common way of confounding the heretics was to perform a public exorcism. Jean de Bours, bishop of Laon, performed such an exorcism on a possessed girl that was so successful a number of Huguenots became Catholics. One of them was the author of the notorious *Histoire de l'hérésie de ce siècle*, Florimond de Robertet.[36]

Despite the presence of these militants, the members of the episcopate had been very slow to react to the appearance of Protestantism in the realm. Even after Calvin had given the movement an effective organization and a great deal more popular appeal, the clear majority of prelates in office failed to meet the responsibility of eradicating heresy imposed on them by their office. Only after the religious issue had burst into open violence in 1560 did the bishops in any number appear among the ranks of those actively involved in opposition to the Huguenots. The prelates, however, as often appear as victims of the violence as perpetrators of it. The efforts of the involved bishops in behalf of the Catholic cause were collectively of less value than the presence of one Catholic captain like Blaise de Monluc.

Although they were among those who had the most to lose if Protestantism won control of France, the bishops made a very small contribution to the struggle to prevent it from happening. A major cause for that state of affairs was likely the chronic absenteeism of the bishops who as a consequence had little or no knowledge of the strength of the Huguenot movement in their dioceses. Bishops often found it difficult to bestir themselves even when their property was seized or ruined and their revenues seriously diminished. The same problems in the upper levels of the Church administration that had been major reasons for the initial appearance of the Reformation were also factors in the failure of the bishops to react strongly to its success. Accounting for this indifference of so large a part of the prelacy is difficult, but one explanation is that the high rank of so many bishops made them feel more secure in their privileged status and less terrified at the prospect of a Huguenot victory. Certainly what leadership the clergy offered to the anti-Protestant movement came far more from the vicars and cathedral chapters. One must not attribute too much to the potential influence of the episcopate in the confessional struggle, but the absence of what was, to use Hugh Trevor-Roper's phrase, the general staff of the Church clearly was a factor in what success Protestantism achieved in France.[37] That success culminated in the most serious crisis that the French Church and its episcopate faced in the sixteenth century—the succession of the Protestant prince, Henri de Navarre, to the French throne.

CHAPTER IX

THE BISHOPS AND
THE SUCCESSION OF HENRI IV

Since so few French bishops can be identified as anti-Protestant activists, it is not surprising that even fewer prelates provide evidence of having been involved in the *Sainte Union*, the Catholic League, when it was organized on a national level in 1576. Often the most zealous episcopal opponents of the Protestants were also ardent royalists who firmly believed that they were serving the crown as well as the Church in their activities to counter the Huguenots. The theory of Gallicanism, as loosely defined as it was, did regard the king as the head of the Church, and for the Gallicans, the League had too strong a taint of ultramontanism. The League's Manifesto of 1576 declared that the "associates will swear full prompt obedience and service to the chief who will be appointed."[1] Most bishops would have been suspicious of an organization that quite explicitly demanded allegiance to the head of a party and not to the king. Thus, the League of 1576 had only a few partisans in the episcopacy.

Active in this early Catholic League was the only member of the Guise family then in the French episcopate, Louis II Cardinal de Guise of Reims, brother of the Duc de Guise, the *chef* of the League. His uncle, Louis I Cardinal de Guise, who had retired from the episcopacy in 1562, was as active in the League as a man known as the "Cardinal of Bottles" could be.[2] Two firebrands in the hierarchy, Aymar Hennequin of Rennes and Urbain de Saint-Gelais of Comminges, who already had notable reputations for their anti-Protestant activities, were deeply involved in the League.

Both recruited for the movement among the notables of their regions and were denounced to the court for their zeal. The only bishop, however, who was noted explicitly as swearing the oath of the League, although others likely did so, was Claude de Bauffrement of Troyes.[3] Other prelates considered to be Leaguers in 1576 were the Cardinal de Pellevé of Sens and Louis de La Haye of Vannes.

When in 1577 Henri III declared himself head of the Catholic League and rescinded some of the concessions he had made to the Huguenots in 1576, the raison d'être of the League largely disappeared. Its mostly noble membership now saw the organization as another device for royal control and taxes. Although it is far from certain, it is probable that there was no organized League from 1578 to 1584.

The situation suddenly changed in 1584 with the death of Henri III's younger brother, Duc d'Alençon, the last Valois prince. Following the strict interpretation of the French law of succession, the Salic law, the next in line for the throne was Henri de Bourbon, the king of Navarre and *chef* of the Huguenots. Confronted with the real prospect of a Protestant sitting on the throne of Saint Louis, the zealous Catholics quickly reorganized the League. The new League was really two organizations, one a revival of that of 1576, largely noble in membership, and the other an urban-based movement with particular strength in Paris, Nantes, and Toulouse. The two parts of the League often acted independently of one another and sometimes at cross-purposes. The Duc de Guise functioned as effective head of both parts, but after his assassination in December, 1588, his brother, Duc de Mayenne, found it increasingly difficult to coordinate the goals and activities of the two factions. From 1584, but especially after 1589, the more zealous bishops active in the League served as intermediaries between the two Leaguer groups.

From the beginning of the revived League, several bishops played key roles. Nicolas de Pellevé of Sens, already noted as active in 1576, served as the League's representative at the papal court. An ally of the Guises from the start of his career, his zeal in promoting the League's interests at the Holy See caused Henri III to order that his ecclesiastical revenues be confiscated and given to the poor. The Huguenots consequently referred to him as "Cardinal Pélé" (skinned).[4] His ally in the curia was the Cardinal de Vaudémont, the young brother-in-law of Henri III, who briefly held a French bishopric and died in 1587.[5]

Another prominent prelate who early appeared in the ranks of the Leaguers was Pierre d'Espinac of Lyon. One of the leaders of the French clergy, who had presided over the Assembly of the Clergy at Melun in 1579, he was for a time much in favor at the royal court. Henri III included him in the *conseil d'état* in 1577. According to d'Espinac's biographer, his influence over the king prompted the jealousy of Henri's principal *mignon*, the Duc d'Epernon. The result was a battle of words and pamphlets in which the archbishop encouraged the rabid Leaguer preacher Jean Boucher of Paris to write a strong polemic against d'Epernon. The duke was so incensed that he commissioned a reply that, among other things, accused the prelate of incest. When the prelate's position at the court became untenable, he not only returned to Lyon but became as well a committed Leaguer and one of its most formidable advocates. He was called "the brains and effective head" of the party and the "right-hand man of the Duc de Guise."[6]

Aymar Hennequin of Rennes, whose nomination Henri III had tried to withdraw in 1574 but could not because it had already proceeded too far, was a member of an important *robin* family of Paris. The Hennequins contributed several members to the League, but Aymar was the most zealous. The Leaguer nobles of Brittany were said to have paid him for his impassioned sermons in support of the League.[7] A close ally of his was the Sorbonnist, Arnaud Sorbin of Nevers, long established as an ardent anti-Huguenot. In 1586 he wrote a poem supporting the League's position in the dispute over Henri de Navarre's excommunication. Another former court preacher who played a major role in the Parisian League was Guillaume Rose of Senlis, seated in 1584. His eloquence had procured for him an appointment as royal preacher, which he used to blast Henri III for his misconduct during Mardi Gras of 1583.

In one of the twists of mind that so characterized Henri III, instead of demoting Rose, he raised him to the see of Senlis.[8] Joining the League in 1585, Rose became one of its most valuable polemicists.

Other bishops active in the first years of the League of 1584 were Louis de Brézé of Meaux, Charles de Rouci of Soissons, Urbain de Saint-Gelais of Comminges, and Alessandro di Bardi of Saint-Papoul. The first of them met with the Duc de Guise and his brother the Cardinal at Reims in 1585 to map Leaguer strategy for Champagne.[9] Brézé may well have had a grudge against the throne because of complications surrounding his appointment to Meaux. He spent most of his time at Paris (until his death in late 1589) where he was a conspicuous figure at Leaguer councils. In addition Antoine de Sennetaire of Le Puy was satirized in the anti-Leaguer "Bibliothèque de Madame de Montpensier" of 1587, indicating a reputation as a Leaguer.[10]

The key Leaguer prelate, however, was a quiet, unassuming old man of more than sixty years, more interested in wine cellars than high politics, the Cardinal de Bourbon. One of the great pluralists of several decades earlier, he had resigned his episcopal benefices and most of his abbeys by 1584. Charles de Bourbon's importance lay in the fact that he was Henri de Navarre's uncle and thus could serve as the League's candidate to succeed Henri III. Although he had no real reputation as a politician, he took rather enthusiastically to the possibility of being the royal successor and was quite active in his own behalf. In anticipation of being king, or perhaps to overcome the objection that as a cleric he had no legitimate son, he received a dispensation from the clerical state to marry. The Leaguer writers, however, made the effective use of the fact that he was a churchman by declaring him the new Melchisedech, both king and priest.[11]

Henri III's inability or, as the Leaguers believed, unwillingness to destroy the Huguenot party was only one of the reasons why the Leaguer clerics were hostile to him. They objected as well to his heavy taxes on ecclesiastics and his highly erratic and often scandalous personal life. Nonetheless, he did have considerable support in the episcopate. Henri's principal ally among the prelates was the archbishop of Bourges, Renaud de Beaune. An ambitious and politically astute churchman, he was chancellor for the Duc d'Alençon until 1580 when he was ousted for suspected financial chicanery. Unlike his grandfather Jacques de Semblançay who was executed in 1527 on the same charge, Renaud was able to retain royal favor and gain a seat in the royal council.[12] Another close ally among the bishops was the Cardinal de Joyeuse, archbishop of Narbonne since 1582 and the brother of Henri's favorite, the Duc de Joyeuse. In 1584 the cardinal went to Rome where he remained for five years as the most vocal supporter of the French king in the curia. After the death of Cardinal Ludovico d'Este in 1587, Joyeuse became cardinal protector of French affairs at the Holy See. However, he demonstrated that his loyalty was to Henri III personally by returning to Toulouse and leading the League in Languedoc after Henri's assassination in 1589.[13]

Another prominent royalist or Politique, as the supporters of the king were called, Claude d'Angennes of Le Mans, had begun his episcopal career with a solemn oath of Catholicism at his formal entry into his first bishopric, Noyon, and was called the chief and protector of Catholics in Noyon. By 1585 he had become an ardent Politique. An anonymous Leaguer pamphlet accused him of heresy himself because of his support for Henri III's policy of toleration for the Protestants. At Tours Archbishop Simon de Maille de Brézé ordered the clergy of the diocese "to pray and preach for the king." The king commissioned Nicolas Fumée of Beauvais to discover the real purpose of the League. Jacques Amyot, the noted poet whose past flirtation with Protestantism had caused the curia to balk briefly at his nomination to Auxerre in 1570, was a close personal friend of the king, as was Pontus de Tyard of Chalon-sur-Saône, another humanist. The latter was said to have kept Chalon loyal to the king in 1585 at a time when Dijon and other neighboring cities were joining the League. In Languedoc the Leaguers refused to accept Horace de Birague of Lavaur as a deputy to the Estates of 1588 and insisted on replacing him with Saint-Gelais of Comminges.[14] Several bishops such as Jean de Monluc of Valence, Sebastien de L'Aubespine of Limoges, and the Cardinal de Birague, bishop of Lisieux, who had been members of the royal council and had served the monarchy zealously, had died by 1585. Henri did not replace them in the royal council or in his inner circle so that the number of prelates who advised him had been reduced considerably in the crucial four years before 1589.

Perhaps the absence of these trusted and astute advisors at court helps to explain the series of royal blunders that led up to the Day of Barricades of May, 1588, when the League drove Henri III out of Paris at the same time as Leaguer uprisings in several other cities occurred. The king's response to his humiliation was to call a meeting of the Estates general for Blois in September. Twenty-six prelates were present as deputies of the First Estate. Seventeen were either already identifiable as Leaguers or would be in the future while nine were or would be Politiques. [15]

Since the League had strong support from the deputies from the lower clergy, it was able to elect its candidates, the Cardinals de Bourbon and de Guise, as presidents of the First Estate. The Leaguers forced Henri to swear again the Edict of Union (first sworn in July, 1588) that declared that the Catholicity of the monarch was the first fundamental law of the realm and no heretic could gain the throne. The Leaguers among the deputies of all three estates also forced the king to grant significant concessions in extending the assembly's authority over taxation. [16]

The Leaguer prelates, however, appear to have had only a small role in these activities; the Politique bishops were far more active and visible. The most prominent of the royalist churchmen at Blois was Renaud de Beaune of Bourges. His oratorical skills, strong personality, and the confidence of the king enabled him to have a broad impact on the assembly. His speeches indicate that he was first of all a royalist, prepared to support the king in virtually any decision that he made. He was not yet a true Politique (defined as one who was prepared to tolerate the presence of Protestants in the realm for the sake of political unity) in that he was willing to swear the Edict of Union after Henri did. As de Beaune said in an address before the king, "when all your subjects will recognize only one God, one Catholic religion and one king, then the people will multiply, justice flourish, peace be found in the land."[17] The assassinations of the two Guises in late December, 1588, seem to have upset the archbishop little. With the Cardinal de Guise dead and the Cardinal de Bourbon in prison, de Beaune presided over the rump Estates and gave a closing address on January 16 that was very favorable to Henri: "Let all good and loyal Frenchmen pray to God that he will conserve for a long time our sweet and agreeable king."[18]

Claude d'Angennes was more controversial than de Beaune because he openly supported the succession of Henri de Navarre. He declared in an address to the estates that while heresy must be hated, the heretics themselves ought to be loved and redeemed by instruction and good example rather than being forced to accept the truth by the sword. The First Estate and the Sorbonne voted to censure him for his pernicious errors. D'Angennes also published a pamphlet defending his refusal to swear the League's Oath of Union because the law of the Church did not permit the taking of arms against the king. A satirical poem circulated during the estates vilifying him and his positions.[19]

The execution of the Guises on royal orders was the key event of the Estates of Blois. According to one account of the event, the Leaguer leaders had held a council several days earlier at which the duke was urged to leave Blois for his safety. But d'Espinac of Lyon persuaded him to stay because of the bad appearance that abandoning Blois would have created.[20] So the opportunity remained for Henri to accomplish the deed that ignited the final and most dangerous phase of the wars of religion. The Cardinal de Guise was executed the day after his brother's death, and the Cardinal de Bourbon and the archbishop of Lyon were thrown into prison. The king apparently intended to execute the latter as well, but his nephew and several Politique prelates successfully appealed for his life.[21] The shedding of the Cardinal de Guise's blood was of great importance for the more legal-minded Leaguers. It enabled them to claim that Henri had incurred immediate and automatic excommunication, which deposed him as the king of a Christian people. That accordingly justified the revolt of the French Catholics, especially the Parisians, who were far more enraged by the death of the Duc de Guise.

In Paris the League, led by the radical element known as the *Seize*, created a Council of Forty, comprising representatives from much of France, with pretensions to ruling the kingdom. Its members included four bishops: Guillaume Rose of Senlis, Aymar Hennequin of Rennes, Nicolas de Villars of Agen, and Louis de Brézé of Meaux. Villars had been a magistrate of the Parlement of Paris before his appointment as bishop of Agen only six months before. Hennequin was the principal celebrant of the funeral mass in Paris for the martyred Guises.[22]

In the provinces the Leaguer response to the death of the Guises was often equally strong. The bishop of Evreux, Claude de Saintes, long noted as a zealous Catholic, is said to have "carried his diocese to rebellion." He sold his house in Paris and gave the money to the League.[23] In Provence, Brittany, and Languedoc, provincial estates met under Leaguer auspices that demanded the release of Leaguer deputies to the Estates of Blois held by the king and appropriated money for the Leaguer armies. Bishops presided over these estates and at least five other bishops were in attendance. Two Leaguer bishops of Brittany, Hennequin of Rennes and Charles d'Espinay of Dol, brought in noted Leaguer preachers to whip up the zeal of their dioceses.[24]

But the royalist bishops were not inactive in support of their party in the first months of 1589. Shortly after the Leaguers had met in Languedoc, the Politiques gathered at Carcassone with four bishops present.[25] In Brittany the Politique estates included two prelates. Claude d'Angennes had the most difficult task assigned to a royalist bishop: the king sent him to Rome in February to explain the deaths of the Guises. Accompanied by the Cardinal de Joyeuse, d'Angennes argued before Sixtus V that the king had not been able to consider the special status of the cardinal in the face of his enemies. Sixtus asked to see Henri's request for a pardon, which the envoys did not have. After a second meeting during which Sixtus insisted on such a request, they agreed to forge one in the hope of delaying a bull of excommunication against the king.[26]

The ruse was not successful as the pope issued an order in July for Henri to come to Rome within thirty days or be excommunicated.

There was no opportunity to test Sixtus's resolve to excommunicate Henri. A Dominican lay brother assassinated the king on August 1, 1589, before the thirty days had elapsed. As traumatic as the Guises' deaths had been for much of the hierarchy, the death of Henri III crystallized the divisions already present within the episcopate. According to the prevalent interpretation of the Salic law, Henri de Navarre was now king of France, and Henri III on his deathbed had commanded his supporters to recognize Navarre as sovereign. The League, nonetheless, proclaimed the existence of a prior fundamental law of Catholicity, which gave the throne to the Cardinal de Bourbon. For most French Catholics it appeared to be a choice between loyalty to the Church or the Crown, although some held out the hope that Navarre would convert, which would have solved their dilemma. It was an issue about which few of the bishops could remain silent or inactive. Nor could Gallicanism with its tradition of both autonomy from Rome and Catholic orthodoxy do anything to inform the decisions of the individual bishops.

Upon Henri III's death several bishops who had aided him against the League became Leaguers themselves rather than recognize Henri de Navarre. The most notable were the Cardinal de Joyeuse, who returned from being Henri III's spokesman in Rome to take an active part in the League's government in Languedoc and the defense of Toulouse, and Jacques Amyot of Auxerre, the noted humanist. Amyot's support of the king had gained him the hatred of the Leaguers who controlled Auxerre, and they found the bishop's change of heart highly suspect. The party's preachers did not stop their attacks on him. One preacher, swinging a halberd, was reported to have shouted that Amyot was evil, worse than Henri de Valois himself. The people were said to have been ready to cut off Amyot's head and to proclaim the leading Leaguer cleric present as bishop. Instead the League procured his excommunication on the grounds that his support for Henri III was heretical. That made Amyot a relapsed heretic because of his earlier flirtation with

TABLE VI

PARTY AFFILIATION OF FRENCH BISHOPS, 1589–91

	Total	Leaguers		Politiques		Unknown	
Nobles of the Sword	47	27	57%	16	34%	4	9%
New Nobles	20	10	50	9	45	1	5
Commoners	16	7	44	6	37	3	19
Foreigners	12	4	33	4	33	4	33
Uncertain Status	4	3	75	1	25	0	0
Total	99	51	52%	36	36%	12	12%

Protestantism. A year later the papal legate Cardinal Cajetan lifted the excommunication. Despite Amyot's serious problems with the fanatics of the League in Auxerre, it appears that he was sincere in his opposition to the succession of Henri IV and should be considered a moderate Leaguer until his death in 1593.[27]

One can assess the division in the episcopacy over the question of whether to accept Henri de Navarre as king by tabulating party affiliation of the bishops based on evidence of a concrete act of support for one party or a clear statement of allegiance in a contemporary chronicle. Fifty-one of the ninety-nine bishops in office at the end of 1589 can in this way be identified as Leaguers; thirty-six as Politiques; and there is insufficient evidence available to classify twelve of them in a party. The large number of vacant sees by late 1589 was a result of the virtual cessation of royal nominations and papal confirmations after May, 1588.

It is clear that the nobles of the sword in the episcopate were considerably stronger in support of the League than were bishops who fell into other social categories. Because of their high status by birth, the sword bishops likely felt a greater sense of independence from the monarchy and assumed that an episcopal office was their due for which they had little need to thank the king. Usually willing to join an antimonarchical party, which the League was despite its protests to the contrary, the nobles among the prelates

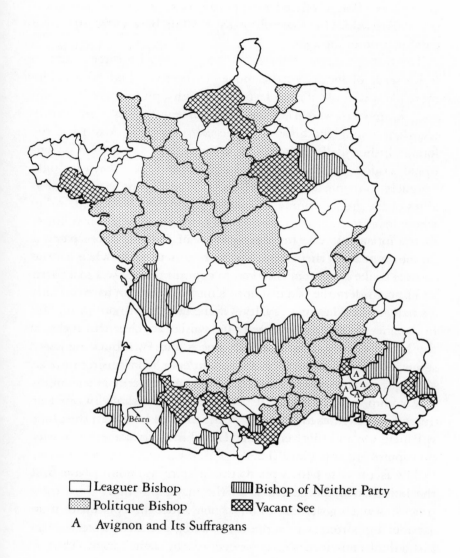

Béarn

☐ Leaguer Bishop   ▥ Bishop of Neither Party
▦ Politique Bishop   ▧ Vacant See
A   Avignon and Its Suffragans

MAP IV

PARTY AFFILIATION OF FRENCH BISHOPS, 1589–90

saw that the League offered an opportunity to assert the interests of their class as well as defending their Church, a most attractive combination of motives.

The bishops in the other social categories had greater reason to feel a sense of loyalty to the monarchy because their offices were more likely a result of royal favor. Although a plurality of the *robins* and commoners were Leaguers, the percentage was significantly less than among the bishops of the *noblesse de race*. A third of the foreign bishops, all of whom were Italians, were Leaguers. Conventional wisdom suggests that the Italians should have been strongly Leaguers, but most were members of families long established as allies of the French throne. A number came from banking families whose loans to the crown would have made them eager for stability in the monarchy. The high proportion of Italians whose party is unknown reflects their tendency to return to Italy when serious trouble broke out before they had to commit themselves to a party.

The consideration of a bishopric's income seems to have had only a small impact on party loyalty. Of the twenty bishoprics highest in income, Politiques possessed nine while Leaguers held eight; of the lowest twenty, Leaguers held eleven and Politiques possessed seven. Geographical location appears to have had a greater impact. Politique bishops were concentrated in the west-central part of the realm from Paris to the Loire valley and in Languedoc while Leaguers dominated the bishoprics of the east, center, southwest, and Brittany. Only in Provence and Dauphiné was there fairly even division of episcopal loyalties.

The factor that best explains this pattern appears to have been the influence of the governors in the major provinces.[28] In those provinces when governors who had held office for a decade or more actively supported one or the other party, a clear majority of the bishops of the provinces belonged to the same party. Thus in Brittany, Burgundy, and Champagne, the governors for the preceding decade were members of the House of Guise, and the League had the support of thirteen of the nineteen bishops while only three were Politiques. On the other hand, in Languedoc, where Henri de Damville had been governor since 1563, thirteen of the twenty-two bishops were Politiques, while six were Leaguers. Only in the joint provinces of Guyenne-Gascony where Henri de Navarre had been governor since 1562 does this pattern not fit. The sixteen prelates of that region included eight Leaguers, three Politiques, and four of uncertain affiliation. However, the circumstance of Navarre's Protestantism likely reduced his influence over the bishops.

Elsewhere, in Normandy and Provence, there were several short-term governors prior to 1589, and the political divisions among their prelates were nearly equal (four Politiques and three Leaguers in Normandy and four Leaguers and three Politiques in Provence). In Dauphiné, which was similarly divided, a long-term governor had been replaced in early 1588. In the region of the Ile-de-France and the Orléanais where royal influence was strongest, five of the seven bishops were Politiques. There is no apparent pattern for the remaining seventeen bishoprics in the small provinces of one or two sees. Also supportive of the above pattern is the fact that those bishops who were in office before their provincial governors were installed were less likely to belong to the same party as the governors. The above pattern is suggestive that the long-term governors had an effect on the loyalties of the bishops. If one grants that point, then the conclusion follows that the governors had considerably more influence over the episcopate than has been generally acknowledged. The loss of control over episcopal appointments in the reigns of Charles IX and Henri III previously noted may have extended further than other evidence has suggested.

While the affiliation of the provincial governors likely had some bearing on that of the bishops, which party controlled the cathedral city seems to have had little correlation with the affiliation of the bishop. In several cities the Leaguers who had seized control of the city forced the bishop to take their party's oath, but that did not necessarily assure the loyalty of the prelate. It may have been a factor in the case of Charles de Bourgneuf of Saint-Malo who was pressured into taking the Leaguer oath because his brother was a noted Politique captain. Bourgneuf eventually became a member of the Leaguer council for Brittany.[29] On the other hand three bishops, Philippe Du Bec of Nantes, Nicolas Fumée of Beauvais, and Pierre de Gondi of Paris later renounced their oaths to the Leaguer cause. Du Bec was the bishop of the city that rivalled Paris as the most ardently Catholic center in France, and his suspected Politique sympathies brought out a mob in early 1589 to force him to swear to the League's oath. The oath, formulated by the Parisian radicals, pledged its swearers to live and die in the Catholic faith, and to defend it with life and goods against those who supported heresy in the realm.[30] Du Bec took the oath but was one of the very first churchmen to recognize Henri de Navarre as king of France in August, 1589. He was forced to flee from the wrath of the Leaguers a month later. Two years later the Leaguer Parlement of Brittany sitting at Nantes would declare him *infamé*, and it sought to deprive him of his benefices.[31]

Gondi of Paris, who had been loyal to Henri III, wavered in the direction of the League after the king's assassination, but his earlier stand convinced the Leaguers of the need to persuade him to take their oath. He undertook several missions for the League, at least for its moderate wing, such as accompanying d'Espinac of Lyon to ask Henri de Navarre to lift the siege of Paris during the summer of 1590. The mission failed, but Gondi, perhaps persuaded by Henri's arguments, did not return to Paris. He quickly gained a reputation as a dedicated royalist and was sent as Henri's representative to Rome in 1592. The pope refused to allow him into the Papal States.[32]

Numerous bishops were forced to flee from their episcopal cities because they were aligned with the party that lost control of the cities. Several of the most prominent bishops of both parties were among those who sought refuge elsewhere. Ironically the two most zealously Leaguer cities, Paris and Nantes, both had Politique bishops who fled from them. The leading Politique bishop, de Beaune of Bourges, joined Claude d'Angennes of Le Mans, Alfonso del Bene of Albi, and Antoine Hébrard of Cahors in refuge at Tours. Pompey Pérille of Apt moved his residence to a nearby town to escape the Leaguers. Several Leaguers also were forced out of their sees; d'Espinac of Lyon, who was the leading churchman in the League, Charles d'Escars of Langres and his brother Anne d'Escars of Lisieux, and Côme Clausse of Châlons-sur-Marne sought refuge in Paris.[33]

Five bishops, not fortunate enough or perhaps not prudent enough to escape to their party's strongholds, were taken prisoners by the opposition. The only Politique so affected was Nicolas Fumée of Beauvais, captured in November, 1589, on the orders of the head of the League, the Duc de Mayenne, because he had recognized Henri de Navarre as king. Fumée was taken before the papal legate in Paris and the death sentence demanded because of his betrayal of the Catholic cause. But the legate refused to condemn him, and Mayenne released him for 900 écus in ransom.[34]

Four Leaguer prelates fell into the hands of the Politiques. Both Guillaume d'Avançon, Archbishop of Embrun, and Elezar Rastell of Riez were taken prisoners in 1590, but the circumstances of their release are unknown. At Rodez Bishop François de Corneillan led the Leaguers in an attempted takeover of the city in hope, so it was said, of his gaining seignorial rights over the entire city. The uprising failed, and he was thrown into prison.[35] The most serious case involved the zealot Claude de Saintes of Evreux. Long holding a reputation as a fiery anti-Huguenot, de Saintes was an early and ardent Leaguer. He refused the sacraments to the people of his diocese who were supporters of Henri de Navarre, and he had enthusiastically praised the assassination of Henri III in a pamphlet that fell into Politique hands. Captured and handed over to the royalist Parlement sitting at Caen, he was condemned to death for lèse-majesté. The Cardinal de Vendôme and several other Politique prelates, not wishing to see one of their fellow bishops so debased, interceded with Henri IV on his behalf, and Henri commuted the sentence to life imprisonment. De Saintes died in prison before the end of 1591.[36]

Except for the executed Cardinal de Guise, de Saintes came the closest to being a casualty of the conflict over the royal succession that the episcopate suffered from 1585 to 1595. That fact is quite remarkable in view of the tremendous range of political and military activities in which the bishops were involved for the two parties. One of the most active was Henri de La Marthonnie of

Limoges. Bishop for less than two years before the assassination of Henri III, he was not active in the League until then. Quickly he became a very zealous partisan. The Politiques controlled the city, but the Leaguers planned a coup. La Marthonnie was asked to lead it because it was "better that he, the bishop, command than a stranger." The uprising was begun on October 15, 1589, as the Leaguers rushed through the city shouting: "Mort aux Huguenots! Tue! Tue! Vive la Croix!" While the greater part of the populace supported them, the Leaguers were able to take control of only a part of the city. A Politique counterattack forced the bishop and his men back to the citadel from which La Marthonnie escaped on October 22. Limoges remained in Politique control for the rest of the civil war.[37]

In Provence Antoine Couppes of Sisteron raised a company of soldiers to defend the nearby city of Digne for the League.[38] Just to the north in Grenoble, an animated defense of the city led by its Leaguer prelate François Fléard failed to hold the city as the Politiques captured it in late 1590.[39] To the west, in Languedoc, Urbain de Saint-Gelais of Comminges, convinced that Joyeuse, the archbishop of Toulouse, was a Politique because of his support for Henri III, put on armor and, carrying a halberd, led 300 armed monks and clergy to seize the archbishop's palace. The superior of a local religious house urged him on to take the leading role, saying: "It is your duty, Holy Prelate, as another Moses, to place yourself at the head of all faithful to accomplish a goal so holy and so approved by God." The Leaguer Parlement of Toulouse declared him governor of Toulouse. But in November, 1589, the Cardinal de Joyeuse returned from his service for Henri III in Rome as an ardent Leaguer. He became the League's *chef* for all of Languedoc. After two years, however, his zeal began to falter, and Saint-Gelais returned as governor, now called "the king of Toulouse."[40] In Brittany the bishop of Dol, Charles d'Espinay, whose revenues Henri III had sequestered in 1588 for his role in the League, led the defense of that Leaguer-controlled city after his brother, the local Leaguer commander, was killed in 1591.[41]

While the military activity of the Leaguer bishops was the most blatant of the services that they rendered their party, the range of other services they provided was very broad. Several prelates, in addition to those already mentioned, served as governors of League-held cities, most prominently d'Espinac for Paris. Bishops went on numerous diplomatic missions to Rome and Spain. The archbishops of Aix, Embrum, and Sens made several trips to Rome as Leaguer envoys, while in 1592 Anne d'Escars of Lisieux went to the Holy See as the special representative of the Duc de Mayenne to convince the pope to back his election as Catholic king of France. The bishops of Riez, Avranches, and Lodève were entrusted with diplomatic missions to Madrid. Other services included the writing of polemics by Rose of Senlis, de Saintes of Evreux, and Génébrard of Aix. Several bishops, including the archbishop of Bordeaux, Antoine Prévost, refused to allow their clergy to include prayers for Henri de Navarre in the canon of the Mass, citing the incongruity of mentioning in the Mass a confessed heretic.[42]

Although the services that the Leaguers in the hierarchy rendered were numerous, varied, and, on the local level, often quite effective, one can argue that the role of the Politique bishop was more significant. Their recognition of Henri de Navarre as sovereign and their presence at his court helped Navarre give credibility to his claim that he did not intend to destroy Catholicism, and they provided continued hope that he would convert.[43] Upon Henri III's assassination in August, 1589, only a handful of bishops immediately recognized Navarre as king. Archbishops Renaud de Beaune of Bourges and Simon de Maille of Tours and bishops Charles Miron of Angers, Nicolas Fumée of Beauvais, Nicolas de Thou of Chartres, Claude d'Angennes of Le Mans, and Philippe Du Bec of Nantes were the only bishops known to accept the Huguenot prince as their king without hesitation. Information on this point is, however, limited.

The roll of royalist prelates grew rapidly in late 1589. Among the most important were the two cardinals Lenoncourt and Vendôme. The latter, Navarre's cousin, sent him a letter in October recognizing him as king.[44] The importance of Vendôme's decision became clear in May, 1590, when the Cardinal de Bourbon, the League's candidate for the throne, died, still a prisoner of his nephew. Vendôme, or the Cardinal de Bourbon as he was now known, had a claim to the throne as a Catholic Bourbon, although it was clearly inferior to that of the Protestant Bourbons, Navarre and Henri II de Condé. His prior recognition of Navarre made it impossible for the League to turn to him as its candidate after the death of the elder cardinal.

In February, 1590, Vendôme and Lenoncourt issued a call for a meeting of the French episcopate to bring about Henri's conversion: "The honor of God and love of the Fatherland obliges us to put our hand to work so worthy." The papal legate warned that such a meeting would be an illegal usurpation of the rights of the papacy, and the Leaguer prelates followed the advice of the bishop of Fréjus who maintained that, although every good Frenchman longed for Navarre's conversion, the bishops must obey the injunction of the legate.[45] The meeting apparently never occurred, and the entire proposal was highly speculative since Navarre had given no assurances that he would convert.

The royalist prelates took a more forceful step in 1591 in order to counter a new bull of excommunication issued against Henri by Gregory XIV. The pope had declared Navarre deprived of his possessions and threatened his supporters among the clergy with excommunication.[46] The bishops met first at Mantes in June, where five of them—the archbishop of Bourges and the bishops of Bayeux, Beauvais, Chartres, and Nantes—signed the Edict of Mantes in which Henri proclaimed religious toleration for Catholics and Huguenots. The Politiques reassembled at Chartres in September and published a statement signed by nine prelates —the above five along with the cardinals of Lenoncourt and Bourbon and the bishops of Angers and Le Mans. The document denounced the papal bull as the work of known enemies of France who controlled the papacy. Since Gregory was acting against the interests of France, his acts were not binding on the French Church. The hint of schism in the official statement apparently was much stronger in the discussions among the bishops present. De Beaune of Bourges was said to have proposed that he be declared patriarch of France in order to establish a Church discipline independent of Rome.[47] This threat of schism was repeated frequently until Henry received papal absolution in 1595.

The Leaguers were so enraged by the activities of many Politique bishops that they proposed to replace them by good Leaguer clerics. For example, the Leaguers of Chalon-sur-Saône renounced Pontus de Tyard as their bishop, but in 1591 he received a letter from Rome to disseminate several papal bulls, making it clear that the pope still considered him to be bishop.[48] In particular the Leaguers wanted to replace the Politiques who had signed the Edict of Mantes, at least those three whose cathedral cities the League controlled—de Beaune by Rose of Senlis, Du Bec of Nantes by Jean Dadre, a theologian of Rouen, and Fumée of Beauvais by the Parisian preacher François Feuardent. The Leaguers actually made an effort to defrock Du Bec and Fumée. The Leaguer Parlement of Nantes declared Du Bec *infamé*, deprived him of his benefices, and asked for a new bishop. The papal legate appointed a "grand vicar" to administer the see; it is not clear whether he tried to take up his duties. At Beauvais the cathedral chapter ordered that the bishopric be declared vacant because of the automatic excommunication that Fumée was said to have suffered for his support for the Protestant prince. The Leaguers also sought to replace the "traitor" Pierre de Gondi in Paris. There were also instances of Navarre and Mayenne appointing administrators for dioceses they controlled to replace bishops of the other party who had fled.[49]

The military and diplomatic services that the Politique bishops rendered to the royalist cause were not as numerous as those of the Leaguers. Reports of a Politique bishop dressed in armor and leading troops are limited to Louis de Moulinat of Sées. Some bishops demonstrated their loyalty to the monarchy by ordering the Te Deum sung in the churches of their sees after each of Henri's victories, by attending royalist assemblies and provincial estates, and by going on diplomatic missions. But the three bishops whom Henri sent to Rome at different times were not received at the papal court.

In addition to the partisans of the two factions in France, there was the group of twelve bishops whose party affiliations cannot be determined. Some fled to places of refuge in France or Italy. While several bishops did take part in some activity in support of a party before fleeing to Italy, others like Antoine Gaume of Saint-Paul-Trois-Châteaux and Silvio di Santa Croce of Arles did not. Still others like Pierre de Baume of Saint-Flour simply disappeared for several years with no evidence of where they went. It is possible that several of these bishops did support one side or the other, but their activity was not sufficiently notable to make their way into the contemporary chronicles.

For nearly four years the bishops of both sides largely held firm. Death did more than did defections to reduce their ranks. The only clear change of allegiance between 1590 and 1593 was that of the well-respected d'Escars of Langres, who announced his recognition of Henri IV in September, 1591.[50] The lack of movement from either party, across all social levels, demonstrated the need for a dramatic move to break the stalemate. The League made its move in January, 1593, when the Duc de Mayenne convoked the long-delayed meeting of the Estates general to elect a Catholic prince as king of France. When the Leaguer deputies met in Paris in late March, there were thirteen bishops present as well as three of Mayenne's recent appointees. Pellevé of Reims and d'Espinac of Lyon were chosen presidents of the estates. It was, however, the bishop of Senlis, Guillaume Rose, who made the greatest impact, partly because of his denunciation of the proposal to elect as sovereign of France Philip II's daughter, granddaughter to Henri II, partly because of his refusal to join a delegation to meet with the Catholic royalists at Suresnes in April. Péricard of Avranches then joined d'Espinac as the Leaguer prelates present at Suresnes, while de Beaune of Bourges was the sole Politique bishop. The Leaguers had refused to accept d'Angennes of Le Mans as a member of the Politique delegation because of his reputation as a supporter of toleration.[51]

The two archbishops, serving as spokesmen for their respective parties, made the most of the opportunity to present their points of view in a debate-like format. They ranged through Scripture, history, Church law, and French law to demonstrate their respective stands: that the successor according to the Salic law was the God-chosen sovereign of France and that a heretic could not be king. De Beaune was able to maneuver d'Espinac into declaring that the League's only objection to Navarre was his religion. This set the stage for de Beaune's triumphant announcement on May 17 that Henri intended to call on the French episcopate to instruct him in Catholic doctrine. D'Espinac could only sputter that he hoped that the conversion was sincere and not a trick to fool the Catholics into accepting Navarre as king.[52] The announcement began a notice-able shift among the Leaguer bishops.

In July, 1593, a number of clerics including eleven bishops arrived at Saint-Denis to instruct Henri. Two of these prelates, however, were his recent appointees, and one was the retired bishop of Digne, whose nephew, the incumbent, was in Paris for the Leaguer Estates. D'Escars of Langres was the only former Leaguer present. Following several days of doctrinal discussion, during which Henri surprised the bishops by his knowledge of Catholic doctrine, they attended Henri as he solemnly abjured his Protes-tant beliefs. The archbishop of Bourges, speaking in the name of the French Church, then lifted the ban of excommunication. The Politiques acknowledged that such cases ordinarily had to be decided by Rome but maintained that Henri's was an exception because the pope had no power to excommunicate a French prince. Further-more there was a need for haste because the king was in constant danger of death.[53] From Rome and the League came angry cries that the Politiques were aiming at a schism, an accusation that was not silenced until Henry was absolved by Clement VIII in 1595.

Once Henri had attended Mass, numerous Leaguer prelates rallied to his cause. The bishop of Orléans declared, "I now conclude that it is necessary to fall under Spanish domination or under the legitimate rule of the king."[54] Yet not all were of the same opinion, for some Leaguers still held out. In November, 1593, the League held a meeting of the Estates of Languedoc at which three bishops and the vicars of four others were present, and similar assemblies in Brittany and Provence in early 1594 each had two bishops in attendance.[55] Despite the holdouts, the momentum of support was clearly in Henri's favor, and in February, 1594, he took another step toward securing complete control of the realm by arranging his coronation at Chartres. Nine bishops were noted as present including two former Leaguers. Because of vacancies and Leaguer holdouts, only one of the six ecclesiastical peers was present, Clausse of Châlons, a former Leaguer.[56] Death had taken four of the Politiques involved in the meetings of 1591, who were thus denied the pleasure of seeing the vindication of their cause.

At the end of March Henri entered Paris in triumph. The royal entry into the capital city marked the effective end of both the wars of religion and the League, although a number of Leaguers carried on the military and ideological battle for several more years. D'Espinac of Lyon wrote a letter of submission to the king dated March 13, 1594, and Génébrard, the archbishop of Aix, seated by the League and confirmed by Rome, submitted on November 15, 1595. Guillaume Rose fled to a monastery in Spanish Flanders, but shortly Henri allowed him to return to his diocese. Despite this gesture the bishop remained unreconciled and frequently attacked Henri in his sermons. In 1598 Rose was the most vocal of the several prelates who opposed the Edict of Nantes. The Parlement of Paris censured him for his opposition. Even papal absolution of Henri did not quiet the last Leaguers immediately. The governor of Burgundy in 1595 accused Pierre Saulnier of being a better Spaniard than royal servant. It was not until June, 1596, that de L'Estang of Lodève acknowledged Henri as king, and the Leaguer appointee in Vannes, Georges d'Aradon, continued to make use of a clause in his documents: "until there is a Catholic king in France." In September, 1596, Clement VIII sent him a stern admonition that now France did indeed have a Catholic monarch.[57]

Because of the real possibility that a Protestant would hold the throne and nominate bishops, the League had mounted the last serious challenge to the Concordat of Bologna. At the Estates of Blois in 1588, Leaguer deputies led the demand for a return to canonical election for consistorial benefices. A large number of the League's polemical works condemned the Concordat and claimed that it was responsible for many of the woes facing the Church and the realm. The most notable of these works was from Gilbert Génébrard, the noted Hebraist whom the League had placed in the archdiocese of Aix. Not only was it a sharp and clear defense of canonical election, it also blamed the unhappy fate of the House of Valois and, in particular, of Henri III, on François I's usurpation of the rights of the clergy. Génébrard stated that the first step toward the restoration of peace and religion would be the abrogation of the Concordat.[58] Several instances of canonical election took place after 1588. At Reims, with the violent death of the Cardinal de Guise, the cathedral chapter proceeded to elect Nicolas de Pellevé, already archbishop of Sens. Henri III appointed his relative, the Cardinal de Lenoncourt. The papacy accepted Pellevé's election and granted his bulls. Other sees where the chapters chose new bishops under Leaguer auspices were Aix and Nîmes. In four other sees the chapters elected candidates but failed to get them approved at Rome. For their part the Politique bishops who met at Mantes in 1591 insisted the existence of the Concordat of Bologna required the conversion of Henri de Navarre in order for him to fulfill properly its obligations.[59]

The controversy over the succession of Henri de Navarre was essentially a conflict between two parts of the establishment — the Church and the monarchy. Certainly no one in the sixteenth century was more a part of the elite than a bishop. The division within the episcopacy, when considered along with the divisions in other institutions such as the Parlements, helps to demonstrate that the League was not primarily based on social discontent. The crisis over the succession of Henri IV cut across class lines rather than along them. The number of Leaguer bishops from the nobility of the sword must be juxtaposed with the urban radicals of the Paris Sixteen to show the breadth of social levels active in the League. Even in Paris where the movement showed greater evidence of social antagonism, the zealous bishops remained among its leaders.[60]

While the Leaguer bishops served their party well, providing a sense of legitimacy to the League and acting as leaders in many of its activities, the Politiques were of even greater value to their party. Their presence in the royal party made it impossible for the informed Frenchman to see the dispute as strictly one of Catholic against Huguenot. They provided at least a limited guarantee of Henri's pledge in 1589 to protect the Church and maintain the religious status quo, and, after his adjuration, of his sincerity. The royalist prelates had a significant if not altogether clear role in Henri's decision to convert and by absolving him of excommunication gave the act of his attendance at Mass a validity and acceptability far greater than was otherwise possible. As consecrated bishops who absolved the king and who were prepared to lead a schismatic French Church if necessary, they helped to put pressure on the papacy to grant its own absolution two years later. Without the Politique bishops the political situation in France might well have remained as stalemated as the military conflict was in 1593.

For most French prelates the ancient adage, *une foi, une loi, un roi*, largely summed up their alliances since the French clergy in its Gallicanism largely equated the monarchy with leadership in the Church. The possibility of the monarchy being occupied by a heretical prince must have been thoroughly traumatic to them. The deep split in the episcopate over recognizing Henri as king in 1589 makes it clear that the resolution of the dilemma was very difficult. Nothing in the French tradition had prepared them for it. Yet the small number of prelates whose party affiliation cannot be determined indicates that it was a decision that most felt obliged to make.

It is instructive to compare the deep division in the episcopate in 1589 to the near unanimity among the bishops in opposition to the Civil Constitution of the Clergy of 1790. Only four bishops holding dioceses along with three titular prelates took the oath of the Civil Constitution.[61] The threat to the prestige, revenues, and powers of a bishop that the Civil Constitution posed, while very real, was nonetheless not as dangerous as the establishment of Protestantism in France would have been. The history of the Reformation until 1589 certainly would have suggested to contemporaries that the establishment of the Reformed religion would have followed the installation of an unconverted Henri IV as king regardless of his pledges to the contrary. The major difference between the two situations is that in 1589 the bishops were forced to choose between monarchy and Church whereas in 1790 the Civil Constitution was seen as a threat to both. To have taken the oath in 1790 was to have given recognition and loyalty to a new government whose legitimacy was clearly in question. In 1589 the Politiques could argue that it was God's unknowable purpose to make Henri de Navarre the royal successor since He had willed the deaths of the last Valois kings without sons to follow them.

Ironically the partisan bishops serve well as the exemplars for both their respective parties. The League's prelates demonstrated the essential character of the League—to protect the privileges and unique status of the Catholic Church in France. No one better enjoyed these privileges and needed more to protect them than a bishop. On the other hand, who better serves as the epitome of the term Politique than a bishop who supported Henri de Navarre—a high churchman who was willing to subordinate the interests of the Church for the sake of the monarchy and recognize a Protestant on the throne of Saint Louis? Certainly the Politiques argued that religion and the Church would be better served if there were peace in France and the laws of the realm were observed, but their first motivation was essentially political. To use a contemporary's definition of the Politiques, these bishops wanted to "join religion to the state and not the state to religion."[62] When the Catholicism of the Bourbon dynasty was ensured by Henri's abjuration, the hierarchy quickly swung back to its former position of strong support for the monarchy, because the distinction between religion and the state, seemingly made necessary by Henri's Protestantism, was no longer needed.

CHAPTER X

THE RETURN OF STABILITY

T he conversion of Henri IV and his subsequent triumph over the League that secured his control over the realm put him in a unique position in regard to the French hierarchy. Far more than any other king, even more than François I at the implementation of the Concordat of Bologna, Henri had the opportunity to remake the episcopacy according to his own perception of what it ought to have been. The opportunity arose because of the serious disorder in which the Church found itself at the end of the civil wars. Chronic absenteeism; the destruction of cathedrals, episcopal palaces and other Church property; uncertainty over the legitimacy of numerous prelates; and a vacancy rate of over one-third created what was surely the most serious crisis in the French episcopacy during the centuries it fell under the Concordat.

Nonresidency, always rampant in the sixteenth century, had become even more pervasive. The more zealous partisans of both sides were absent from their sees from as early as 1584 to as late as 1598. Numerous bishops had had to flee from their episcopal cities because they belonged to the party that had lost control of the city or because they wished to escape the ravages of civil war. Some sought refuge in Italy never to return. Several Leaguers fled from France upon the victory of Henri IV but returned over the next three or four years. In the Midi the Huguenots occupied at least twelve dioceses and refused to allow their bishops to enter them. And evidence of the whereabouts of a number of bishops is impossible to find. It appears possible that as few as 10 percent of the French bishops were in residence in 1594.

The problem of the ruin of churches and ecclesiastical property, already very serious before 1588, was exacerbated in the last period of civil war. In the diocese of Gap the visitation of Pierre de Paparin in 1600 revealed that some 80 percent of the seventy-plus churches that he visited were badly damaged or ruined. At the parish of Rabou, for instance, Paparin found no curate, no repository for the Blessed Sacrament, no baptismal font, no sacred oils or chalice, and no roof on the church. Leaguers and Politiques alike converted churches and clerical buildings into fortresses, or tore them down for tactical reasons, or wrecked them in the battles for control of the cities. For instance, in the battle for Limoges, the Politiques destroyed the episcopal palace and a dwelling owned by the bishop. At Montpellier the reconstructed bishop's residence was again razed in the fighting.[1] After peace was restored, chapters and bishops often found themselves in heated dispute over their proper share of the costs of rebuilding or repairing the cathedrals.[2]

The two problems of contested legitimacy of many bishops and the vast number of vacancies were often related because numerous contested nominations were not made permanent. Both the League and Henri de Navarre had attempted to place their candidates in episcopal sees between 1589 and 1594. The Duc de Mayenne, acting as lieutenant general of realm for the League, had made a number of nominations, several of which Rome confirmed. Papal confirmation gave them a hold on the bishopric that was most difficult to dislodge. Thus Henri accepted Anne de Murviel as bishop of Montauban as part of the treaty between the king and the Duc de Joyeuse in 1596.[3] Mayenne's cousin, the Duc de Mercoeur, the Leaguer *chef* of Brittany, made two nominations for that province. One of them, the appointment of Georges d'Aradon to Vannes, received curial approval, and he took permanent possession of the see. The Cardinal de Bourbon, acting as king for the League, named Gérard Bellanger to Fréjus. He received the papal bulls but never took possession of the see. In several Leaguer-controlled cities the cathedral chapters moved to fill episcopal vacancies by canonical elections. Of these chapter candidates, Rome confirmed three.

For his part Henri IV had made numerous appointments, although not for every vacancy, to assert his right as king prior to papal absolution in July, 1595. Rome refused to grant the bulls of office to any of his candidates before 1595, and a number of them were never confirmed. Even after his absolution long delays in procuring bulls from the curia were common, in part because papal suspicions about Henri's sincerity resulted in greater care in examining his recommendations.

To add to the confusion, in seven dioceses both sides had candidates for the episcopal chair. The first such case had occurred in 1589 in Reims shortly after the death of the Cardinal de Guise. Henri III had appointed the Cardinal de Lenoncourt, while the League transferred Nicolas de Pellevé from Sens to Reims. Since Reims was under the control of the League and Pellevé received the papal bulls, the Leaguer took possession of the archdiocese. The deaths of both candidates before 1595 prevented any further conflict. An interesting example of dual candidates occurred at Nîmes in 1594 where the Duc de Montmorency named Pierre de Valernod twelve days after the incumbent's death, who shortly received royal assent, while the League and the Joyeuses supported Louis de Vervins to whom the incumbent had resigned the see two months earlier. Although Vervins was the chapter's candidate as well, Valernod was able to use effectively the accusation that Vervins had been an extensive purchaser of ecclesiastical property sold in the royal alienations. Valernod was confirmed in 1598, but Vervins became archbishop of Narbonne in 1600.[4] Other examples of dual nominations included Coutances, where the Politique outlived his Leaguer rival and eventually won confirmation, and Grasse, where neither the Leaguer nor the Politique, who was married with four children, secured the see that passed to a third candidate in 1599.[5]

Henri IV had little success with his nominations before he gained papal absolution. Several Politique candidates were driven out by the Catholic populace, as in the examples of Meaux and Evreux, although in the latter the Politique Jacques Davy Du

Perron eventually secured confirmation and possession. More serious was the refusal of the papacy to confirm Henri's early appointments even after 1595 or inordinate delays in granting the bulls. The most notable example of the former was the case of René Benoist, curate of Paris, who attended the abjuration of Saint-Denis and was shortly thereafter appointed bishop of Troyes. After frequent requests for confirmation, Henri finally abandoned the effort to procure his bulls in 1604. At Dol the Politique Edmond Revol failed to win confirmation; after ten years he passed his claim to his cousin, Antoine, who received the papal bulls in 1603. An usher of Henri's court, Jean Le Breton, was given Bordeaux; after taking the revenues for three years, he resigned to François de Sourdis. The royal nominees to Meaux and Alet both died unconfirmed after waiting several years for their bulls.[6]

The most serious example of the problem of long delays before confirmation was the case of Renaud de Beaune who waited eight years for his bulls transferring him to Sens. When the Leaguer Nicholas de Pellevé transferred from Sens to Reims in 1589, the Politiques refused to recognize him as archbishop of Reims nor would they recognize the candidate elected by the chapter of Sens as archbishop there. When Pellevé died in 1594, Henri treated Sens as a new vacancy and gave the see to de Beaune. Aware of Clement VIII's anger at de Beaune for his uncanonical absolution of Henri and his pretensions of being a French patriarch, the royal council issued an order installing the prelate at Sens without requesting the papal bulls. The chapter agreed to accept him as *archevêque nommé*, and he made his formal entry in April, 1595. After receiving papal absolution, Henri submitted the nomination to Rome. The king and his archbishop probably expected a punitive delay, but they could hardly have expected to wait for seven years.

In 1596 Henri wrote a letter directly to Clement, praising de Beaune's services to the Church and the monarchy. But it failed to produce the bulls nor did two further letters to the pope sent in 1597 and 1598. In the latter year the affair was complicated by the Edict of Nantes in which the members of the curia saw de Beaune's hand. After 1600 relations between Rome and Paris improved considerably, especially after Henri asked Clement to serve as god-father for his first son. In April, 1602, Clement finally issued the bulls for de Beaune's transfer to Sens.[7] Despite the long delay, the archbishop, with his notoriety, fared little worse than several other nominees such as Bertrand d'Echaux, whom Henri named as bishop of Bayonne in 1593 but who was confirmed only in 1599.

Part of the responsibility for these problems did rest with Henri IV since some of his early appointments hardly met even the loose standards of the time. He gave the see of Fréjus to one of his military commanders in 1594 who in turn passed it on to Bartholomew Camelin for a pension of 3,666 écus. Clement VIII protested this transaction but under pressure from Henri confirmed Camelin in 1599.[8] The see of Noyon involved a similar transaction where one candidate sold the appointment to another, who subsequently exchanged it with a third cleric for an abbey. The latter, Charles de Balsac, eventually received the papal bulls. Henri also accepted the seating of the ignorant local curé François Yver as caretaker bishop of Luçon for the Richelieu family.[9]

The correspondence between Henri and his agents in Rome indicates that the problem of disputed appointments was a matter of considerable concern to the king, but they were few compared to the number of vacancies. Henri had a unique opportunity in 1595 to create a French episcopacy of his own design, yet he did not move with undue haste in filling the vacancies. The number of empty sees, which in 1594 numbered six archbishoprics and thirty bishoprics without prelates confirmed by Rome, remained high until after 1600. Despite the large number of vacancies that Henri IV had to fill upon securing his throne, the average number per year of bishops appointed in his reign was less than for previous reigns.

This analysis shows that Henri IV appointed commoners at a rate higher than any other king of the *Ancien Régime*, although their proportion of the episcopacy still remained quite low and was not significantly higher than under Charles IX. The *anoblis* were also represented in higher numbers compared to previous reigns. The increases in these two social categories were made largely at

TABLE VII

SOCIAL ANALYSIS OF BISHOPS SEATED BY HENRI IV, 1589–1610

(N = 109)

Noblesse de Race		Anoblis		Commoners		Foreigners		Unknown Social Origins	
43	40%	25	23%	16	15%	6	5%	19	17%

the expense of the *noblesse de race*. The number of bishops of that status was the lowest of any reign until 1789. The proportion of foreigners had also declined, and three of those listed in that category were third-generation French residents. Perhaps they ought not be listed as foreigners at all.

It is clear that Henri chose his prelates from a wider range of families and social groups than did his predecessors. But the statistics (see appendix III, table V) on bishops following relatives in bishoprics or with close relatives in other sees are a little misleading since several prominent families like the Guises with a tradition of providing prelates did not have family members in the hierarchy at the time Henri named their scions.[11] Nonetheless Henri's appointments did include bishops from numerous families not previously represented in the episcopacy, and his reign began a period of about a century when prelates from recently ennobled families comprised as much as a third of the episcopate.

Several explanations have been postulated for this pattern of episcopal appointment. J. Michael Hayden argues: "Members of the new nobility were appointed at a fairly consistent rate throughout his reign, while the Third Estate appointments were concentrated between the years 1597 and 1602. The reason for Henri's action was quite possibly an attempt to win the loyalty of all segments of the population after the Wars of Religion rather than just the loyalty of the old nobility." Hayden further suggests that "perhaps it could be said that Henry IV's ecclesiastical policy was part of a larger plan to rearrange the social structure of France or to break down the old structures in preparation for absolutism."[12]

Louis Prunel, who in his work on reform in the French Church does not attempt to do a social analysis of the episcopal appointments under Henri IV, nonetheless has noted the presence of a large number of *roturiers* and *anoblis*. He proposes that it was because of the king's search for good bishops that he chose men from those two social classes. Prunel cites Henri's words to the clerical assembly in 1605 that "I glory to see that the bishops I have established are better than those of the past" and his pledge to Cardinal de Grivy that he would "fill the sees with capable and pious subjects." Prunel suggests that his largely successful search for good bishops resulted in the nomination of clerics from lower social status. [13]

Third, Michel Peronnet describes the change in social character of the episcopacy in the early seventeenth century in terms of Cardinal de Richelieu's depiction of the bishop as a servant of the king with the function of administering the religious sector for him. Thus the rulers of this period, beginning with Henri IV and including Marie de Medici and Louis XIII, looked for their bishops in the same class from which they chose other administrators—the service nobility which was largely made up of new nobles. Richelieu was clearly opposed to the appointment of commoners. [14]

There is, however, still another explanation for the pattern of episcopal nominations under Henri IV: the king wanted to reward those who had supported him in his fight for the throne. In response to Hayden's argument, the analysis of the party affiliation of the bishops in 1589 presented in the previous chapter suggests that Henri did need to pay attention to winning the loyalty of the *noblesse de race* since bishops of that status were Leaguers in higher proportion than those from the other categories. An analysis of the division among the magistrates of the Parlement of Paris in 1589 supports that conclusion. [15] If the king did have a sense of the need to gain the loyalty of different social classes, he could hardly have ignored the sword nobles.

The proposition that Henri in the years before 1602 (Hayden's cutoff point) was largely interested in rewarding supporters regardless of social status is, it is true, based on evidence of party affiliation

for less than half of the appointments in that period. Many of the
new prelates did not have previous positions of sufficient importance to make their way in the contemporary chronicles. But if
those nominees whom Rome refused bulls are also included, the
pattern becomes clearer. The vast majority of episcopal nominees
for whom party loyalty can be determined were Politiques, and a
considerable number of them were commoners.

Two of the three Parisian curés who attended the king's abjuration received bishoprics.[16] Both were commoners, as was Seraphim
Blanchy, appointed to Angoulême, who revealed a plot to kill the
king in 1593. A well-known Politique of the Third Estate who
received a miter was Arnaud d'Ossat of Rennes. Three of the
Politiques in the Parlements appointed to bishoprics were
commoners. Henri chose from his supporters among the magistrates frequently—a total of nine including two from the Leaguer
Parlement of Paris who served his interests in 1593. An *anobli*
magistrate of the Parlement of Toulouse, Guitard de Rattes, whose
house was pillaged and who was condemned to death by the Leaguer Parlement because of his support for Henri, was named to
Montpellier in 1596. The king also looked to the court preachers
and *aumôniers* who were with him before 1594; five of their company were promoted. A commoner among them was Jean Bertaut,
given Sées. He had complimented Henri on his victories and was
present at his coronation.[17]

Politiques also predominated among Henri's early appointments
from the higher social classes. The first cleric to salute him as
king, René de Daillon Du Lude, was named to Bayonne in 1593.[18]
The Politique Pierre Valernod, an *anobli* whose case has already
been mentioned, received Nîmes. At Luçon the Richelieu family
was permitted to hold on to the bishopric because the Cardinal's
father was a dedicated Politique. A number of Henri's bishops were
relatives of prominent Politiques. The son of Chancellor Pomponne
de Bellièvre (given Lyon) and the nephew of Philippe Du Bec of
Nantes (given Saint-Malo) fell into that category as did Jean-Pierre
Camus, the reforming bishop of Belley, whose father was a prominent Politique of Paris, and six other candidates.

In contrast the list of known Leaguers who received bishoprics from Henri before 1602 is quite short—a total of six. Two of them were clients of the Cardinal de Joyeuse—Louis de Vervins who received Narbonne in 1600 and Jean Daffis, his vicar, given Lombès in 1598. A long-time Guisard among Henri's bishops seated before 1602 was Godefroy de Billy of Laon. He, however, like two other Leaguers, received his bishopric through a resignation *in favorem*. Late in Henri's reign the appointment of former Leaguers increased considerably as the old animosities were forgotten or forgiven. While these figures and examples are not entirely conclusive, they suggest a pattern whereby Henri favored his friends whether commoner or noble.

An analysis of Henri's episcopal appointments before and after 1602 bolsters this thesis. Sixty percent of the commoners and 64 percent of the new nobles seated in the episcopacy during Henri's reign received their bishoprics before 1602; and 53 percent of all his appointments were made before then. Thus it is plausible to conclude that because most of those of his supporters who were to be rewarded with bishoprics had received them by 1602, Henri's pattern of appointments after 1602 returned closer to that of his predecessors.

Once in the episcopacy, however, many of the newly established families, especially from the new nobility, were able to create dynasties for themselves through the devices of resignation *in favorem* or the appointment of relatives as coadjutors with the right of succession. Because many of these families held positions close to the monarchy, they helped to establish the pattern of bishops from the service nobility which Peronnet has noted. Peronnet also notes that "the *anoblis* received more easily the appointment of a coadjutor (usually a relative) than the nobles of the sword and often assured a transition before the nomination of a bishop without a link to the diocese."[19] The effort to gain a coadjutor on the part of the *anobli* bishops may well reflect the desire of these newly established families to ensure their families' future control of their sees in a manner by then more in favor with the papacy than resignation *in favorem*. Being both less secure and more enterpris-

ing than the nobles of race, the new nobles worked more actively to
pass their bishoprics on to their relatives.

The analysis of the qualifications of Henri IV's bishops calls into
question Prunel's thesis that the king dipped into the lower social
orders in order to create an episcopate filled with capable and pious
subjects. It is true that he did appoint a number of bishops who
proved to be zealous reformers and did offer French sees to men
such as Pierre Cotton, Pierre Du Bérulle, and François de Sales
who refused them. But one is hard put to find in his bishops a
pattern of nominations of well-qualified candidates that differs in a
significant way from those of his predecessors. The proportion of
appointees with university degrees was less than for the reign of
Charles IX. Of the previous four kings only Henri III nominated
men at a higher rate who were not yet ordained priests, and both
kings' nominees had about the same proportion of candidates who
were under the age of twenty-seven.[20] There was only a small
decrease in the number of bishops who held commendatory benefices
at the time of their consecration. It is true that the percentage of
Henri IV's bishops who resigned did decline noticeably, and the
proportion of prelates chosen from religious orders was up
substantially. Nonetheless, the qualifications of Henri IV's bishops
when analyzed in this manner appear only a little better than those
from Henri III's reign and actually inferior to those in Charles
IX's.[21]

These statistics, however, belie the fact that there was a real
qualitative change in the French episcopacy after 1600. Although
Henri IV followed his predecessors in steadfastly refusing to publish the entire canon of Tridentine decrees, he did urge the French
clergy to reform the Church on several occasions. Likely more of an
influence was the example of reforming Italian bishops, especially
Carlo Borromeo of Milan, who had several disciples placed in
French sees. Another source of Borromeo's influence was the publication in 1582 of the decrees of his reform synods; for example,
d'Espinac of Lyon ordered 100 copies for his clergy.[22] Spain and the
Spanish Lowlands also provided examples of reform through the
implementation of most of the Tridentine decrees. Philip II had

accepted the council's legislation "without prejudice to the rights of the crown," and that action was supported by several reform synods in Spain and the Lowlands. The Dutch revolt slowed the process in that region, although the independent bishopric of Liège had successfully enforced the Tridentine reform by 1570. Occasional German bishoprics such as Salzburg, Würzburg, and Trier also had gotten well along in the process of reform, but for most of Catholic Germany, it was delayed until well into the seventeenth century.[23] For the most part France was surrounded by lands where Tridentine reform was well under way by 1600. There was, therefore, something of a moral imperative for French bishops to follow suit.

Thus many of Henri IV's early episcopal nominees whose career profiles promised little in religious zeal proved to be active reformers. Several authors such as Prunel attribute to Henri IV a real desire to appoint reforming bishops, and he likely was aware of the bent of mind of the clerics of the court whom he raised to the hierarchy even if they did not meet all of the requirements of the Concordat of Bologna. The king was willing to take the advice of François de Sales who procured French sees for several of his disciples like Pierre de Fenouillet of Montpellier. On the other hand some of the more zealous reformers like Pierre de Valernod of Nîmes and Nicolas de Briroy of Coutances were clients of the local magnates about whose characters Henri probably knew nothing before their appointments.

Conforming to the standards of the Concordat or the Council of Trent did not indicate that a new bishop would be a zealous pastor of his diocese. Some bishops who lacked several of the prerequisites for appointment proved to be zealous reformers, while some who were completely in adherence with the Concordat and had impressive credentials for episcopal office proved to be quite incompetent and desultory. For example Jean Camus was appointed to Belley at the age of twenty-five without a university degree holding a commendatory abbey yet became one of the glories of the French Catholic Reformation. Similarly one of the century's most irregular nominations of one of the least promising candidates resulted in the seating of a truly zealous bishop. Upon the death of Pierre de Paparin of Gap in 1600, his relatives concealed the fact of his death until they had forged a resignation *in favorem* for Charles-Solomon Du Serre, the brother of the wife of a nephew of the dead prelate. Only twenty-five years old at the time, Du Serre had recently converted from Protestantism, and his morals were less than upright. Yet he proved to be an ardent reformer once installed in his see, making visitations of his parishes, rebuilding churches, and carrying on an active campaign to convert the Huguenots.[24] Conversely Jean Granier of Montpellier (1602–8), royal *aumônier*, theologian, and member of a religious order, was an absentee prelate who was embroiled in a bitter dispute with the chapter over his refusal to contribute to the repair of the cathedral.[25]

Likewise it was possible for a prelate who was not in residence to have been an effective reformer and a bishop regularly in his see to have been uninterested in reform. François de La Rochefoucauld, bishop of Clermont, was a member of the royal council yet worked actively to reform his clergy by bringing in the Jesuits and the Capuchins and by publishing the statutes of reform approved by a diocesan synod in 1599. The opposite case was presented by Louis de Vigne of Uzès who was usually in his diocese but appears to have done little to reform his clergy.[26] Considerable reform was accomplished in some dioceses without the direction of the bishop, and his support did not always translate into effective reform. But the reforming elements in the see usually found their task considerably easier if the bishop applied his authority and talent to the cause.

Henri IV's bishops do show considerable improvement in fulfilling a number of the obligations which Trent imposed on the episcopacy. Nearly 40 percent held at least one diocesan synod and several did so on a nearly semiannual basis.[27] Information on pastoral visitations is less complete, but it is clear that far more bishops made tours of their dioceses or visited some parishes than did so previously. Evidence is available to indicate that, at a minimum, 12 percent of Henri's nominees made an effort to visit their parishes.[28] Episcopal residency also increased substantially. Some

45 percent of the bishops seated under Henri IV were regularly present in their sees; information is not available for another 23 percent; and only 32 percent can be clearly identified as absentee bishops. Even the young bishop of Luçon, Armand de Richelieu, was an activist bishop in residence for several years before the affairs of the court drew him away.

Early in his reign Henri IV largely paid attention in choosing the bishops to rewarding loyalty and friendship and gave rather little thought to the religious fervor and zeal of his candidates. Thus a larger number of *roturiers* and *anoblis* than usual appeared in the episcopal rolls, and their career profiles differed little from previous reigns. Several zealous bishops did receive sees as did a number of incompetents, but that appears to have been largely a hit-or-miss matter on Henri's part. After 1602, however, the appointments did become more systematic. The proportion of nobles of the sword returned to close to 50 percent, and adherence to the requirements of the Concordat improved to an extent. It appears that, despite some obvious failures, Henri did make an effort later in his reign to identify episcopal nominees who would be reformers.

By 1610 most of the problems confronting the episcopacy that had resulted from the wars of religion had been overcome. The task of repairing the cathedrals was proceeding at a good pace, despite the numerous lawsuits to force bishops to help finance the work. The number of vacancies had been reduced to the routine occurrences, and the number of bishops who were unconsecrated or of questionable legitimacy had declined to the usual frequency. Except for the Béarnais sees, the bishops could reside in all the French dioceses, admittedly with some risk in several of them.

In several sees of the Midi like Castres, Montpellier, and Montauban, however, the bishop could not reside in the cathedral city but was forced to live in another town in the diocese. In largely the same sees, the monarchy was forced occasionally to reduce the décimes because the Huguenots still held extensive Church property. With the return of the religious strife in the south in 1619, the destruction of churches and clerical property was repeated on a smaller scale until the government victory in 1629. Personal violence to several bishops also occurred. At Vence Guillaume Du Blanc was saved from a conspiracy to murder him in 1598 when an altar boy, idly running his hand over the episcopal chair during a long sermon, dislodged its back and uncovered a cache of gunpowder. Guitard de Rattes narrowly escaped from a Huguenot riot in Montpellier in 1600 when he tried to retake possession of his cathedral.[29] Three years later Frédéric de Ragueneau of Marseille was assassinated by the villagers of one of his fiefs. The murder appears to have been the result of a quarrel between the seigneur and his tenants, but the possibility of religious motivation remains strong. In 1614 the bishop of Riez, Charles de Saint-Sixt, was poisoned because of his interference in the affairs of the city, which was largely Protestant.[30]

Nonetheless for most of France sectarian violence was a thing of the past by 1610. Having returned largely to stability, the episcopacy could concentrate on the great task of reforming itself and the French Church. And the monarchy could devote its attention to what Peronnet refers to as the regularization of the episcopacy — the appointment of bishops of more uniform background, education, and training. The implementation of such a policy began in the last years of the reign of Henri IV and continued through the seventeenth century, creating the stereotype prelate of the *Ancien Régime*.[31]

CHAPTER XI

CONCLUSIONS

Over a period of sixty-three years five French kings placed 377 bishops in the episcopate. Anyone who is familiar with social structure of sixteenth-century France will not be surprised that half of those prelates were from the *noblesse d'épée*.[1] Because most of the foreigners placed in the French hierarchy were from families of similar status, almost 60 percent of the bishops came from the established elite. Since the second half of the sixteenth century is often seen as the period of the rise of the *noblesse de robe*, it is more of a surprise that the *anoblis* constituted only 16 percent of the bishops under study. Likely most surprising is the fact that the proportion of the *roturier* bishops, at 13 percent, was so close to the new nobles. It is certainly true that many of these commoner prelates were members of prominent and wealthy families, some of which eventually passed into the *noblesse de robe*, but in the sixteenth century their commoner status was still so obvious that the contemporary records took specific note of it.

That more than one of every ten bishops seated in this era was a commoner, as small a proportion as this is, contrasts sharply with the much smaller numbers of *roturier* bishops in the late Middle Ages and the next two centuries of the *Ancien Régime*. Over half of the commoners found in the episcopate of the *Ancien Régime* were appointed in these six decades.[2] Since the appointments of the reign of Henri II followed much the same pattern as the previous reigns, he had little part in the changing social makeup of the episcopate. It was during the reign of Charles IX that the substantial change occurred. The number of bishops from the old nobility dropped well below 50 percent while those of commoner status went over 10 percent. However, the pattern of episcopal appointments of the next two kings show that more powerful factors than the influence of one person were at work. It is true that under Henri III, bishops of old noble status were again more than half of the nominees, but commoner appointees remained over 10 percent as well. In the last year of Henri III's reign, because of the much higher rate of resignations by noble bishops and because many vacancies were left unfilled, the proportion of commoners in the episcopate was nearly 20 percent. *Anobli* prelates, who in the eyes of much of the population were nearly as declassé as the *roturiers*, constituted another fifth of the ranks of bishops. Henri IV continued the practice of making numerous episcopal nominations from the ranks of commoners and new nobles to the point that his appointments from the nobility of the sword constituted just 40 percent of the total.

A number of factors unique to the period had combined to give the *roturiers* an unprecedented number of bishoprics. These factors included the special consideration given to humanists, the rapid rise of a number of families that were not yet legally noble, and Henri IV's policy of rewarding his supporters from every social level; but certainly the most important one was the religious wars of the era. The monarchy's desperate need for money required that the sons of parvenu bankers receive bishoprics to buy the loyalty of those families. The sectarian fighting, especially in the Midi, demanded that all the sons of the local Catholic nobles serve as warriors and not as churchmen as some would have in more peaceful times. And as the kingdom seemed to be slipping from the control of the monarchy, so also the king appeared to be losing his grip over the appointment of prelates. Periods of near anarchy tend to be times when established barriers of all sorts begin to break down. For several decades, therefore, the social origins of the episcopate had changed significantly with the lower levels of French society much more strongly represented. The opportunities for social mobility in the Church appeared to be expanding, as they were within the government bureaucracy. But the apparent opening of the ranks of the upper clergy was largely illusory. Within several years after peace was established in 1598, Henri IV returned to the pattern of episcopal appointment of prior to 1559, and the number of commoners in the episcopate declined sharply. While the *anoblis* continued to gain bishoprics in good numbers throughout the seventeenth century, the number of *roturiers* declined to the same levels as during the reigns of François I and Henri II. The high incidence of commoners was an aberration that largely reflected the crisis in French society in the second half of the sixteenth century. Furthermore, in the next century intellectuals were not lionized as the humanists had been, and the commoners among them did not have the standing to gain episcopal chairs. These factors help to explain the decline in commoner prelates after 1610.

Having been elevated to the ranks of the elite by appointment to a bishopric, some commoners found that they did not hold the same respect and authority that their social betters in the episcopacy did. To what extent they lost some of their effectiveness as bishops because of their social status is difficult to determine, but it is clear that there was considerable hostility to the commoner bishops within the ranks of the nobility. Given the mind-set of the early modern French nobles, it would have required a change of attitude most difficult to effect for them to accept commoner bishops on a regular basis. The wealth, authority, and honors of most bishops were so vast that it seemed proper that only a noble should enjoy them. An occasional exception could be tolerated; but if the proportion of commoners among the bishops had become permanently higher, there likely would have been a serious backlash once France had been stabilized.

In the long term the return to an almost exclusively noble episcopate hurt the French monarchy by closing off an opportunity for social mobility for the bourgeoisie. Yet it may have had a beneficial impact on the episcopacy by enhancing its ability to conserve its properties and revenues after 1600. Speaking of Elizabethan England, Lawrence Stone has argued: "No longer was the episcopacy closely linked by blood and social position to the nobility. . . . Men of lowly origins, they were now defenseless against the rapacity of their betters. And so when the summons for surrender came, the majority of the bishops, for all their squeals of dismay, nevertheless gave in without undue obstinacy."[3] It is true that the French bishops, when called on by the monarchy for financial support, also gave only limited resistance. The French monarchy, however, found that using the episcopacy to reward service and buy loyalty from the nobility of even the highest ranks could prove as profitable as plundering the bishoprics, with far less opposition. To make an episcopal office attractive to the scions of the great families, the revenues and honors of the bishops had to remain high. Thus the financial demands actually declined for much of the seventeenth century. One explanation for the great increase in the percentage of bishops from the *noblesse de race* in the eighteenth century is that the net income of a large number of bishoprics had climbed to the point that even the smaller sees had become suitable prizes for the best noble families.

In the late sixteenth century, however, the decline in the proportion of prelates from the nobility of the sword should presumably have resulted in an improvement in fulfilling the educational requirement of the Concordat of Bologna. The French kings clearly interpreted the clause waiving that requirement for the nominees of prominent families to apply very broadly to the nobility. But the change in social composition of the episcopate did not result in a significant improvement in that regard. Only a third of the 377 bishops had training in law or theology; the lawyers outnumbered the theologians by a ratio of nearly three to one. Among the *anoblis* the ratio was fifteen to one, but that statistic is not unexpected. A law degree, especially one in civil law, was more likely to lead to ecclesiastical advancement than a degree in theology. This pattern appears to reflect the monarchy's use of a bishopric to reward royal officers who were far more often lawyers than theologians as well as the extensive legal obligations of the bishops.

It is not surprising that only 30 percent of the bishops of the status of sword nobles had the required university training, but it is unexpected that even a smaller proportion of *anoblis* did, given that they did not have the standing that the old nobles did and that they were largely associated with the law courts. Although the *roturiers* at 60 percent had by far the best record in meeting the Concordat's educational prerequisite for episcopal office, nonetheless the other 40 percent did not have the required degree. Some of the latter were humanists whose intellectual achievements met the spirit of the Concordat if not the letter, but many were not. Their nomination and confirmation indicate the extent to which both monarchy and papacy were willing to disregard the Concordat's clause. It was further demonstrated in the fact that foreign (almost entirely Italian) nominees had the worst record of any social group, many of whom the popes appointed. Last, one can not attribute the lack of the proper degrees to the clause of the Concordat exempting members of those religious orders that prohibited taking those degrees, since only two members of such orders appear in the roll of bishops.

The Concordat of Bologna had given the French monarchy effective control over the bishoprics. Clearly François I, and to a lesser extent his successors, used the episcopacy as a means of rewarding diplomats, important royal officials, and even military captains. It was a way of providing them with an income and freeing the royal treasury of the burden of paying them as they deserved. The king's ability to reward faithful service by appointing the official himself, a member of his family, or even a family client to a bishopric was especially useful in tying the Italian and French bankers more closely to the throne. As the collator of the episcopal benefices, the king could grant pensions to laymen as a way to repay loans from those bankers.

The kings, however, had less success in their efforts to use the bishops as instruments of direct royal authority in the provinces. It is true that prelates appear frequently as provincial governors, lieutenants, and other royal officials in the provinces. The bishops given these posts appear to have served the monarchy more zealously than lay nobles holding such offices did. The appointment of nearly half of the bishops to dioceses outside of the natural zones of influence of their families suggests at first glance an attempt on the part of the monarchy to use the episcopate to extend its authority. Yet it is unclear whether there was such an effort, since the king often appointed an individual to a specific diocese merely because it had become vacant at the time when the king had decided to reward him with a see. Furthermore, the chronic absenteeism, often caused by the monarchy's use of the bishop for royal service elsewhere, reduced the effectiveness of any royal effort to exploit the episcopate as an instrument of royal control in the provinces. In addition local episcopal dynasties and control over various bishoprics by the local nobility resulted in numerous appointments that served those families and the forces of particularism better than the central government.

Nonetheless the monarchy was quite successful in seating bishops loyal to it. The depth of loyalty to the institution of the monarchy among French bishops was well demonstrated by the support that so many gave to Henri de Navarre in 1589; opposition to the Huguenot prince was clearly stronger in the lower clergy. Some bishops served the monarchy so completely that they were identified more as the king's men than as churchmen. While the monarchy probably made less effective use of its control over episcopal nominations to enlist the bishops as instruments of royal authority than it could have, the Concordat did serve the kings well.

The kings gained particular benefit from their control of episcopal placement through the financial advantage it provided. The wealth of the Church and its leaders aroused the envy and avarice of most other Frenchmen. The envy and the outrage of the men of the Third Estate regarding the wealth of the clergy was clearly revealed at the Estates of Orléans where the proposals of the *Tiers* to seize much of the clergy's wealth would have reduced the bishops to little more than modestly paid government officials. These schemes failed to be implemented because the monarchy was not prepared to deplete the Church of its resources so drastically, certainly not for the benefit of other institutions.

The monarchy itself did successfully impose heavy financial

demands on the clergy. Royal exactions on the clergy in the form of the forced sale of property, the multiple décimes, and the steeple taxes were so high in the period from 1561 to 1589 that if they had continued for another decade or two, which would have been likely had Henri III not been assassinated, the end result might well have been what the deputies of the Third Estate had been seeking. As it was, the clergy permanently lost about 5 percent of its real estate (somewhat higher in the Midi) to the forced alienations. The loss, though hardly devastating, was a noticeable one. More importantly the décime was standardized at 1,300,000 livres annually, which at the turn of the seventeenth century constituted about 8 percent of the clergy's estimated gross income. The bishops paid somewhat less than that proportion. With increasing episcopal revenues and a drop in the size of the décimes to 660,000 l later in the seventeenth century, the impact of the annual gift to the monarchy became increasingly less burdensome even with large special subsidies voted by the clerical assembly to aid the monarchy at times of war.[4] But in the decades after 1561 with the twofold attack on their revenues and property by monarch and Huguenot, it must have appeared to many bishops that the entire financial structure of the episcopacy, carefully built up over so many centuries and so jealously guarded, was headed for ruin. Yet the bishops offered little opposition to the monarchy's demands. What objection was made came largely from the cathedral chapters and diocesan assemblies presided over by vicars.

The lack of a strong response to royal financial exactions on the part of the prelates was not only a consequence of their loyalty to the crown; it also reflected the major justification—the eradication of Protestantism—the monarchy gave for demanding clerical taxes. The monarchy stated that it was proper that the churchmen contribute heavily to the effort to destroy the Reform movement since its success would injure them more than any other group. But the bishops bore much of the responsibility for the presence of the Protestants since a significant factor in the rise of Protestantism was the blatant negligence of their duties by most bishops in the first two-thirds of the sixteenth century. Even a conscientious vicar could not truly replace the bishop in effective direction of the clergy. The absenteeism, the lack of training, the ignorance, the moral turpitude of so many bishops were reflected by the diocesan clergy. The unedifying lifestyle of so many prelates was one of the factors in the success of the Reformation, since many of the more sensitive people in French society could no longer tolerate the fact that so many of the shepherds of the flock of Christ were more truly wolves.

Once Protestantism did begin to appear in the realm, many bishops did little or nothing to counter its presence. Few prelates used the authority of their offices to stem the rise of the Protestant party. The early response of the episcopate to the appearance of a rival religion in France was so feeble that both François I and Henri II made attempts to move jurisdiction over heresy from the bishops to the Parlements, which the prelates energetically resisted. Even after the violence and destruction of the first civil war began, often directed against bishops and their property, a near majority of the bishops remained uninvolved in the anti-Protestant effort.

Consistent with this lack of zeal against the Huguenots on the part of much of the episcopate was the support that more than a third of the bishops rendered to Henri de Navarre before his conversion. Drawn out of loyalty to the institution of the monarchy, seduced perhaps by the personality of Henri himself, and motivated in some cases by opportunism, bishops provided a substantial part of the leadership of the Politique party. A large minority of the French bishops were willing to see a Protestant sit on the throne of Saint Louis, although one may presume that most harbored hope that Navarre would become Catholic.

Obviously one cannot really assess the extent to which the successful enthronement of Henri de Navarre without converting to Catholicism would have proven disastrous for the Catholic Church and its episcopate. But even the repeated and apparently sincere assurances from Navarre that he would respect the position of the Church would not likely have prevented the deterioration of its power and influence under a Protestant monarch. Men of ambition would have converted to Protestantism, likely including a good number of bishops, just as there was a flock of conversions to Catholicism from Henri's Protestant entourage after 1593. When considered in that light, the large faction of Politiques among the prelates hardly served the interests of their Church.

Considering the role of the bishops in creating the atmosphere in which Protestantism arose, it would appear that France remained Catholic despite the bishops, not because of them. Nonetheless the episcopate did make a contribution to the Church's continued domination of French society, even if that contribution was considerably less than might have been expected of the hierarchy. The most significant way that the episcopate had an impact on the maintenance of Catholicism was largely a passive one. The power, wealth, and prestige of the episcopal office bound many important families and individuals to the Church through their desire to retain the positions that so enhanced their standing. Clearly one cannot measure this factor in any systematic way, but the Protestant rejection of the traditional office of bishop did cost the movement considerable support, both within the episcopate itself and among the nobles. Holding a bishopric in the family was nearly as attractive as seizing its properties and rights and far less troublesome.

The contrast between the ultimate failure of Protestantism in France and the ease of the Anglican settlement in England, which kept the episcopacy, is instructive, even if the English monarchy reduced the wealth of the episcopate and the proportion of nobles among the bishops. Both monarchies found their control of the bishops valuable, and one factor in Navarre's decision to convert was to gain acceptance of his episcopal appointments, which were not recognized either by Rome or by the French people. Henri IV may have called James I "the wisest fool in Christendom," but he was certainly shrewd enough to recognize the wisdom behind James's "No bishop, No king."

The involvement of French bishops in the succession crisis of 1589–93 was the most concerted effort they put forth in the sixteenth century. None of the other problems they faced—the Reformation, the financial demand of the monarchy, the loss of jurisdiction from their tribunals—aroused the passion and vigor that their involvement in the two parties of the succession dispute brought forth. Nearly all of the prelates were involved to some degree in one of the two factions. Both factions ironically made a contribution to keeping the monarchy Catholic. The Leaguer bishops did so by providing talent and leadership to a party lacking both after the assassination of the Guises. The League's stubborn refusal to accept Henri de Navarre as king while he remained a Protestant was the key factor in his decision to convert. On the other hand the Politique bishops provided a measure of assurance that Navarre's pledges to maintain Catholicism were sincere, thus keeping a number of Catholic nobles in his party. More importantly they gave evidence of the sincerity of his conversion in 1593 and accepted his abjuration, enabling most French Catholics to accept him as king and ensuring the continued Catholicism of the monarchy.

Only after that crisis had passed and the growth of Protestantism was stemmed did the prelates begin to reform the episcopacy. The very danger that Protestantism and in particular the presence of the Huguenot successor posed to the Church had to have been a factor in that reform. Philip Benedict has suggested that "by jolting the Catholic Church out of its inertia, the political crisis may well have provided the initial push that was needed for the Counter-Reformation to get underway."[5] The French hierarchy provides further evidence for this thesis in that a number of bishops who had not demonstrated any interest in reform before 1589 emerged as reformers after the civil wars. The anarchy and disruption in so many dioceses in the previous decades likely made it impossible for some reform-minded prelates to begin to implement meaningful reform earlier, while others may have been caught up in the spirit of reform as it began to appear in the French Church after 1595. But for still others the terrifying prospect of a Protestant wearing the crown must have awakened a zeal for reform in order to secure the Catholicism of the realm. Two prelates who fit the pattern of latecomers to the Catholic Reformation were Côme Clause of Châlons-sur-Marne and Pierre de Paparin of Gap.

Both had been seated around 1570, and neither had demonstrated any interest in reform until the last years of his life after 1595. Paparin for instance died shortly after an extensive visitation of his diocese had exhausted him.[6]

The relationship between the Catholic League and Church reform that Benedict proposes finds support as well in the caliber of episcopal appointments that the Leaguers made in sees they controlled. Génébrard of Aix, Muriel of Montauban, and Valernod of Toulouse were Leaguer nominees whose reputations for zeal and reform were well above that of the run of the episcopate. Nonetheless it is true that Henri IV named the first significant number of reforming bishops.

To what extent the failure of the French episcopate to begin to reform itself immediately upon the conclusion of the Council of Trent would have stemmed the growth of the Huguenot party is, of course, difficult to answer. The close coincidence of the end of the council with the outbreak of the wars of religion indicates that the immediate implementation of the Tridentine decrees and the reform of the clergy would not have prevented the first civil wars. Perhaps the French Church needed the forty years of religious war and the threatened loss of its unique status to persuade the high clergy to reform. But the considerable success of numerous reforming bishops after 1600 suggests that an episcopate quickly conforming to the reforms of Trent might have helped reduce the agony of the wars of religion.

The Protestant challenge to the very office of bishop was the most serious aspect of a vast crisis that confronted the French episcopate in the second half of the sixteenth century. The financial demands of the monarchy on the clergy, the significant albeit temporary change in the social composition of the episcopate, and the challenges to its legal jurisdiction and temporal powers would have created critical problems for the bishops even without the presence of the Huguenots. But the long-term impact of the episcopate's crisis was not nearly as powerful and extensive as numerous Frenchmen, many Catholics of the Third Estate as well as the Protestants, had advocated. Except for a considerable loss in the range of its legal jurisdiction and the permanent imposition of a royal tax, there was very little change in the office of bishop. The Tridentine reform movement corrected some of the worst abuses in the episcopacy when it began to have a real effect on the French Church after 1600, but it did not change the basic style of the office or reduce its power and revenues. If indeed one can describe the Protestants and many of the Leaguers as revolutionaries, seeking fundamental change in the political and social structures of France, then the study of the episcopate demonstrates that they did not have any success in achieving their goals. For the bishops emerge from this period of multiple crises as much as part of the elite of the kingdom as they had been before 1547. Some of the small details of the French social structure had changed in the six decades between 1547 and 1610, but the broad pattern was the same, with the bishops still at the very top.

If the events of the late sixteenth century did result in rather little real change in the nature of the episcopal office, what consequence did they have on the episcopate? As was true for most of the institutions of the French kingdom that survived the sixteenth century, the problems did not transform the episcopacy but strengthened it. The limited reforms of the early seventeenth century eliminated some of the most glaring abuses without changing the office; and they strengthened the moral prestige of the bishops. The clear need for a better class of bishops resulted in the nomination of a more uniform type of prelate with more extensive university training and a somewhat better sense of duty to the pastoral activities of the bishop. The bishops were partially compensated for the successful imposition of a royal tax by the existence of the national assembly of the clergy that continued to meet regularly throughout the *Ancien Régime*. The assembly gave the clergy the means to deal with the monarchy as a national corporate body, a privilege no other class in France had. The episcopate emerged from the religious wars certainly not purified, since many of the same ills that beset it were still present in 1789, but clearly tempered and strengthened for the duration of the *Ancien Régime*.

THE MONETARY SYSTEM

I n the sixteenth century, the French monetary system was, as were those of all of Europe, very complicated and confusing. The *écu d'or soleil*, also known as the *écu au soleil*, was the principal and largest gold coin in circulation in France. It had roughly the same value as the *scudi* of the papal curia. Most accounts, however, were expressed in terms of the *livre tournais*, a monetary unit of account. Its rival, the *livre parisis*, had largely disappeared by 1547. All references to the livre in this work are to the tournais. The livre (l) was divided into 20 *sols* (s), which in turn were divided into 12 deniers (d), 240 d to the livre. No such coins actually existed. In 1519 the écu was pegged at two livres. It rose to 2.25 l in 1533; to 2.50 l in 1550 (at which time the *henri* replaced the écu for ten years); and was set at 3 livres in 1575. The monetary reform of 1577 declared that the écu was to be the unit of account as well as a real coin, but most accounts continued to be expressed in livres. Henri IV returned to the livre as the unit of account in 1602. Silver coins included the *franc*, worth one livre, and the *teston* and *quart d'écu*, both worth one-fourth of an écu or 15 s at the rate established in 1577. There were also a number of coins of silver mixed with copper used largely for retail trade. The most common coin in circulation was the *douzain*, worth 12 d.[1]

ROLL OF BISHOPS SEATED,
1547 – 1610,
AND A METHODOLOGICAL NOTE

I make no pretensions that the following roll of bishops and their terms of offices and social status is completely accurate. There are far too many difficulties that preclude that possibility. A major one is that there is no central source of information about the bishops of the sixteenth century. The papal constitution of 1591 requiring far more detailed information about episcopal candidates did not begin to take effect until after 1600. Once it did, dossiers containing extensive information on the appointees began to accumulate in French archives, now collected in the "Minutier central des notaires Parisiens" of the Archives Nationales. For the period under study, however, data about the social background, education, and prior careers of the bishops must be gleaned from many sources. For many of the prelates the data are limited. The most authoritative sources are the "Acta consistorialia," the minutes of the consistorial meetings at which episcopal nominations were approved.[1] Unfortunately the "Acta" for the sixteenth century are uneven, varying greatly in detail from one pope to another, from the mere mention that the cardinal protector presented the French candidates for bishoprics and abbeys to a full description of the candidates' credentials.

The editors of the *Hierarchia Catholica medii aevi*[2] have compiled the episcopal rolls for the sixteenth century using information from the "Acta consistorialia." They provide the date of papal confirmation but are often inaccurate on the end of episcopal terms. Further information on the prelates can be drawn from the *Gallia*

Christiana,[3] the *Dictionnaire de biographie française*, and a myriad of local, provincial, and diocesan histories in print. Nonetheless, little is known about a large number of sixteenth-century bishops beyond their dates in office and social status. For a smaller number even the latter point is unavailable. Thus compiling accurate statistics about the French episcopate before 1600 is most difficult, and any tables that are constructed to indicate the social status and career profiles of bishops seated in the century are open to some correction.

The best sources for determining whether a bishop was of the status of *noblesse d'épée* are La Chenoye-Desbois, *Dictionnaire de la noblesse*,[4] Moreri, *Le grand dictionnaire historique*,[5] and the Cabinet des Titres of the Bibliothèque Nationale, especially the Cabinet D'Hozier. They, however, are heavily dependent on the *recherches* of the late seventeenth century, which were done to establish noble status and to eliminate pretenders and place them on the tax rolls. Their reliability is somewhat suspect, because they were manipulated by bribery and other chicanery and often do not include old *petite-noblesse* families that had died out by the time of the *recherches*. Thus it is possible that a few of the bishops whom I have placed in the category of unknown social origins were from such families. Several families explicitly placed in the *noblesse de race* by sixteenth-century sources do not appear in the *Dictionnaire de la noblesse*.

The above sources also include most *anobli* families. The concept that holding certain offices ennobled the incumbents appeared in the late fourteenth century, and *anobli* families will be defined as those gaining noble status after 1400. Additional sources include various studies of the Parlements, in particular François Bluche, "L'origine des magistrats du Parlement de Paris au XVIIIe siècle,"[6] Edouard Maugis, *Histoire du Parlement de Paris*,[7] and A. Floquet, *Histoire du Parlement de Normandie*.[8]

I have classified as *roturiers*, the unprivileged, only those bishops for whom I have found explicit statements in the sources of the commoner origins of such bishops or the occupations of their fathers. In the sixteenth century, however, a large number of merchant and financier families were in a state of transition, holding government offices and seigneuries and fancying themselves as sieurs but not yet reorganized as noble by the crown and most of French society. Many such families would in the next century be included in the *noblesse de robe*. But others who were "living nobly" in the sixteenth century could not prove their claim to noble status in the *recherches* of the next century, although family members appointed to the episcopate prior to the *recherches* may well have been considered to be noble at the time of the nomination. Placing bishops from both types of families in a social category is hazardous, and they account for a large proportion of the category of unknown social origins. It is likely that only a few prelates I have placed in that category were true commoners since contemporary sources appear to emphasize the social origins of a *roturier* bishop. But for several bishops from the small sees of the Midi, any information beyond the dates of their terms in office is completely lacking. In three cases the *recherches* failed to include the bishops in question as members of noble families despite the circumstantial evidence such as geography that suggests that they were. An example is that of the two Isnards of Glandèves who are not listed as members of noble Isnard family of Provence.[9] Finally the category of bishops of uncertain social origins includes several cases where I could not resolve clear contradictions in the sources over social status.

The data for the career profiles of the bishops (appendix 3) have been drawn from a vast number of sources; the most useful is the *Hierarchia Catholica*. Certain categories such as bishops who held benefices in *commendam* or who resigned with a pension are less definitive than others, but all categories including those of social status do involve an element of uncertainty.

The roll of bishops below does not include those nominees whom Rome refused to confirm, unless, as in several cases, they administered the see for more than a year and took its revenues. The roll does include those who were confirmed but never consecrated. The list of bishops was established largely from Eubel, *Hierarchia Catholica*. Information on virtually every bishop can be found in the *Gallia Christiana*, and most prelates of noble status are noted in La Chenoye-Desbois, *Dictionnaire de la noblesse*. The work noted for each bishop will indicate the principal printed source of additional information for that bishop. For a small number of bishops I found no work that provided any additional information beyond that in Eubel and the *Gallia Christiana*.

ABBREVIATIONS USED IN THE ROLL

N	*noblesse d'épée*
A	*anobli* or new noble
R	*roturier* or commoner
F	foreigner
U	uncertain social status
ANG	*Acta Nuniaturae Gallicae*
DBF	*Dictionnaire de biographie française*
De Vic	De Vic et al., *Histoire de Languedoc*
DGHE	*Dictionnaire d'histoire et de géographie ecclésiastique*
Fisquet	Fisquet, *La France pontificale*
Picot	Picot, *Les Italiens en France*
Taillandier	Taillandier, *Histoire ecclésiastique et civile de Bretagne*

Full bibliographical citations for the other works cited are found in the bibliography.

Name	First See	Date of Confirmation
Aillebout, Charles d'	Autun	1573
Alamani, Giovanni	Bazas	1555
Alamani, Luc	Mâcon	1583
Albon, Antoine d'	Lyon	1564
Albret, Pierre d'	Comminges	1561
Ambroise, Adrien d'	Tréquier	1604
Amyot, Jacques	Auxerre	1570
Angennes, Charles d'	Le Mans	1559
Angennes, Claude d'	Noyon	1578
Angennes, Jacques d'	Bayeux	1604
Annoncourt, Jean d'	Poitiers	1555
Aradon, Georges d'	Vannes	1593
Auraisin, Andre d'	Riez	1570
Auraisin, Claude d'	Castres	1551
Aussan, Hector d'	Couserans	1549
Avançon, François d'	Embrum	1560
Avançon, Guillaume d'	Grenoble	1561
Balaguier, François de	Bazas	1565
Balaguier, Jean de	Bazas	1563
Balsac, Charles de	Noyon	1597
Bandello, Matteo	Agen	1550
Bardi, Alessandro di	St-Papoul	1564
Barrau, Bertrand de	Pamiers	1583
Barrault, Pierre de	Lodève	1566
Bauffrement, Claude de	Troyes	1562
Beaumanoir, Charles de	Le Mans	1610
Beaune, Martin de	Le Puy	1557
Beaune, Renaud de	Mende	1581
Bellanger, Bernard	Fréjus	1592
Bellièvre, Albert de	Lyon	1599
Bellièvre, Charles de	Lyon	1604
Benoist, René	Troyes	1593
Bertaut, Jean de	Sées	1607
Bertier, Jean de	Rieux	1602
Bertrand, Jean	Comminges	1551
Bertrand, Pierre	Cahors	1558

Social Status	Principal Source of Information
U	DBF, I, 1573
F	O'Reilly, *Histoire de Bazas,* p. 203
F	DBF, I, 1103
N	DBF, I, 1263–64
N	DBF, I, 1322
N	Taillandier, II, lxxviii
R	Cioranescu, *Amyot*
N	DBF, II, 1087–88
N	DBF, II, 1090–93
N	DBF, II, 1095
N	
N	DBF, III, 197
N	Fisquet, V, article Riez
N	ANG, XIV, 603
N	Lafaille, *Annales de Toulouse,* II, 290, 301
A	DBF, IV, 808
A	DBF, IV, 810–12
N	O'Reilly, *Histoire de Bazas,* p. 206
N	O'Reilly, *Histoire de Bazas,* p. 205
N	DBF, IV, 1523
F	Picot, p. 86
F	Picot, p. 87
N	Lanhandis, *Annales de Pamiers*
A	Martin, *Histoire de Lodève,* II, 13–16
N	DBF, VI, 918
N	Pialin, *Eglise du Mans,* V, 425
A	DBF, V, 1159
A	Baumgartner, "Renaud de Beaune"
R	Busquet, *Histoire de Provence,* p. 381
A	DBF, V, 1539
A	DBF, V, 1559
R	Pasquier, *Un curé de Paris*
R	Grente, *Bertaut*
A	DBF, VI 157
N	DBF, VI, 274–75
N	DBF, VI, 283

Name	First See	Date of Confirmation
Billy, Godefroy de	Laon	1601
Birague, Horace de	Lavaur	1583
Birague, René de	Lisieux	1583
Bizet, Tristan de	Saintes	1550
Blaigny, Gabriel de	Noyons	1588
Blanchy, Seraphim	Angoulême	1593
Bochelet, Bernardin	Rennes	1558
Bonard, François	Couserans	1581
Boni, Carlo Di	Angoulême	1567
Bonzi, Giovanni di	Béziers	1598
Bonzi, Tommaso di	Béziers	1576
Bouchard, Guy	Périgueux	1554
Boucher, Etienne de	Quimper	1560
Bouliers, François de	Fréjus	1579
Boulogne, Antoine de	Digne	1602
Bourbon, Charles I de	Lectoure	1569
Bourbon, Charles II de	Rouen	1597
Bourdeille, François de	Périgueux	1576
Bourges, Jérôme de	Châlons-sur-Marne	1556
Bourgneuf, Charles de	St-Malo	1586
Bourguignons, César de	Limoges	1547
Bours, Jean de	Laon	1564
Breslay, Réné de	Troyes	1605
Brézé, Louis de	Meaux	1553
Brichanteau, Benjamin	Laon	1608
Brichanteau, Crispin	Senlis	1560
Briçonnet, Claude	Nîmes	1554
Briroy, Nicolas de	Coutances	1597
Broullat, Jacques de	Arles	1550
Bussy d'Amboise, Gentian de	Tarbes	1554
Camelin, Barthélemy	Fréjus	1599
Camus, Jean	Bellay	1609
Canignani, Alessandro	Aix	1576
Caracciolo, Antonio	Troyes	1551
Carafa, Carlo	Comminges	1556
Carles, Lancelot de	Riez	1550

Social Status	Principal Source of Information
N	DBF, VI, 483
F	DBF, VI, 509
F	DBF, VI, 509
R	
N	DBF, VI, 559
R	
A	Sutherland, *Secretaries of State,* pp. 19–20
U	DeVic, IV, 382
F	Picot, p. 103
F	Bellaud, *Les évêques italiens,* pp. 215–367
F	Bellaud, *Les évêques italiens,* pp. 160–214
U	Lavergne, *Histoire de Périgueux,* p. 186
N	DBF, VI, 1202
N	ANG, IX, 82; XII, 852
R	DHGE, X, 10
N	DBF, VI, 1393–94
N	DBF, VI, 1395
N	DBF, VI, 435
U	Barthelémy, *Diocèse de Châlons,* pp. 204–6
A	DBF, VI, 1490
F	Aulagne, *La Réforme dans Limoges,* p. 2
R	DBF, VI, 1043
R	DBF, VII, 219–20
N	DBF, VII, 265
N	Fisquet, XV, article Laon
N	DHGE, IX, 45
A	Martin, *Histoire de Lodève,* II, 2–16
N	DBF, VII, 347–48
N	Degert, "Le procès," p. 70
N	DBF, VII, 724
R	DBF, VII, 975
A	DBF, VII, 1014
F	Dolan, *Entre tours,* pp. 193–94
F	Roserat de Melun, *Caracciolo*
F	ANG, XIV, 95–99
A	DBF, VII, 1151

Name	First See	Date of Confirmation
Cavalesi, Raymond	Nîmes	1573
Chauvigné, Rolland de	St-Pol-de-Leon	1554
Chevalier, Pierre	Senlis	1561
Clause, Cosme	Châlons-sur-Marne	1574
Clause, Henri	Châlons-sur-Marne	1608
Clause, Jean	Senez	1561
Clause, Nicolas	Châlons-sur-Marne	1572
Clermont, Théodore de	Senez	1551
Coquelet, Claude	Digne	1587
Corneillan, François de	Rodez	1582
Corneillan, Jacques de	Rodez	1560
Cospéan, Philippe	Aire	1606
Cossé, Arthur de	Coutances	1560
Couppes, Antoine	Sisteron	1582
Cous, Antoine de	Condom	1604
Crequi, Antoine I de	Nantes	1553
Crequi, Antoine II de	Nantes	1561
Cros, Antoine de	St–Paul	1599
Daffis, Jean	Lombès	1598
Daillon du Lude, René de	Luçon	1553
Danès, René	Lavour	1557
Dax, Antoine	Alet	1564
Deodel, Etienne	Grasse	1573
Dinet, Casper	Mâcon	1602
Doc, Jean	Laon	1552
Donadieu, François de	Auxerre	1594
Donadieu, François II de	St–Papoul	1608
Donnaud, Pierre de	Mirepoix	1587
Douglas, Valentin	Laon	1581
Du Bec-Crespin, Jean	Nantes	1596
Du Bec-Crespin, Philippe	Vannes	1559
Du Bellay, Eustache	Paris	1551
Du Blanc, Guillaume I	Toulon	1571
Du Blanc, Guillaume II	Grasse	1589
Du Bourg, Jean	Rieux	1566
Duchemin, Jean	Condom	1581

Social Status	Principal Source of Information
R	Menard, *Histoire de Nîmes*, V, 449
N	Taillander, II, xlii
A	Maugis, III, 214
A	Galpern, *Religions of Champagne*
A	Barthelémy, *Diocèse de Châlons*, p. 249
A	DBF, VIII, 1397
A	Barthelémy, *Diocèse de Châlons*, p. 237
N	DBF, VIII, 1494
R	Fisquet, XIII, article Digne
N	DBF, IX, 672
N	DBF, IX, 623
R	DBF, IX, 755
N	Marchand, *Charles de Cossé*, 40, 437–38
F	
N	
N	DBF, IX, 1206
N	DBF, IX, 1206
R	DBF, IX, 1205
A	DBF, IX, 1474
N	DBF, IX, 1503
F	Picot, pp. 111–12
N	DBF, I, 351
N	DBF, X, 1085
A	LaRochette, *Evêques de Mâcon*, III, 470–71
N	DBF, XI, 412
N	DBF, XI, 503
N	DBF, XI, 503
N	DBF, XI, 530
N	ANG, VIII, 694
N	DBF, XI, 886
N	Catta "Evêques de Nantes" pp. 23–70
N	ANG, XIV, 348–50
R	Doublet, "Guillaume Du Blanc"
R	Doublet, "Guillaume Du Blanc"
N	ANG, XIII, 231
U	DBF, XI, 1218

Name	First See	Date of Confirmation
Dugny, Philibert	Autun	1551
Dulis, Eustache	Nevers	1606
Du Perron, Jacques Davy	Evreux	1592
Du Plessis de Richelieu, Armand	Luçon	1606
Du Plessis de Richelieu, Jacques	Luçon	1586
Du Puy, Bernard	Agde	1583
Du Sault, Jean	Dax	1598
Du Serre, Charles	Gap	1600
Du Tillet, Jean	St-Brieuc	1565
Du Vair, Pierre	Vence	1602
Ebrard de St. Supplice, Antoine	Calors	1579
Eschaux, Bertraud d'	Bayonne	1599
Elbene, Alfonso d' I	Albi	1588
Elbene, Alfonso d' II	Albi	1608
Elbene, Bernardo d'	Lodève	1559
Epinac, Pierre d'	Lyon	1577
Erlault, Antoine	Chalon-sur-Saône	1561
Escars, Anne d'	Lisieux	1584
Escars, Charles d'	Poitiers	1560
Escoubleau, François d'	Bordeaux	1599
Escoubleau, François d'	Maillezais	1605
Escoubleau, Henri d'	Maillezais	1572
Esparbes, Joseph d'	Pamiers	1605
Espinay, Charles d'	Dol	1558
Este, Ludovico d'	Auch	1559
Farnese, Alessandro	Tours	1553
Fauçon, François de	Orléans	1550
Faur, Pierre de	Lavaur	1581
Fenouillet, Pierre	Montpellier	1608
Fléard, François de	Grenoble	1575
Fleyres, Pierre de	St. Pons	1587
Foix de Candale, Amanieu de	Carcassone	1554
Foix de Candale, Christophe de	Aire	1570
Foix de Candale, François de	Aire	1576
Foix de Carming, Paul de	Toulouse	1577
Fonsec, Jean de	Tulle	1551

Social Status	Principal Source of Information
N	DBF, XI, 1493
U	Fisquet, XX, article Nevers
A	DBF, XII, 339–41
N	Tresory, *Richelieu*
N	Tresory, *Richelieu*, pp. 6–9
R	Jordan, *Histoire d'Agde,* p. 379
A	Degert, *Evêques de Dax,* p. 270
N	DBF, XII, 855
A	DBF, XII, 917
A	Radouand, *Guillaume Du Vair*
N	ANG, XIII, 576
N	DBF, XII, 1110
F	DBF, XII, 1181
F	DBF, XII, 1181
F	Picot, p. 49
N	Richard, *La Ligue et les papes*
R	DBF, XII, 1382
N	DBF, XI, 1235
N	DBF, XI, 1235
N	Peyrous, "La réforme de Cardinal de Sourd
N	Peronnet, *Les évêques,* I, 483
N	Peronnet, *Les évêques,* I, 483
N	De Vic, IV, 432
N	Busson, *Charles d'Espinay*
F	Picot, p. 26
F	Picot, pp. 8–11
F	Bouges, *Histoire de Carcassone,* pp. 316–17
N	DBF, XI, 1376
R	DBF, XIII, 995
A	ANG, XIII, 223
N	De Vic, IV, 421
N	O'Reilly, *Histoire de Bazas,* p. 205
N	Harrie, *François Foix,* p. 55
N	Harrie, *François Foix*
N	Didier, *Paul de Foix*
N	Balzac, *Historiae tutelensis,* p. 216

Name	First See	Date of Confirmation
Fossé, Jean de	Castres	1554
Fouré, Jacques	Chalon-sur-Saône	1573
Fournier, Pierre	Périgueux	1561
Foy, Jean de	Poitiers	1568
Frejoso, Janus	Agen	1555
Frémiot, André	Bourges	1603
Fumée, Nicolas de	Beauvais	1573
Garidelli, Audiano	Vence	1576
Gaume, Antoine	St. Paul	1585
Gaurdon, Flotard de	Tulle	1582
Gaurdon, Louis de	Tulle	1560
Gaurdon, Jean de	Tulle	1599
Gelas, Claude de	Agen	1609
Gelas de Leberon, Charles de	Valence	1574
Gelas de Leberon, Pierre de	Valence	1598
Génébrard, Gilbert	Aix	1591
Girard, Robert de	Uzès	1574
Glandèves, Toussaint de	Sisteron	1606
Gondi, Henri de	Paris	1597
Gondi, Pierre de	Langres	1565
Gontaut, Robert de	Condom	1565
Granier, Jean de	Montpellier	1607
Grenon, Jean	Grasse	1566
Gribaldi, Vaspasien	Vienne	1569
Grimaldi, Louis	Vence	1560
Guillart, Charles de	Chartres	1553
Guise, Louis I de	Reims	1574
Guise, Louis II de	Reims	1605
Hallegoet, Guillaume de	Tréguier	1587
Helais, Jacques de	Langres	1562
Hennequin, Aimary	Rennes	1573
Hennequin, Jérôme	Soissons	1587
Héroet, Antoine	Digne	1552
Humières, Charles d'	Bayeux	1548
Hurault, Denis	Orléans	1582
Hurault, Paul	Aix	1599

Social Status	Principal Source of Information
R	ANG, II, 257–58
R	
R	Lavergne, *Histoire de Périgueux,* p. 92n
N	ANG, XII, 358
F	Picot, p. 168
A	DBF, XIV, 1190
A	DBF, XIV, 1439
F	DBF, XV, 436
R	DBF, XV, 779
N	Baluze, *Historiae tutelensis,* pp. 261–62
N	Baluze, *Historiae tutelensis,* pp. 257–58
N	Baluze, *Historiae tutelensis,* p. 270
R	Barrière, *Histoire du diocèse d'Agen,* II, 380
N	DBF, XV, 956
N	DBF, XV, 956
R	Dolan, *Enre tours,* pp. 247–48
U	De Vic, IV, 303
N	
F	Salmon, *Cardinal de Retz,* pp. 11–21
F	Salmon, *Cardinal de Retz,* pp. 11–21
N	Du Tems, *Le clerge de France*
U	La Roque, *Evêques de Montpellier,* pp. 124–26
U	Busquet, *Histoire de Provence,* p. 317
F	
N	Busquet, *Histoire de Provence,* p. 313
A	Degert, "Procès," p. 105
N	Fournon, *Ducs de Guise*
N	Fournon, *Ducs de Guise*
N	Taillandier, II, lxxvii
N	
A	ANG, XII, 609
A	Maugis, *Parlement de Paris,* III, 257
A	Fisquet, XII, article Digne
N	Fisquet, XVI, article Bayeux
A	Duchateau, *Histoire de Orléans,* p. 261
A	Hayden, *Estates of 1614,* p. 243

Name	First See	Date of Confirmation
Hurault, Philippe	Chartres	1598
Iharse, Salviate I d'	Tarbes	1580
Iharse, Salviate II d'	Tarbes	1602
Isnard, Clémens	Glandèves	1593
Isnard, Octave	Glandèves	1605
Jacomel, Tommaso	Toulon	1566
Jarnate, Balthas de	Embrun	1548
Jaubert, Jean de	Bazas	1606
Joyeuse, François de	Narbonne	1581
Kernevenoy, Claude de	Tréguier	1566
La Baume, Prosper de	St–Flour	1573
La Brosse, Jean de	Vienne	1561
La Croix Chevrières, Jean de	Grenoble	1607
La Guesle, Francois de	Tours	1597
La Haye, Jean de	Vannes	1574
La Haye, Louis de	Vannes	1575
La Marthonnie, Geoffroi de	Amiens	1576
La Marthonnie, Henri de	Limoges	1587
Lancrau, Pierre de	Lombès	1566
Langues, Jérôme de	Couserans	1593
Lanjelier, Nicolas	St–Brieuc	1564
L'Archiver, François	Rennes	1602
La Rochefoucauld, Antoine de	Angoulême	1607
La Rochefoucauld, Francois de	Clermont	1585
La Saussaye, Mathurin de	Orléans	1564
La Tour, Antoine de	Tulle	1587
La Tour, François de	Quimper	1578
L'Aubespine, Gabriel de	Orléans	1604
L'Aubespine, Jean de	Limoges	1583
L'Aubespine, Sebastien de	Limoges	1558
Laurens, Gasper de	Arles	1605
Laurens, Honoré de	Embrun	1601
Lauro, Thomas de	Vabres	1588
La Vallette, François I de	Vabres	1561
La Vallette, François II de	Vabres	1600
Le Baron, Charles de	Valence	1574

Social Status	Principal Source of Information
A	Hayden, *Estates of 1614*, p. 250
N	Monlezun, *Histoire de Gascogne*, V, 490
N	Hayden, *Estates of 1614*, p. 243
R	
R	
F	
N	Fisquet XII, article Embrun
N	O'Reilly, *Histoire de Bazas*, p. 212
N	Vaissière, *Messieurs de Joyeuse*
N	Taillandier, II, lxxv
U	
U	
A	Bligny, *Grenoble*
N	
U	Taillandier, II, xxxix
U	Taillandier, II, xxxix
N	
N	Guibert, *La ligue à Limoges*
N	Courrage, *Lombèz*
F	Monlezun, *Histoire de Gascogne*, V, 515
R	Taillandier, II, lxxvii
R	Taillandier, II, xi–xii
N	
N	Delumeau, *Diocèse de Clermont*, pp. 122–24
N	Duchateau, *Histoire d'Orléans*, pp. 167–69
N	Baluze, *Historiae tutelensis*, pp. 266–69
N	Taillandier, II, xxiv
A	Duchateau, *Histoire d'Orléans*, pp. 270–72
A	Sutherland, *French Secretaries*, pp. 20–22
A	Sutherland, *French Secretaries*, pp. 20–22
A	
A	Fisquet, XV, article Embrun
U	De Vic, IV, 310
N	*Histoire ecclésiastique*, I, 337
N	De Vic, IV, 312
N	Colombet, *Eglise de Vienne*, VII, 201

Name	First See	Date of Confirmation
Le Cornu de La Courbe, Nicolas	Saintes	1576
Le Cririer, Antoine	Avranches	1561
Le Cririer, Auguste	Avranches	1575
L'Estang, Christophe de	Lodève	1580
L'Estrange, Francois	Alet	1560
Le Fevre, Jean	Vannes	1566
Le Gouverneur, Guillaume	St—Malo	1610
Le Gras, Jean—Baptiste	Tréguier	1572
Le Henneyer, Jean	Lodève	1557
Le Maingre, Etienne	Grasse	1604
Le Meignen, Henri	Digne	1560
Lenoncourt, Philippe de	Châlons-sur-Marne	1550
Le Sueur d'Esquetal, Payen	Coutances	1549
Levis, Charles de	Lodève	1604
L'Hostel, Jean de	Viviers	1575
Lingendes, Jean de	Sarlat	1602
Liscoet, Charles de	Quimper	1582
Lisle, John	Coutances	1592
Lorraine, Charles de	Castres	1583
Lustac, Jean de	Périgueux	1548
Maille de Brézé, Simon de	Viviers	1552
Marcilly, Charles de	Autun	1586
Marcilly, Pierre de	Autun	1558
Marconnai, Melchior de	St-Brieuc	1601
Marillac, Bertrand de	Rennes	1566
Marillac, Charles de	Vannes	1550
Martel de Basquerille, Etienne	Coutances	1552
Marteli, Ugolino di	Glandèves	1568
Martin, Jacques	Vannes	1599
Martin, Jacques	Senez	1601
Martin, Jean	Périgueux	1600
Matz, Jean de	Dol	1557
Maugiron, Ayman de	Glandèves	1557
Maury, Jacques de	Bayonne	1579
Medici, Guilio de	Béziers	1561
Mesnier, Jean	Noyon	1594

Social Status	Principal Source of Information
U	
U	
U	
A	Peronnet, *Les évêques*, I, 504
U	De Vic, IV, 297
R	Peronnet, *Les évêques*, I, 498
R	Tuloup, *St. Malo*, p. 188
R	Peronnet, *Les évêques*, I, 698
R	Osmont, "Jean le Henneyer"
N	Barbiche, *Lettres de Henri IV*, p. 124
R	Doublet, "Guillaume du Blanc," pp. 176–89
N	Fisquet, XX, Auxerre
N	Marchand, *Charles de Cossé*, p. 437
N	Peronnet, *Les évêques*, I, 449
N	Peronnet, *Les évêques*, I, 497
R	
N	Pocquet, *Histoire de Bretagne*, V, 159
F	Heron, *Diocèse de Coutances*, p. 188
N	De Vic, *Histoire de Languedoc*, IV, 211
N	Lavergne, *Histoire de Périgueux*, p. 84
N	De Vic, IV, 318
N	Abord, *Histoire d'Autun*, II, 41.
N	Abord, *Histoire d'Autun*, I, 228–29
N	Taillandier, II, lxxii
N	Vaissier, *Charles de Marillac*
N	Vaissier, *Charles de Marillac*
N	Marchand, *Charles de Cossé*, p. 438
F	Picot, *Les italiens*, pp. 112–13
A	Taillandier, II, xxxvii
U	Héron, *Diocèse de Coutances*, p. 203
U	Lavergne, *Histoire de Périgueux*, p. 286
N	Taillandier, II, lxvii
N	
R	Monlezun, *Histoire de Gascogne*, V, 374
F	Bellaud, *Les évêques italiens*, pp. 90–160
U	

Name	First See	Date of Confirmation
Miron, Charles	Angers	1588
Montano, Horatio	Arles	1598
Montiers, Jean de	Bayonne	1551
Monluc, Jean I de	Valence	1553
Monluc, Jean II de	Condom	1571
Monte, Christoforo del	Marseille	1550
Monte, Innocente del	Mirepoix	1553
Morenne, Claude de	Sées	1600
Morvillier, Jean de	Orléans	1552
Moulinat, Louis de	Sées	1564
Murviel, Anne de	Montauban	1600
Neuville, Rolland de	St-Pol	1563
Noailles, Charles de	St-Flour	1609
Noailles, François de	Dax	1556
Noailles, Giles de	Dax	1562
Nogaret, Jean de	Toulouse	1605
Nogaret, Louis de	Toulouse	1608
Olivier, Seraphin	Rennes	1599
Ormy, Claude I d'	Boulogne	1566
Ormy, Claude II d'	Boulogne	1600
Orsini, Giovanni	Tréguier	1548
Ossat, Arnauld d'	Rennes	1596
Paparin, Pierre de	Gap	1572
Pellevé, Nicolas de	Amiens	1555
Pellevé, Robert de	Pamiers	1553
Péllissier, Jean	Apt	1607
Péricard, François	Avranches	1588
Péricard, Georges	Avranches	1583
Péricard, Guillaume	Evreux	1608
Pérille, Pompey de	Apt	1588
Pisani, Francesco	Narbonne	1551
Plas, Leodegard de	Lectoure	1599
Pobel, Thomas	St. Paul	1578
Polverel, Etienne	Alet	1607
Polverel, Pierre	Alet	1603
Pompadour, Godefroi de	Périgueux	1551

Social Status	Principal Source of Information
A	Félebien, *Histoire de Paris,* III, 777
F	
N	Monlezun, *Histoire de Gascogne,* IV, 497
N	Regnaud, *Jean de Monluc*
N	Regnaud, *Jean de Monluc*
F	Ricard, *Les évêques de Marseille*, pp. 100–2
F	ANG, IX, 50–55
R	Fisquet, XVIII, article Sées
A	Baquenault, *Morvillier*
A	Fisquet, XVIII, article Sées
N	Marcellin, *Histoire de Montauban,* II, 95
N	Taillandier, II, xliv
N	
N	Degert, *Evêques de Dax,* pp. 215
N	Degert, "Procès," p. 77
N	Lafaille, *Annales de Toulouse,* II, 536
N	Lafaille, *Annales de Toulouse,* II, 536
R	Taillandier, II, xi
A	ANG, XIV, 33
A	
F	Picot, *Les italiens,* p. 28
R	D'Ossat, *Lettres,* Intro.
A	Fisquet, V, article Gap
N	Didier, *Paul de Foix,* p. 116
N	Lahandis, *Annales de Pamiers*
U	Bozé, *Histoire d'Apt,* p. 305
A	Fisquet, XVIII, article Avranches
A	Peronnet, *Les évêques,* I, 506
A	Fisquet, XVII, article Evreux
F	Boze, *Histoire d'Apt,* p. 296
F	Ancil, *Nonciatures de Paul IV,* lvii
N	De Vic, IV, 371
N	
A	De Vic, IV, 424
A	De Vic, IV, 424
N	Laverne, *Histoire de Périqueux,* p. 180

Name	First See	Date of Confirmation
Pontac, Arnaud de	Bazas	1572
Pontlevoy, Pierre de	Maillezais	1561
Popian, Simeon de	Cahors	1608
Potier, Réné	Beauvais	1592
Premblay, Antoine	Mende	1581
Prés de Montpezat, Jacques de	Montauban	1556
Prévost, Antoine	Bordeaux	1561
Ragueneau, Frédéric	Marseille	1572
Ragueneau, Pierre	Marseille	1556
Raimbaud de Simiane, Jean	Vence	1555
Raimond, Jean	St–Papoul	1601
Rastel, Elezar de	Riez	1577
Rattes, Guiford de	Montpellier	1596
Revol, Antoine de	Dol	1603
Revol, Edmund de	Dol	1593
Robin, Gérard de	Lodève	1606
Rochechouart, Aymar de	Sisteron	1573
Rodolfi, Filipo	Albi	1568
Romanis, Bertrand de	Fréjus	1565
Rose, Antoine	Senlis	1601
Rose, Guillaume	Senlis	1584
Rouchon, Raymond de	St–Flour	1599
Rouci-Sissone, Charles de	Soissons	1557
Rouille, Pierre de	Montpellier	1570
Rousseau, Charles de	Mende	1609
Rousset, François	Uzès	1595
Rouxel, François	Lisieux	1599
Rovere, Hieronimus della	Toulon	1560
Ruzé, Guillaume	St–Malo	1570
Saint-Belin, Godefroi de	Poitiers	1577
Saint-François, Bernardin de	Bayeux	1573
Saint-Gelais, Urbain de	Comminges	1570
Saint-Martyn, Pierre de	Vannes	1572
Saint-Nectaire, Antoine de	Clermont	1567
Saint-Romain de Chaumont, Jean de	Aix	1551

Social Status	Principal Source of Information
N	Tamizey, *Arnaud de Pontac*
N	Peronnet, *Les évêques,* I, 483
U	
A	Delettre, *Evêques de Beauvais,* III, p. 274
U	
N	Marcellin, *Histoire de Montauban,* II, 75–77
N	Evennett, "Pie IV et les bénéfices"
N	Ricard, *Histoire de Marseille,* p. 105
N	Ricard, *Histoire de Marseille,* p. 104
N	Bozé, *Histoire d'Apt,* pp. 291–99
U	
N	Fisquet, IV, article Riez
A	LaFaille, *Annales de Toulouse,* II, 518
U	Taillandier, p. lxxxv
U	Taillandier, p. lxxi
U	Alzieu, *Un diocèse*
N	L'Estoile, *Mémoires,* I, 375
F	Picot, p. 101
U	Lambart, *Guerres de Religion*
N	
N	Labitte, *La Démocratie,* p. 299
U	
N	Fisquet, XIV, article Soissons
U	LaRougue, *Histoire de Montauban*
U	
U	
N	Fisquet, XVI, article Lisieux
F	Picot, p. 173
R	Tresvaux, *Histoire d'Angers,* p. 364
A	
N	Maugis, *Histoire de Parlement,* III, 286
N	Brontin, *Réforme pastorale,* p. 159
U	Taillandier, II, xxxvi
N	Delumeau, *Clermont,* p. 122
N	Dolan, *Entre tours,* pp. 245–47

Name	First See	Date of Confirmation
Saint-Sixte, Charles de	Riez	1599
Saintes, Claude de	Evreux	1574
Sala, Jacques	Viviers	1554
Salignac, François de	Sarlat	1567
Salignac, Louis de	Sarlat	1579
Salviati, Antonio	St–Papoul	1561
Salviati, Lorenzo	St–Papoul	1549
San Severino, Aymero di	Agde	1561
San Vitale, Eucherim	Viviers	1565
Santa Croce, Prospero di	Arles	1567
Santa Croce, Silvio di	Arles	1574
Saulnier, Pierre	Autun	1588
Savonières, Mathurin de	Bayeux	1583
Selve, Jean de	St–Flour	1567
Sennetaire, Antoine de	Le Puy	1561
Septres, Giles de	Toulon	1599
Serres, Jacques de	Le Puy	1597
Simiane, François de	Apt	1577
Simonetta, Nicolo	Quimper	1548
Soissonde, Jean de	Bayonne	1566
Sorbin, Arnaud	Nevers	1578
Spifame, Giles	Nevers	1559
Strozzi, Lorenzo	Béziers	1547
Suau, Jean	Mirepoix	1555
Subject, Antoine de	Montpellier	1573
Sulla, René de	Luçon	1578
Thome, François	St-Malo	1573
Thou, Nicolas de	Chartres	1573
Tiercelin, Jean–Baptiste	Luçon	1562
Trapes, Léonard de	Auch	1599
Turricella, Jacopo	Marseille	1605
Tyard, Cyrus de	Chalon-sur-Saône	1594
Tyard, Pontus de	Chalon-sur-Saône	1571
Urre, Pierre d'	Viviers	1571
Uterlou, Adam d'	Mende	1586
Valliart de Gueles, Germain	Orléans	1586

Social Status	Principal Source of Information
U	De Vic, IV, 397
R	L'Estoile, *Mémoires*, III, 101
F	Picot, p. 81
N	
N	
F	Picot, pp. 85–87
F	Picot, pp. 85–87
F	Jordan, *Histoire d'Agde*
F	De Vic, IV, 417
F	Picot, pp. 89–90
F	Picot, p. 90
R	Drouot, *Mayenne*, I, 62
R	Fisquet, XVIII, article Bayeux
N	
N	De Vic, IV, 410
U	
N	De Vic, IV, 410
N	Bozé, *Histoire de Apt*, p. 294
F	Picot, p. 48
R	Peronnet, *Les évêques*, I, 498
R	ANG, XIII, 767
A	Delmas, "Le procès de Jacques Spifame"
F	Bellaud, *Les évêques italiens*, pp. 17–62
R	Peronnet, *Les évêques*, I, 493
R	Oroux, *Histoire ecclésiastique de la cour*, II, 15
N	Du Tressay, *Histoire de Luçon*, II, 124
R	Tuloup, *Saint-Malo*, p. 155
A	Maugis, *Histoire de Parlement*, III, 209
A	Du Tressay, *Histoire de Luçon*, II, 89
U	
F	Picard, *Histoire de Marseille*, p. 108
N	Drouot, *Mayenne*, I, 63
N	Kushner, "Pontus de Tyard"
N	De Vic, IV, 415
U	De Vic, IV, 396
A	Duchâteau, *Histoire d'Orléans*, pp. 277–78

Name	First See	Date of Confirmation
Valerio, Giovanni	Grasse	1550
Valernod, Pierre de	Nîmes	1598
Vassé, Jean de	Lisieux	1580
Vercelli, Alfonso	Lodève	1570
Vergier, Claude de	Lavaur	1600
Vervins, Louis de	Narbonne	1600
Vialart, Antoine	Bourges	1572
Vieuxpont, Jean de	Meaux	1602
Vigor, Simon	Narbonne	1563
Vigne, Louis de	Uzès	1598
Villars, Jérôme de	Vienne	1598
Villars, Nicolas de	Agen	1587
Villars, Pierre I de	Mirepoix	1561
Villars, Pierre II de	Mirepoix	1576
Viole, Guillaume	Paris	1564
Visandon, Jean de	Tulle	1599
Vitellozzi, Giovanni	Carcassone	1567
Yver, François	Luçon	1599

Social Status	Principal Source of Information
F	ANG, VI, 317
A	Sauzet, *Contre-Réforme*, pp. 52–64
N	ANG, II, 33
F	Martin, *Histoire de Lodève*, II, 16
U	DBF, IV, 440
N	Sauzet, *Contre-Réforme*, pp. 52–54
A	Brimont, *Le XVIᵉ siècle en Berry*, II, 161
N	Barbiche, *Lettres de Henri IV*, p. 6
R	Didier, *Paul de Foix*, p. 207
U	De Vic, IV, 303
N	Collombet, *Eglise de Vienne*, III, 231
N	Maugis, *Histoire de Parlement*, III, 207
N	Collombet, *Eglise de Vienne*, III, 206
N	Collombet, *Eglise de Vienne*, III, 217
A	Maugis, *Histoire de Parlement*, III, 206
N	Baluze, *Historiae tutelensis*, p. 3
F	Bouges, *Histoire de Carcassone*, p. 330
R	Du Tressay, *Histoire de Luçon*, II, 158–62

SOCIAL AND CAREER ANALYSIS OF FRENCH BISHOPS BY REIGN, 1547 – 1610

TABLE I
SOCIAL AND CAREER ANALYSIS OF BISHOPS SEATED DURING THE REIGN OF HENRI II, 1547 – 1559

	Noblesse de Race	Anoblis	Commoners
Total Bishops (N)	44 55%	9 11%	3 4%
Held Law Degree	10 23%	2 22%	0 0%
Held Theology Degree	1 2%	0 0%	1 33%
Cleric of the Court	2 4%	1 11%	1 33%
Member of Religious Order	3 7%	0 0%	1 33%
Member of a Parlement	3 7%	1 11%	1 33%
Followed Relative in Diocese	8 18%	1 11%	0 0%
Close Relative Elsewhere in Episcopate	3 7%	0 0%	0 0%
Not Yet 27 Years of Age at Appointment	3 7%	0 0%	0 0%

TABLE I (continued)

Foreigners	Uncertain Social Origins	Total
22	2	80
28%	2%	100%
3	1	16
14%	50%	20%
1	0	3
5%	0%	4%
2	0	6
9%	0%	8%
2	0	6
9%	0%	8%
0	1	6
0%	50%	8%
3	0	12
14%	0%	15%
0	0	3
0%	0%	4%
2	0	5
9%	0%	6%

TABLE I (continued)

SOCIAL AND CAREER ANALYSIS OF BISHOPS
SEATED DURING THE REIGN OF HENRI II,
1547 – 1559

	Noblesse de Race	Anoblis	Commoners
Not Yet a Priest at Appointment	6 14%	2 22%	0 0%
Kept Benefices at Appointment	14 32%	2 22%	0 0%
Resigned with a Pension	9 21%	5 55%	1 33%
Resigned, No Pension Indicated	3 7%	0 0%	1 33%
Former Canons	5 11%	1 11%	0 0%

TABLE II

SOCIAL AND CAREER ANALYSIS OF BISHOPS
SEATED DURING THE REIGN OF CHARLES IX,
1560 – 1574

	Noblesse de Race	Anoblis	Commoners
Total Bishops (N)	41 43%	15 16%	12 13%
Held Law Degree	13 32%	5 33%	8 67%
Held Theology Degree	0 0%	1 7%	3 25%
Cleric of the Court	3 8%	0 0%	6 50%
Member of Religious Order	4 10%	1 7%	2 16%

TABLE I (continued)

Foreigners	Uncertain Social Origins	Total
2	0	10
9%	0%	12%
5	1	22
23%	50%	28%
13	1	29
59%	50%	36%
0	0	4
0%	0%	5%
1	1	8
5%	50%	10%

TABLE II (continued)

Foreigners	Uncertain Social Origins	Total
16	11	95
17%	11%	100%
3	2	31
19%	18%	33%
2	2	8
12%	18%	8%
3	2	14
19%	18%	15%
0	0	7
0%	0%	7%

TABLE II (continued)

SOCIAL AND CAREER ANALYSIS OF BISHOPS
SEATED DURING THE REIGN OF CHARLES IX,
1560 – 1574

	Noblesse de Race	Anoblis	Commoners
Member of a Parlement	4 10%	2 13%	0 0%
Followed Relative in Diocese	8 20%	4 26%	1 8%
Close Relative Elsewhere in Episcopate	6 15%	3 20%	0 0%
Not Yet 27 Years of Age at Appointment	1 3%	1 7%	0 0%
Not Yet a Priest at Appointment	8 20%	3 20%	1 8%
Kept Benefices at Appointment	17 41%	5 33%	2 16%
Resigned with a Pension	6 15%	1 7%	1 8%
Resigned, No Pension Indicated	4 10%	1 7%	1 8%
Former Canons	8 20%	0 0%	4 33%

TABLE II (continued)

Foreigners	Uncertain Social Origins	Total
0	1	7
0%	9%	7%
3	2	18
19%	18%	19%
0	0	9
0%	0%	9%
0	0	2
0%	0%	2%
1	0	13
6%	0%	14%
6	2	32
38%	18%	34%
1	1	10
6%	9%	11%
2	1	9
12%	9%	9%
1	2	15
6%	18%	16%

TABLE III

SOCIAL AND CAREER ANALYSIS OF BISHOPS
SEATED DURING THE REIGN OF HENRI III,
1574 – 1589

	Noblesse de Race	Anoblis	Commoners
Total Bishops (N)	40 53%	11 14%	11 14%
Held Law Degree	8 20%	5 45%	3 27%
Held Theology Degree	3 8%	0 0%	3 27%
Cleric of the Court	1 3%	0 0%	2 18%
Member of Religious Order	7 18%	0 0%	3 27%
Member of a Parlement	7 18%	1 9%	0 0%
Followed Relative in Diocese	8 20%	3 27%	1 9%
Close Relative Elsewhere in Episcopate	5 12%	0 0%	0 0%
Not Yet 27 Years of Age at Appointment	4 10%	1 9%	0 0%
Not Yet a Priest at Appointment	13 33%	3 27%	1 9%
Kept Benefices at Appointment	15 38%	2 18%	2 18%
Resigned with a Pension	4 10%	1 9%	1 9%
Resigned, No Pension Indicated	2 5%	0 0%	1 9%
Former Canons	7 18%	1 9%	3 27%

T A B L E III (continued)

Foreigners	Uncertain Social Origins	Total
9	5	76
12%	7%	100%
0	1	17
0%	20%	22%
1	2	9
11%	40%	12%
0	0	3
0%	0%	4%
3	1	14
33%	20%	18%
1	0	9
11%	0%	12%
1	0	13
11%	0%	17%
3	0	8
33%	0%	11%
1	0	6
11%	0%	8%
3	0	20
33%	0%	26%
3	2	24
33%	40%	32%
0	1	7
0%	20%	9%
0	0	3
0%	0%	4%
1	2	14
11%	40%	18%

TABLE IV
SOCIAL AND CAREER ANALYSIS OF BISHOPS
SEATED DURING THE PERIOD 1547 – 1589

	Noblesse de Race	Anoblis	Commoners
Total Bishops (N)	132 50%	36 14%	27 10%
Held Law Degree	31 23%	12 33%	11 41%
Held Theology Degree	4 3%	1 3%	7 26%
Cleric of the Court	7 5%	2 6%	9 33%
Member of Religious Order	15 11%	1 3%	6 22%
Member of a Parlement	14 11%	4 11%	1 3%
Followed Relative in Diocese	24 18%	8 22%	2 6%
Close Relative Elsewhere in Episcopate	14 11%	3 9%	0 0%
Not Yet 27 Years of Age at Appointment	8 6%	2 6%	0 0%
Not Yet a Priest at Appointment	28 21%	8 22%	2 6%
Kept Benefices at Appointment	49 37%	9 25%	5 19%
Resigned with a Pension	31 24%	9 25%	4 15%
Resigned, No Pension Indicated	16 12%	1 3%	3 11%
Former Canons	21 16%	2 6%	7 26%

TABLE IV (continued)

Foreigners	Uncertain Social Origins	Total
47	20	262[a]
18%	8%	100%
6	4	64
13%	20%	24%
4	4	20
9%	20%	8%
5	3	25
11%	15%	10%
5	1	28
11%	5%	11%
1	3	25
2%	15%	10%
7	2	42
16%	10%	16%
3	0	20
7%	0%	8%
3	0	13
7%	0%	5%
6	2	46
13%	10%	18%
14	6	83
30%	30%	31%
17	3	64
36%	15%	24%
2	3	25
4%	15%	11%
3	5	38
7%	25%	15%

a This total includes eleven bishops nominated during the reign of François II.

TABLE V

SOCIAL AND CAREER ANALYSIS OF BISHOPS
SEATED DURING THE REIGN OF HENRI IV,
1589 – 1610

	Noblesse de Race	*Anoblis*	Commoners
Total Bishops (N)	43 40%	25 23%	16 15%
Held Law Degree	11 28%	7 28%	4 25%
Held Theology Degree	7 18%	0 0%	4 25%
Cleric of the Court	1 3%	2 8%	3 19%
Member of Religious Order	6 15%	5 20%	3 19%
Member of a Parlement	0 0%	3 12%	1 6%
Followed Relative in Diocese	14 35%	4 16%	0 0%
Close Relative Elsewhere in Episcopate	1 3%	5 20%	0 0%
Not Yet 27 Years of Age at Appointment	7 18%	3 12%	0 0%
Not Yet a Priest at Appointment	10 25%	6 24%	0 0%
Kept Benefices at Appointment	10 25%	5 20%	4 25%
Resigned with a Pension	1 3%	3 12%	2 12%
Resigned, No Pension Indicated	2 5%	1 6%	2 12%
Former Canons	9 21%	2 8%	4 25%

TABLE V (continued)

Foreigners	Uncertain Social Origins	Total
6	19	109
5%	17%	100%
3	7	32
50%	37%	29%
0	2	11
0%	11%	10%
1	1	8
17%	5%	8%
2	6	22
33%	32%	20%
1	1	6
17%	5%	6%
1	3	22
17%	16%	20%
0	0	6
0%	0%	6%
0	0	10
0%	0%	9%
1	4	20
17%	21%	18%
0	4	23
0%	21%	21%
0	0	6
0%	0%	6%
0	0	5
0%	0%	5%
0	1	16
0%	5%	15%

TABLE VI

SOCIAL AND CAREER ANALYSIS OF BISHOPS

SEATED DURING THE PERIOD 1547 – 1610

	Noblesse de Race	*Anoblis*	Commoners
Total Bishops (N)	176 47%	62 16%	47 13%
Held Law Degree	42 24%	19 31%	16 34%
Held Theology Degree	11 6%	1 2%	11 23%
Cleric of the Court	8 5%	4 7%	12 26%
Member of Religious Order	22 12%	6 11%	10 21%
Member of a Parlement	14 8%	7 11%	2 4%
Followed Relative in Diocese	38 22%	12 19%	2 4%
Close Relative Elsewhere in Episcopate	15 9%	8 13%	0 0%
Not Yet 27 Years of Age at Appointment	15 8%	5 8%	0 0%
Not Yet a Priest at Appointment	38 22%	14 23%	2 4%
Kept Benefices at Appointment	59 34%	14 23%	9 19%
Resigned with a Pension	32 18%	12 19%	6 13%
Resigned, No Pension Indicated	18 10%	2 3%	6 13%
Former Canons	30 17%	4 7%	11 24%

TABLE VI (continued)

Foreigners	Uncertain Social Origins	Total
53	39	377[a]
14%	10%	100%
9	11	97
17%	28%	26%
4	7	34
8%	18%	9%
6	4	35
12%	10%	9%
7	7	52
13%	18%	14%
2	4	29
4%	10%	8%
8	5	63
16%	13%	17%
3	1	27
6%	2%	7%
3	0	23
6%	0%	6%
7	6	67
13%	15%	18%
14	11	107
26%	28%	28%
17	4	71
33%	10%	19%
2	3	31
4%	8%	8%
3	6	54
6%	15%	15%

a This total includes the six bishops successfully installed by the Catholic League.

GLOSSARY

Annates   A portion of a year's income from a vacant consistorial benefice owed to the pope when he filled the vacancy. Strictly speaking, bishops did not pay the annates but a fee of similar amount called the *Common Services* for the promulgation of their bulls of office.

Anobli   New noble, generally used for a family that had been ennobled since 1400. The term is more appropriate for the sixteenth century than *noblesse de robe* since many new nobles had received their patents of nobility for reasons other than service in the royal courts.

Aumônier   Almoner. The term was used for the chaplains of the courts of the kings and princes.

Benefice   A Church office with an income irrevocably attached to it.

Benefice in *commendam*   A benefice held in trust. The holder had the right to receive the income of the benefice without being obligated to perform its duties. The Council of Trent declared that only the benefices of abbeys and priories of men could be held in trust. Benefices that involved the care of souls such as bishoprics and curates could not be held in trust.

Collation   The right to fill a vacant benefice.

Confidence   The practice by which someone who could not hold a benefice, particularly a bishopric, whether because of lay status or the prohibition against pluralism, could nevertheless draw the income from it through the placement of a client as its incumbent.

Consistorial benefice   A benefice for which the appointment of its occupant had to be approved in papal consistory. The term referred to the bishoprics and the abbacies of the major monasteries.

Décime   The royal tenth, in theory a gift of a tenth of its annual income that the clergy agreed to give the king. In fact it was a royal tax but was usually less than a tenth.

Dîme   The tithe, a tenth of agricultural production owed to the Church.

It was collected before any other obligations were to be met. It also was usually less than a tenth.

Economat   See *régale*.

Indult   A papal decree making an exception to a general law.

Noblesse d'épée   Nobility of the sword, the old nobility whose status had been established by military service in the Middle Ages. Virtually synonymous with *Noblesse de race* but slightly less encompassing.

Officialité   The bishop's court, where cases such as heresy that fell under episcopal jurisdiction were tried.

Pays d'obédience   Those provinces over which the king of France had gained sovereignty after the Pragmatic Sanction of 1438. The term usually referred to Provence and Brittany in the sixteenth century but was not synonymous with *pays d'état*.

Pension   A portion of the income of a benefice (legally no more than a third) taken by someone other than the benefice holder. Often the pensioner was the former incumbent who had resigned, but it could also be a cleric with no connection with the benefice or a lay person.

Régale   The right of the king to govern a diocese while it was vacant. The term usually referred to the king's right to take the revenues of a vacant see. A diocese in that circumstance was said to be *en économat* (under supervision). The king could pass his right to the revenues to another person.

Regression   The right of a cleric to return to a benefice that he had earlier given up, upon the death or resignation of the current incumbent. The right of regression had to be explicitly stated in the document of resignation made by the first cleric and accepted by the new holder.

Rentes   An annuity or bond issued by the crown. The kings after François I issued most of its rentes through the Hôtel de ville of Paris. Certain taxes and tolls that the Hôtel de ville collected for the monarchy were consigned to pay the interest on the rentes and less regularly to repay the principal.

Resignation in *favorem*   A means by which the holder of a benefice could in his resignation from that benefice designate his successor. For the consistorial benefices the consent of the king and the pope was required and usually given.

Robin   A member of the sovereign courts or a family that had a tradition of serving in such courts. A substantial number of *robins* had noble status as *noblesse de robe*.

Roturier   A commoner; anyone who did not belong to the clergy or nobility.

NOTES

ABBREVIATIONS USED IN THE NOTES

ADC	Archives Départementales de la Cher
ADEL	Archives Départementales de l'Eure-et-Loir
ADHA	Archives Départementales des Hautes-Alpes
ADHV	Archives Départementales de l'Haute-Vienne
ADIV	Archives Départementales de l'Ille-et-Vilaine
ADLA	Archives Départementales de la Loire-Atlantique
ADLG	Archives Départementales de la Lot-et-Garonne
ADM	Archives Départementales du Morhiban
ADTG	Archives Départementales de la Tarn-et-Garonne
AN	Archives Nationales, Paris
ANG	*Acta Nuntiaturae Gallicae*
BHR	*Bibliothèque d'humanisme et renaissance*
BN	Bibliothèque Nationale, Paris
BSHPF	*Bulletin de la Société d'histoire du Protestantisme français*
CSPF	*Calendar of State Papers Foreign Series*
DBF	*Dictionnaire de biographie française*
RHEF	*Revue d'histoire de l'église de France*

CHAPTER I

1. Denys Hay, *The Church in Italy in the Fifteenth Century* (Cambridge: Cambridge University Press, 1970), pp. 1–20, appears to argue essentially the same about the Italian bishops for the previous century. Hay is knowledgeable about both the Italian and English Churches but not about the French. He regards the situation in the English episcopacy as rather superior to that of the Italian and generally also regards the French

as better but without a real basis on which to make that assessment.

2. Jules Thomas, *Le Concordat de 1516, ses origines, son histoire au XVIe siècle*, 3 vols. (Paris: Alphonse Picard, 1910). Volume III alone is concerned with the implementation of the Concordat after 1516. Volume I deals with the Pragmatic Sanction of 1438, and volume II is concerned with the negotiations between Leo X and François I.

3. Aubenas, *Histoire de l'église* (Paris, 1951), p. 313; cited in Jean Delumeau, *Catholicism between Luther and Voltaire* (London: Burns and Oates, 1977), p. 158.

4. Edelstein, "Les origines sociales de l'épiscopat sous Louis XII et François Ier," *Revue d'histoire moderne et contemporaine*, XV (1978), 239 ff.; and "The Social Origins of the Episcopacy in the Reign of Francis I," *French Historical Studies*, VIII (1974), 377−92. These articles summarize her doctoral dissertation, "The Recruitment of the Episcopacy under the Concordat of Bologna in the Reign of Francis I" (Columbia University, 1972). Hayden, "The Social Origins of the French Episcopacy at the Beginning of the Seventeenth Century," *French Historical Studies*, X (1977), 27−38.

5. Peronnet, *Les évêques de l'ancienne France*, 2 vols. (Paris: Honoré Champion, 1978). An offprint of Peronnet's dissertation at the University of Lille, the work is badly done, with strikeovers and corrections not removed and multicolored graphs reproduced in black and white, badly reducing their legibility. Its pressrun was very small, and it has been out of print since 1979. While there is some duplication between my work and Peronnet's, especially in the analysis of social origins of the bishops, I believe that the inaccessibility of the book and some differences in my data and Peronnet's dictate incorporating that material into this study.

6. For example, in 1515 Claude de Seyssel, then bishop of Marseille, later archbishop of Turin, wrote: "In France the church offers another means, common to all the estates, for attaining to a high and worthy station. In this matter the practice in France is and has always been that by virtue and knowledge those of the two lesser estates may attain to great ecclesiastical dignities as often as or more often than those of the first, even to the rank of cardinal and sometimes to the papacy." *The Monarchy of France*, trans. J. H. Hexter (New Haven: Yale University Press, 1981), pp. 63−64.

7. See chapter II for a discussion of the Gallican Crisis of 1551 in which Henri II came close to a break with the papacy, with the apparent support of the French hierarchy.

8. On Gallicanism see the authoritative work of Victor Martin, *Les origines du Gallicanisme*, 2 vols. (Paris, 1939). The discussion in Norman Ravitch, *Sword and Mitre* (The Hague: Mouton, 1966), pp. 14–20, is too thoroughly formed by the controversies of Louis XIV's reign to be very pertinent for the sixteenth century.

9. See Ravitch, pp. 14–16; and H. O. Evennett, *The Cardinal of Lorraine and the Council of Trent* (Cambridge: Cambridge University Press, 1930), pp. 24–27, for the distinction between the two types of Gallicanism. The definitive statement of Gallican principles was the Four Articles of 1682, in Ravitch, pp. 217–18.

CHAPTER 11

1. By the reign of Louis XII more than half of the successful episcopal candidates were identifiable as the king's choices. Pierre Imbart de La Tour, *Les origines de la Réforme*, 4 vols. (Paris: Hachette, 1905–35), I, 89–123. For a good summary of the motives for the Concordat, the negotiations that created it, and the resistance to it in France, see R. J. Knecht, *Francis I* (Cambridge: Cambridge University Press, 1981), pp. 51–65.

2. More correctly the Concordat did not mention the annates, explicitly prohibited by the Pragmatic Sanction, which left the way open to the pope to claim them again. L. von Pastor, *The History of the Popes from the Close of the Middle Ages* (St. Louis: Herder, 1952), IX, 421.

3. The principal discussion of the criteria of the Concordat of Bologna is in Thomas, *Concordat*, II, 59–70. See also Pastor, *History of the Popes*, VIII, 418–20. The Concordat also allowed the appointment of members of reformed orders who were not permitted to take academic degrees. It was a loophole rarely exploited.

4. Thomas, *Concordat*, II, 353–57; III, 100–120. See also M. Boulet, "Les élections épiscopales en France au lendemain de Concordat de Bologna," *Mélanges d'archéologie et d'histoire d'école française de Rome*, LVII (1940), 190–234. Since the papal decree quashing elections was a special indult, every new pope had to renew it for every new king.

5. Peronnet, *Les évêques*, I, 486–87. A good example of the disputes over royal nominees was the appointment of Louis de Guillart to Chartres in 1524. ADEL, G, 6, fol. 1–147.

6. Pierre Blet, "Le Concordat de Bologne et la réforme tridentine," *Gregorianum*, XLV (1964), 250–63. Blet finds that the last call for a

return to canonical election was made by the assembly of clergy of 1605.

7. According to Thomas, *Concordat*, II, 339, the age and degree requirements of the Concordat did not apply to Brittany and Provence. "Le roi choisira personnes capables." The dukes of Brittany had their own concordat of 1411 under which the pope named the bishops of the duchy, but the choices had to be favorable to the duke. E. Catta, "Les évêques de Nantes (1500–1617)," RHEF, LI (1961), 25.

8. Conrad Eubel et al., eds., *Hierarchia Catholica medii aevi*, 7 vols. (Münster: Libraria Regensbergiana, 1918–1936), III, article Lescar. Two entries for the sixteenth century contain the phrase "for whom the king of Navarre supplicated." Eubel is the source for all dates of appointment, deaths or resignations, pensions, and benefices held *in commendam* for the bishops under study unless other works are specifically noted. On the sees of Béarn see also Hayden, "Social Origins," p. 30n.

9. BN, Fonds Baluze 285, fol. 40. Orange was returned to the jurisdiction of the Concordat in 1720.

10. Thus the total number of dioceses under the Concordat from 1516 to 1559 was 111 (fourteen archdioceses and ninety-seven dioceses); after 1559 to 1601 it was 110, until Bellay was added. The figures do not include the titular see of Bethléem that had real jurisdiction over a hospital near Clamecy; the incumbent exercised the functions of a bishop in its chapel. Its bishop shows up occasionally on the rolls of French bishops and the décimes. After 1600 the duke of Nevers was its permanent collator.

11. Thomas, *Concordat*, II, 59–156. See, for example, the work of the archbishop of Aix, Gilbert Génébrard, *Liber jure et necessitate sacrum electorum ad Ecclesiam Gallican redintegrationem* (n.p., 1593). On the Parlement's objection to the Concordat as a pro-papal document, see R. J. Knecht, "The Concordat of 1516: A Reassessment," *Government in Reformation Europe 1520–1560*, ed. Henry J. Cohn (London: Macmillan, 1971), pp. 91–112.

12. François Isambert et al., *Recueil général des anciennes lois françaises* (Paris: Belin-Leprieur, 1828), XIV, 64–66; Georges Picot, *Histoire des Etats Généraux de 1355 à 1614*, 4 vols. (Geneva: Megariotis Reprints, 1979), II, 85, 393–94. In their *cahiers* all three estates proposed a return to election of bishops, but each had wanted a different group of electors. The clergy demanded election by the chapters (a return to the Pragmatic Sanction); the nobility, by the local estates; the *tiers*, by the curates.

13. Thomas, *Concordat*, II, 334–41, 388–90); R. Ancel, *Nonciatures*

de France. Nonciatures de Paul IV (Paris: Coffre, 1909), lvi–lvii; ANG, VI, 275–76. For a more extensive discussion of the conflict between Julius and Henri over the pope's attempts to seat his candidates, see Baumgartner, "Henry II's Italian Bishops: A Study in the Use and Abuse of the Concordat of Bologna," *Sixteenth Century Journal*, XI (1980), 49–58. As late as 1586 the papal nuncio Frangipani reported that the monarch had asked for the renewal of the indults for the two provinces, indicating that Sixtus V had been slow about issuing them when he became pope in 1585. ANG, XVI, 319, 325.

14. On the Gallican crisis of 1551, see Romier, "La crise gallicane de 1551," *Revue historique*, 108 (1911), 225–50; 109 (1912), 27–55. Also see M. François, *Correspondance du Cardinal François de Tournon* (Paris, 1946), p. 259; CSPF, Edward, pp. 93–127; ANG, VI, 474–77. On Du Moulin, see BN, fonds français 4737, fol. 18; and Donald Kelley, "The *Fides Historicae* of Charles Du Moulin and the Gallican View of Historical Tradition," *Traditio*, XXII (1966), 347–403; Evennett, *Cardinal of Lorraine*, pp. 38–39; and Marc Venard, "Une réforme Gallicane? Le project de concile nationale de 1551," RHEF, LXVII (1981), 201–25.

15. H. O. Evennett, "Pie IV et les bénéfices de Jean Du Bellay: Etude sur les bénéfices français vacant en curie après le Concordat de 1516," RHEF, XXII (1936), 431. In January, 1560, Pius IV had issued the new indults for the *pays d'obédience* with the understanding that the king would send a letter pledging strict observance of the requirements of the Concordat. The failure of the king to do so helped to reenforce the pope's determination to fill Du Bellay's benefices. Pius claimed the right to fill Arles after the death of the Cardinal de Lenoncourt at Rome because he had not yet signed the indult when the death occurred. ANG, XIV, 317, 320.

16. Abbé Oroux, *Histoire ecclésiastique de la Cour de France*, 2 vols. (Paris, 1776), II, 134; Report of the nuncio Frangipani to Rome, August 30, 1570, ANG, VI, 77–79; Thomas Bouges, *Histoire ecclésiastique et civile de la ville et diocèse de Carcassone* (Marseille: Laffitte Reprints, 1978), p. 332.

17. Noël Didier, *Paul de Foix et Grégoire XIII 1572–84* (Grenoble, 1834); ANG, II, 46–52 and passim. According to Thomas, *Concordat*, III, 198, Gregory XIII appointed Nicolas Le Cornu de La Courbe to Saintes in 1576 with royal approval. Under what circumstances is not clear. La Courbe was the last bishop appointed by Rome in the sixteenth century.

18. The following is based largely on volumes II and III of Eubel, *Hierarchia Catholica*. On the episcopal dynasty of the house of Lorraine, see Joseph Bergin, "The Guises and their benefices, 1588–1641," *English Historical Review*, XCIX (1984), 434–58; and "The Decline and Fall of the House of Guise as an Ecclesiastical Dynasty," *Historical Journal*, XXV (1982), 781–803.

19. Charles Marchand, *Charles Ier de Cossé Comte de Brissac et Maréchal de France 1507–1563* (Paris: Champion, 1889), pp. 437–38. J. B. Laffon, ed., *Le diocèse de Tarbes et Lourdes* (Paris, n.d.), p. 86. Those who held family sees did have to petition the king through the usual channels if the example of Aire in 1570 was typical. The brother holding the bishopric having died, the head of the de Foix family asked the Duc de Montmorency "to do us the favor of requesting of the king the bishopric of Aire . . . for the brother that God has spared me." Cited by Jeanne Harrie, "François de Candale and the Hermetic Tradition in Sixteenth-Century France" (Ph.D. diss., University of California–Riverside, 1975), p. 55.

20. Peronnet, *Les évêques*, I, 483, 632. Peronnet has an extensive discussion of the episcopal dynasties, although his concern is primarily for the dynasties created after 1516 (pp. 626–45).

21. Peronnet, *Les évêques*, I, 494, states that 143 of the 243 bishops (59 percent) seated between 1516 and 1559 "appartiennent à des familles qui ont forni au moins deux évêques." His statistics appear much higher than mine because he included the preconcordatory period, extended the calculations to include cousins within several degrees of blood, and was concerned as well with the first decades of the Concordat when the continued canonical election of many bishops extended the preconcordatory pattern of selection from powerful local families.

22. Thomas, *Concordat*, III, 189, states that it was Du Tillet who was refused his bulls in the exchange of sees, but Eubel, *Hierarchia Catholica*, III, article Meaux, and DBF, XII, 917, attribute the problem to Brézé.

23. On the twenty-day rule, see Marcel Marion, *Dictionnaire des institutions de la France aux XVII et XVIII siècles*, (New York: Burt Franklin, 1968), p. 486. On Mirepoix, see ANG, IX, 50–55; Pastor, *History of the Popes*, XIV, 76. On Lavaur, see Guillaume de Taix, *Mémoires des affaires du clergé de France* (Paris, 1625), II, 164.

24. DBF, XI, 1040. Charles IX named Du Bourg's brother in 1566, but Rome refused to grant his bulls until he went to Rome himself in 1576.

25. Marion, *Institutions*, p. 486.

26. On confidence, see especially ibid., p. 128.

27. M. Mesnard, *Histoire civile, ecclésiastique et littéraire de la ville de Nîmes*, 5 vols. (Paris, 1754), pièces justificatives, number 20.

28. In repeating Paul III's decree of 1547 limiting cardinals to one bishopric, Paul IV decreed that cardinals were to hold the right of regression to only one see. Pastor, *History of the Popes*, XIV, 197–99. See also C. Laplatte, "L'administration des évêchés vacants et la régie des économats," RHEF, XXIII (1937), 161–225; Ferdinand André et al., *Inventaire sommaire des archives départementales de Lozère, Archives ecclésiastiques* (Mende: Privat, 1882), p. 16; Hay, *The Italian Church*, pp. 18–19.

29. Bouges, *Histoire de Carcassone*, p. 328.

30. This chronology is what I have been able to decipher from the entries for 1563 in "Acta consistorialia," BN, Fonds Latin 12560. Apparently Tournon and d'Este had a heated dispute over who had the prior right of regression in 1563.

31. The nominee to Tarbes in 1554. Jean Du Tems, *Le clergé de France* (Paris, 1774), p. 457.

32. DBF, XI, 530; Didier, *De Foix et Grégoire XIII*, p. 116n.

33. ANG, XII, 609.

34. Louis Madelin, "Les premiers applications de Concordat de 1516," *Mélanges d'archéologie et d'histoire de l'école française de Rome*, XIV (1897), 323–85. He argues that the dossiers he studied are likely the originals.

35. The popes tried to use the Jesuits in France to collect information about episcopal nominees. Some Jesuits cooperated; others refused. Communication from Dr. A. L. Martin.

36. Louis Jadin, "Procès d'informations pour la nominations des évêques et abbés des Pays-Bas," *Bulletin de l'institut historique belge de Rome*, VIII (1928), 5–25; François de Dainville, *Cartes anciens de l'église de France* (Paris: J. Vrin, 1956), p. 286.

37. See Appendix II.

CHAPTER III

1. For the *feuille des bénéfices*, see Ravitch, *Sword and Mitre*, pp. 56–59.

2. Peronnet, *Les évêques*, I, 440, 482–83; II, table 59. For an analysis of Louis XII's bishops, see Edelstein, "Les origines sociales de l'épiscopat," pp. 23–47.

3. Imbert de La Tour, *Les origines de la réforme*, 4 vols. (Paris, 1904–35),

II, 140–44. As was noted in chapter two, a number of cathedral chapters were able to continue the practice of canonical elections after 1516. Basing his analysis on when Eubel (*Hierarchia Catholica*, vol. III) first notes a royal nomination for a bishopric, Peronnet finds that 36 percent of the appointments between 1516 and 1559 were made by canonical election. *Les évêques*, I, 483. It was hardly likely, however, that many of these elections were made without consideration of the king's will.

4. Madelin, "Premières applications," pp. 326–31. Concerning the bishops in office in 1516, Peronnet, *Les évêques*, I, 447, found that fifteen of the thirty-five bishops for whom he determined age of appointment were under the age required by canon law (thirty years) and seven were less than eighteen years of age.

5. Madelin, "Premières applications," pp. 326–31.

6. Ibid.; and Edelstein, "The Recruitment of the Episcopacy," p. 182. Edelstein gives the number of bishops seated from the period of 1516 to 1547 as 182, but she includes the two dioceses of Béarn for which the French monarchy did not receive the right to nominate their bishops until 1617 as well as two bishops who had been given sees before 1516 but transferred after that date. I have adjusted her tables to compensate for the net reduction of seven bishops. Peronnet, *Les évêques*, I, 1440, table 59, lists 243 appointments for the period from 1516 to 1559. Peronnet uses blocks of time such as from 1516 to 1559 as well as a year-by-year graph, which is very difficult to read, to present his statistics on the number of bishops seated. He has no specific analysis for the reigns of the kings.

7. Edelstein, "The Recruitment of the Episcopacy," chapters III and IV.

8. Peronnet, *Les évêques*, I, 542, 630–31.

9. Arthur Tilley, *Studies in the French Renaissance* (Cambridge: Cambridge University Press, 1922), p. 165. Any discussion of François I's appointments must bear in mind that Louise de Savoie served as regent for her son from 1523 to 1526. For the most part her episcopal nominations followed the same pattern.

10. Robert Harding, *Anatomy of a Power Elite: The Provincial Governors of Early Modern France* (New Haven: Yale University Press, 1978), pp. 32–36.

11. François de Guise, *Mémoires*, in Michaud and Poujoulet, *Nouvelle collection des mémoires* (Paris: Guyot, 1853), VI, 191; the Venetian ambassador Soranzo, in Eugenio Alberi, *Relazioni degli ambasciatori veneti*, 15

vols. (Florence, 1840), II, 437; Romier, *Origines politiques*, I, 55–56. See also Evennett, *The Cardinal of Lorraine* pp. 10–11. See the letter of Madame de Cossé to the Duc de Guise asking him to request his brother the Cardinal to present her husband's bastard son to the king for the diocese of Coutances in 1559. The son, Arthur de Cossé, did become bishop of Coutances. Cited in Marchand, *Charles de Cossé*, p. 436. See also ANG, VI, 446, ff.

12. Peronnet, *Les évêques*, II, 1440, table 59; 1432, table 54. In his year-by-year graph of the number of appointments, he attributes the total of seventy-four to the years 1548–1559. It is clear that Henri II nominated two bishops in 1547 after becoming king and two who received their bulls in 1560, but I have no way to account for the further discrepancy of two.

13. On Danès, see E. Picot, *Les italiens en France au XVIe siècle* (Bordeaux: Gounouilhan, 1918), pp. 111–12.

14. See Baumgartner, "Henry II's Italian Bishops," XI, 49–58. I have counted as foreigners only those clearly from outside the area of French influence. There were several bishops from Savoy, Lorraine, and Flanders, regions of French culture claimed by the French monarchy.

15. ANG, IX, 50–55; Pastor, *History of the Popes*, XIV, 76.

16. Farnese, who had been archbishop of Avignon before 1553, was said to have had French benefices and pensions worth 30,000 livres in 1558 (ANG, XIV, 105). By then, however, he had fallen out of favor. The extensive movement of the Italian bishops in France may have been a reflection of the widespread practice of exchanging sees in Italy. (Hay, *The Church in Italy*, pp. 17–18).

17. According to Peronnet, *Les évêques*, II, 1436, table 57, Henri's bishops were slightly older at the time of appointment than the bishops from other reigns, but the difference is not great enough to explain the differences in the average length of episcopal career. Peronnet admits that his statistics on age prior to 1598 are based on little more than a quarter of the bishops of the period (I, 446, 473). He has nothing on the average term in office for Henri II's bishops.

18. Attributing nominations for the eighteen-month reign of François II is difficult and risky because of the lack of precise knowledge on when the nominations were sent to Rome. Using as an average a delay of four months from nomination by the king to approval by the curia, I find eleven nominations that were very likely made by François II.

19. See especially Antoine Degert, "Procès de huit évêques Français

suspects de Calvinisme," *Revue des questions historiques*, XXVI (1904), 60–108.

20. According to Peronnet, *Les évêques*, I, 672–75, the number of transfers by incumbent bishops from one see to another was unusually high from 1516 to 1564: the average number of nominations per year for that period was six while the number of transfers was 2.6. For the period from 1564 to 1592, he finds a nomination rate of 5.25 per year while transfers averaged only 0.6. He attributes this dramatic change to the fact that prior to 1564 the kings made such transfers of established bishops to make good their right of nomination against the chapter's right of election, whereas after 1564 the loss of royal control reduced the number of transfers. By choosing 1564 as his dividing point, however, he includes the large number of transfers allowed by Catherine de Medici and thus somewhat skews his statistics. I see little evidence of such a pattern of royal policy in the transfers under Henri II. Almost all of them involved moves from poorer sees to those with more revenues and prestige.

21. M. de La Pijardière, *Histoire de la ville de Montpellier*, 4 vols. (Montpellier: C. Caulet, 1930), III, 259. According to Thomas, *Concordat*, III, 196, Jean de Buz was refused confirmation to Châlons in 1535. He appears to have been the only nominee denied papal bulls before 1559 on grounds other than the struggle over the Concordat.

22. Charles Taillandier, *Histoire ecclésiastique et civile de Bretaigne* (Paris, 1756), p. xxxviii.

23. Edelstein, "The Recruitment of the Episcopacy," p. 173, states that 27 percent of François I's bishops were not "university educated." It is not clear precisely what she means by the phrase, but it strikes me as being too low a figure. See below, chapter XI.

24. Peronnet, *Les évêques*, I, 448.

25. Peronnet gives the average number of nominations per year as 5.6 from 1516 to 1789 and the average term in office as 16 years. Ibid., I, 437, 681. Was Catherine's apparent approval of the movement of bishops a result of her Italian upbringing? Of course one must keep in mind that she came to France at age fourteen.

26. ANG, XIII, 632.

27. Ibid., pp. 615, 778–79.

28. Ibid., p. 233n; DBF, XIV, 721.

29. ANG, XIII, 98, 378, 423, 478, 500.

30. ANG, II, 33, 209, 228, 256, 269–70. It may well be that the correspondence of the nuncios from this period, especially Dandino's,

gives an exaggerated sense of how serious this problem was under Henri III because they paid far more attention to the quality of episcopal nominees than did earlier nuncios. Ivan Cloulas, "Les rapports de Jérôme Ragazzoni, évêque de Bergome, avec les ecclésiastiques," *Bulletin de l'école français de Rome*, LXXII (1960), 518n, notes that "Les sollicitations de la Cour de France pour la nomination à Lisieux avaient été particulièrement pressantes."

31. Other episodes of a similar sort involved the sees of Lavaur in 1578, Périgueux in 1576, Vienne in 1587, Bayeux in 1583, and Pamiers in 1578. In 1580 the king gave the right to fill Laon to one of his captains who wanted to name his brother. Dandino at first opposed the nominations on the grounds that a confidence had been arranged for the 1880 écus of revenue of the bishopric. He later reported that the candidate, Valentin Douglas of a Scottish family settled in Brittany, was a Benedictine of merit (ANG, XIII, 94, 806).

32. A change in the attitude of the papacy clearly was involved, since Dandino had been nuncio for two terms thirty years earlier and had paid almost no attention to abuses in the episcopacy.

33. ANG, VII, 446. Castelli indicated that the theologian Guillaume Rose, later bishop of Senlis, was one of those who confirmed the existence of an arrangement of confidence. This helps to explain the bitter antagonism between Rose and de Beaune in the next decade. It appears that de Beaune did hold Mende in confidence after 1581 because he was offered 10,000 livres for the see in 1586.

34. BN, Fonds français nouvelles 3560, vol. 332. "Remonstrances du Clergé de France prononcée devant le Roy par l'évêque de Bazas."

35. Castelli, ANG, VII, 366, 387, describes the arrangement of confidence held by the Princess de Conti for Bayeux with Bishop Mathurin de Savonnières.

36. In checking the length of the vacancies listed by Pontac against the rolls of bishops in Eubel, *Hierarchia Catholica*, III, it appears that Pontac exaggerated in several cases. The nuncio Salviatti, ANG, XII, 152, listed eleven dioceses that in 1572 had been vacant for a year or more. The longest vacancy was at Rieux, for eight years.

37. Peronnet, *Les évêques*, I, 498. Two of the three examples that Peronnet gives, however, are from the reign of Charles IX.

38. Ibid., I, 1440, table 59. It is not clear what criteria he used to list a bishop as a *roturier* or an *indéterminé*. He lists forty-two *indéterminés* for 1560–88 and nine *roturiers* while I have found twenty-six commoners

and left twenty-nine uncertain.

39. Ibid., I, pp. 489–99, 683–85. It strikes me that Peronnet has exaggerated the number of "lost sees." In 1574 the Sieur de Fourquevaux stated that four sees in Languedoc—Alet, Nîmes, Lodève, and Uzès—were controlled by the Huguenots, and thus one could not expect the bishops to reside in them.

40. *Lettres de Henri III*, ed. Pierre Champion, 3 vols. (Paris: Libraire C. Klinksieck, 1965), III, 416–17. Papal objection to the pluralism involved in the king's proposal kept de Beaune from being confirmed as archbishop of Bourges until 1580.

41. For example, the see of Périgueux in Guyenne was said in 1576 to have lost the greater part of its revenues to war, yet a noble of the sword, François de Bourdeille, was appointed (DBF, VI, 435). On royal compensation for lost revenues, see Ernest Martin, *Histoire de la ville de Lodève*, 2 vols. (Montpellier: Imprimerie Serre, 1900), II, 41.

42. Peronnet, *Les évêques*, I, 489. Peronnet also argues that perhaps the religious wars had persuaded the king to choose a better class of bishops who had theology degrees, would not accumulate benefices, and were more likely to be in residence in their sees. The pattern of rejected nominations makes that unlikely. But in a different sense the argument has some validity. Four of the commoners settled in dioceses where an arrangement of confidence was reported to have existed or a first nomination made had been rejected. The need to prevent the pope from claiming the right to fill the see required that candidates of better qualities be nominated.

43. Claire Dolan, *Entre tours et clochers* (Sherbrooke, Québec: Editions de l'Université de Sherbrooke, 1981), pp. 211–25; Mark Greengrass, *France in the Age of Henri IV* (London: Longman, 1984), pp. 159–62.

44. Peronnet, *Les évêques*, I, 437. This substantially briefer episcopal generation was a result in large part of the numerous resignations, but it was also a consequence of a shorter average lifespan for bishops of the sixteenth century, fifty-five years as compared with over sixty for the next century. The violence of the era was only a small direct factor in that four bishops died violently in the forty years.

45. George Huppert, *Les Bourgeois gentilshommes* (Chicago: University of Chicago Press, 1977), pp. 145–47, is correct in his assessment of the importance of the financier families in the episcopacy, but he exaggerates the number of bishops coming from these families by implying that there were many more than those which he lists.

46. Peronnet, *Les évêques*, II, 1443, table 60. This table indicates that no bishop came from the military between 1559 and 1588, but it is clear that at least two had military careers prior to episcopal appointment, as did two of Henri II's nominees. But I would certainly agree with Peronnet, I, 467, that "en XVIe siècle les carrières pré-épiscopales restent enveloppées d'une certaine obscurité."

47. Robert Kalas, "Wealth, Place and Power in Sixteenth-Century France: The Rise of the Selve and Noailles Families" (Ph.D. diss., New York University, 1982), p. 146.

48. James K. Farge, *Biographical Register of Paris Doctors of Theology, 1500–1536* (Toronto: Pontifical Institute of Medieval Studies, 1980), and a private communication from Dr. Farge. He notes that only three Paris theologians who graduated in 1500–36 received French sees and that 22 percent of the small number of graduates whose social status he could determine were noble. In the seventeenth century the proportion of bishops with theology degrees increased substantially to the point that it was over 90 percent by the late eighteenth century. For the sixteenth century Peronnet states: "On ignore à peu près totalement le cursus universitaire des évêques" (I, 457). It is indeed true that one can find little information about what universities the bishops attended or how many had attended a university without receiving a degree in law or theology. Nonetheless the sources are very explicit about those appointees who had higher degrees.

49. E. J. Long, "Utrum iurista vel theologus plus proficiat ad regimen ecclesia," *Medieval Studies*, 30 (1968), 134–63; Roy Haines, "The Practice and Problems of a 15th century English Bishop: The Episcopate of William Gray," *Medieval Studies*, 34 (1972), 435–61.

50. On the relationship between an education in the classics and social mobility, see Richard Kagan, *Students and Society in Early Modern Spain* (Baltimore: The Johns Hopkins University Press, 1974), esp. pp. 58–61, 88–105. However, the practice of venality in France reduced the close correlation between an education in Latin and social mobility that Kagan found in Spain for the sixteenth century.

51. Huppert, *Bourgeois gentilshommes*, p. 88. Huppert does not provide a date, but Ruzé's term as bishop was 1572–87.

CHAPTER IV

1. Jean Labatut, *Les ducs et pairs de France au XVIIe siècle* (Paris: Presses universitaires, 1972), pp. 239–45, 322–27. Labatut points out how in the seventeenth century the monarch augmented the income of the great nobles if their income was insufficient to meet the level of wealth appropriate for their rank.

2. Marion, *Dictionnaire*, pp. 172–73; Doucet, *Les institutions de la France au XVIe siècle*, 2 vols. (Paris: Picard, 1948), II, 820–29. Marion, p. 171, states that the dîme could be as low as a sixtieth. The dîme on wine in the see of Gap in the sixteenth century was one-eighteenth (ADHA, G, 1427). However, in Rouen in 1541 the dîme on 800 lambs of one region was 80 or 10 percent (ADSM, G, 2605). See also E. Ladurie, *The Peasants of Languedoc* (Champaign: University of Illinois Press, 1974), pp. 78–79, 181–84; and Ladurie and Gay, *Tithe and Agrarian History from the Fourteenth to the Nineteenth Century* (Cambridge: Cambridge University Press, 1982).

3. The practice of alienating the tithes was an ancient one. See Catherine Boyd, *Tithes and Parishes in Medieval Italy* (Ithaca, N.Y.: Cornell University Press, 1952), esp. pp. 129–53.

4. Gerard Cholvy et al., *Le diocèse de Montpellier* (Paris: Beauchesne, 1976) p. 98. Cholvy notes that the bishop of Saint-Pons took between 30 and 40 percent of the entire financial resources of his diocese.

5. Robert Tattegrain, *Du temporel des bénéfices ecclésiastiques sous l'ancien régime* (Paris: Larose et Tenin, 1909), pp. 114, 126–28. At Mende in 1514, a new bishop received 1,500 l from his clergy on the "occasion of his joyous coming." André, *Inventaire sommaire de Lozère*, p. 10. The bishop of Bourges collected 693 l in 1562 for the *droit du synode* (ADC, G, 15).

6. Imbart de La Tour, *Origines*, pp. 244–56. He presents the rate of fees imposed for the various categories of ecclesiastical revenues at the end of the fifteenth century. The income from spiritual revenues for the see of Rouen in 1543 was 19,090 l or 60 percent of the bishop's total revenues. The receipts for that year included 27 l for the reconciliation of excommunicates (ADSM, G, 132, 311). Tattegrain, *Du temporel*, p. 128, also notes that disputes over procurations and other fees often went to the Parlement or resulted in the excommunication of recalcitrant clerics.

7. ADHA, G, 1427, fol. 3–7.

8. E. C. Lodge, *The Estates of the Archbishop and Chapter of Saint-André*

of Bordeaux under English Rule (New York: Octagon Books, 1974) p. 20. G. Moran, "The Catholic Church and the Protestant Party in Languedoc during the Wars of Religion, 1559–1588" (Ph.D. diss., Cornell University, 1978), p. 49. At Rouen in the archbishop received 271 l in 1542 for the registering of wills and the settling of the estates of those dying intestate. ADSM, G, 311. The right of *haute justice* in his seigneurie of Gaillon netted him 72 l. Ibid., G, 632.

9. P. Richard, *La papauté et la ligue française: Pierre d'Epinac, archévêque de Lyon (1573–1599)* (Paris: Picard, 1902), p. 69. ADIV, G, 13. See also Lodge, *Estates*, pp. 123–24, for the various tolls collected for the archbishop of Bordeaux. In 1440 he gained 50 l from a toll on hides and cloth brought into the city.

10. ADLA, G, 5.

11. For example in 1552 the bishop of Vannes received from his temporal 377 *livres de Bretagne* in silver, 294 *perées* of wheat, 1,197 of rye, 674 of oats and 49 capons (ADM, G, 294). In 1522 the bishop of Bourges took in 2,078 *livres tournais* in silver, 12 *muids* of wheat, 25 of rye, 33 of oats, and 14 *pippes* of wine (ADC, G, 15, f. 2).

12. The papal taxes are listed for each see in Eubel, *Hierarchia Catholica*, vols. II and III.

13. The roll of benefices of the *département* of 1516 is found in AN, G8* 1–6. A later copy is in ibid., 243.

14. V. Carrière et al., *Introduction aux études d'histoire ecclésiastique locale*, 3 vols. (Paris: Letouzey et Ané, 1936), III, 250–51, cites the Venetian ambassador that in 1516 the clerical revenues were calculated at half of their value and that the royal assessors had been more lenient on the sees north of the Loire. Doucet, *Institutions*, II, 838–40, states that the décime was in fact "the tenth part of two-thirds of the revenues of all benefices." See A. Cans, *L'organization financière du clergé de France à l'époque de Louis XIV* (Paris: Picard, 1918), pp. 182–84, for a further discussion of this point.

15. The roll of décimes of 1563 is found in BN, Fonds français, 17658, "Taxes des 1,500,000 livres sur les bénéfices de France en l'année 1563." One cannot establish a roll of episcopal incomes from the departmental archives because the source materials do not exist for many, perhaps a majority, of the sees. See the discussion in Jean Meuvret, "La situation matérielle des membres du clergé séculier dans la France du XVIIe siècle," RHEF (1968). Peronnet uses no source from earlier than 1648 in his study of episcopal income (*Les évêques*, I, 565; II, table 66).

The "Declaration des archeveschés, éveschés et abbayes du royaume," BN, Fonds français, 23338, from sometime in Henri IV's reign, appears even more inconsistent compared to known episcopal revenues than the roll of 1563.

16. For the décime of 1563, BN, Fonds français, 17658. For Rouen, ADSM, G, 134, fol. 4; for Gap, ADHA, G, 1427; for Dax, Degert, *Evêques de Dax*, p. 265; for Agen, ADLG, G, d, 3bis.

17. BN, Fonds français, 17,658, does not include the six sees of the *généralité* of Poitiers, since they were excused from the levy of 1563 because of the religious strife there.

18. Ladurie, *The Peasants of Languedoc*, p. 108. In 1524, however, the temporal revenues of the bishop of Chartres were estimated at 20,000 l (ADEI, G, 6, f. l). It is unlikely that his spiritual revenues were that much higher or his total revenues had increased so rapidly that his income exceeded 120,000 l by 1563. It is possible that his décime included several unmentioned monasteries attached to the bishopric.

19. E. Maugis, *Histoire de Parlement de Paris*, 3 vols. (Paris: Picard, 1914), I, 444; Harding, *Anatomy of a Power Elite*, p. 139; BN, Fonds Dupuy, 27, fol. 1.

20. Felicity Head, *Prelates and Princes* (Cambridge: Cambridge University Press, 1980), p. 54, table 3:1. She notes that the *valor ecclesiasticus* was also undervalued by about 10 percent. See C. E. Challis, *Tudor Coinage* (New York: Barnes and Noble, 1939), for a discussion of the rate of exchange. On the Italian sees, see Hay, *The Church in Italy*, pp. 10–12.

21. The "Acta consistorialia" lists those monasteries that a new bishop was allowed to continue to hold *in commendam* and those that he had to give up. This information is repeated in Eubel, *Hierarchia Catholica*. For the difficulty in determining how many abbeys were held in trust by the great churchmen, see the example of the Cardinal de Bourbon in Abbé Delettre, *Histoire du diocèse de Beauvais*, 3 vols. (Beauvais: Desjardins, 843), III, 255.

22. François, *Tournon*, pp. 428–29.

23. Evennett, *Cardinal of Lorraine*, p. 10; André, *Inventaire sommaire de Lozère*, p. 15. Bergin, "The Guises and Their Benefices," p. 38, shows that in 1605 the archbishop of Reims farmed his revenues for only 14,000 l, but Bergin notes that the revenues of all of the Guise-held benefices had declined greatly since the mid-sixteenth century. The contract of a revenue farmer would also call for the farmer to hand over somewhat less than the total revenues available.

24. ANG, VIII, 779. For a discussion of ecclesiastical pensions see BN, Fonds Baluze, 179, fol. 1–11. "Des pensions sur les curés et sur les prebends," dated 1671. The data on pensions that follow are taken largely from Eubel, *Hierarchia Catholica*, vol. III.

25. ANG, VIII, 205.

26. ANG, XIV, 326.

27. In Jacques Lavaud, *Desportes* (Paris, 1936), p. 259; cited by Huppert, *Bourgeois gentilshommes*, p. 147.

28. Tattegrain, *Du Temporel*, pp. 140–42. The practice of leaving out the names of pensioners would suggest the number of lay pensioners was substantially higher than the number that appear in the "Acta consistorialia" and thus in Eubel. Peronnet's description of the system of pensions in the eighteenth century indicates that, although very little had changed in two hundred years, the practice of giving pensions on bishoprics to laymen had disappeared. *Les évêques*, I, 585–87.

29. Guillaume de Taix, *Mémoires,* p. 4; BN, Acquisitions nouvelles françaises, 3560, fol. 332.

30. A. Sicard, *L'ancien clergé de France*, 3 vols. (Paris: LeCoffre, 1893–1903), p. 113.

31. ANG, XIII, 358. There is no indication in Eubel, *Hierarchia Catholica*, III, 274, that de Fay received any reduction in the fees.

32. Martin, *Histoire de la ville de Lodève*, II, 16–17. J. de Lahandis, *Annales de Pamiers* (Toulouse: Le Henneyer et fils, 1882), I, 462.

33. ADHA, G, 1147–1244, passim. As of 1588, the last entry in the litigation, Paparin had paid 2,700 l.

34. Adrien Clergéac, *La curie et les bénéficiers consistoriaux* (Paris: Alphonse Picard, 1911) p. 43. The reduction was a result of the efforts of the Council of Constance to get French support for its solution for the Great Schism. The taxes are listed for each see in Eubel, *Hierarchia Catholica*, vols. II and III. It appears that the sums given for the French sees do not reflect the reduction accorded to the French Church.

35. Clergéac, *La curie*, p. 207; William Lunt, *Papal Revenues in the Middle Ages*, 2 vols. (New York: Octagon Books, 1965), I, 89–94; II, 289–92. Certain fees were fixed, and accordingly a bishop of a poor diocese paid 200 percent or more of the common services for the other fees. As the revenues of the bishopric increased, the percentage of the common services that the other fees were declined to as low as 45 percent. A French bishop with a tax of 100 florins paid 340 florins in all for his bulls; the archbishop of Trier with a tax of 10,000 florins paid a

total of 14,506 florins in 1500. Clergéac, p. 207; Lunt, II, 298–99.

36. Du Tems, *Le clergé de France*, p. 457.

37. As in the cases of Guillaume Rose of Senlis and Pompey Pérille of Apt. ANG, II, 170. The latter did receive his bulls gratis but there is no indication that Rose received a reduction.

38. Lunt, *Papal Revenues*, II, 299, 312; *Recueils des actes, titres, mémoires concernant les affaires du clergé de France*, 12 vols. (Paris, 1721), IX, 947.

39. *Recueils des actes*, IX, 947.

40. Antoine Degert, *Histoire des évêques de Dax* (Paris: Delhomme et Brisquit, 1903), p. 265.

41. ADSM, G, 94–137. The décimes for these years are not listed, perhaps because d'Amboise as a cardinal was exempt.

42. ADHV, G, 63.

43. Brantôme, *Les dames gallantes* (Paris: Garnier frères, 1967), p. 299; Donald Peattie, *Immortal Village* (Chicago: University of Chicago Press, 1945), p. 129; Abbé Bozé, *Histoire de l'église d'Apt* (Apt: Chez Tremallois, 1820), p. 294; Oroux, *Histoire ecclésiastique*, II, 88.

44. Galpern, *Religions of Champagne*, pp. 33, 194.

45. ADC, G, 22, fol. 23; ADL, G, 36, fol. 39; Kalas, "Wealth, Place, and Power," pp. 333, 374; Harrie, "François de Foix," p. 62. Late in his life and in his will, François de Foix of Aire provided endowments for a chair of mathematics, for theology students, and for the poor that totaled 3,833 écus annually.

46. Fisquet, *La France pontificale*, article Arles.

47. Bozé, *L'église d'Apt*, p. 291.

48. Evennett, *Cardinal of Lorraine*, p. 9n.

49. Moran, "Catholic Church," p. 339; Abbé Du Tressay, *Histoire des moines et des évêques de Luçon*, 2 vols. (Paris: Lecoffre fils, 1869), II, 66.

50. P. Gagnol, "Les décimes et les dons gratuits," RHEF, II (1911), 465; Carrière, *Etudes*, III, 260–86.

51. Doucet, *Institutions*, II, 835n. François collected a total of fifty décimes in thirty-two years; Henri II, fifty-one in twelve years.

52. J. Viguier, *Les contracts et la consolidation des décimes à la fin du XVIe siècle* (Paris: H. Jouve, 1906), p. 44; DBF, II, 504. See also the order of François I to the bishop of Coutances to assemble the clergy of the diocese for a "don gratuit" of 10,339 l, August, 1542, to be paid by November. *Catalogue des actes de François I*, 10 vols. (Paris: Imprimerie Nationale, 1887–1910), IV, 364.

53. Carrière, *Etudes*, III, 256.

54. Ladurie, *Peasants*, pp. 174–75, demonstrates that the impetus for these proposals came from the Third Estate of Languedoc where the Huguenots were influential.

55. Picot, *Histoire des etats*, II, 247; Viguier, *Contracts des décimes*, pp. 67–68. The different sources give slightly different variations of the two schemes. In the second plan 48,000,000 l was to be put into rentes to produce 4,000,000 l a year for the clergy, 42,000,000 l was to be used to pay off royal debts, and the remaining 30,000,000 l was to be given to the cities to encourage commerce and repair their fortifications.

56. For further discussion of the Contract of Poissy, see Louis Serbet, *Les assemblées du clergé de France 1561–1615* (Paris: Honoré Champion, 1906), pp. 26–82; Martin Wolf, *The Fiscal System of Renaissance France* (New Haven: Yale University Press, 1972), pp. 121–26; Carrière, *Etudes*, III, 262–63.

57. Rentes were a form of annuity in which the *rentier* bought the income from a source of revenue, which in the case of the king was a toll or tax, for others the rent from property or feudal dues, in exchange for a large sum of money. The annual income served as interest for the principal that was repaid in a lump sum at the end of the contract. The monarchy often left its rentes extend indefinitely. The best known of the rentes were those held for the monarchy by the Hôtel de ville of Paris, but cities or individuals could take them from bishops as well. See, for example, ADIV, G, 13, for contracts of rentes between the bishop of Rennes and several bourgeoisie. The rente was necessary because it was the only form of loan at interest accepted by the Church. For the rentes on the Hôtel de ville see Wolf, *Fiscal System*, pp. 91–93.

58. P. Blet, *Le Clergé de France et la monarchie* (Rome: Grégorienne, 1959), pp. 163–72.

59. Froumenteau, *Le secret des finances de France* (n.p., 1581), p. 72. The Venetian ambassador in 1563 put the income of the whole realm at 15,000,000 écus of which the clergy received 6,000,000 (c. 16,500,000 l). M. Tommaseo, *Relations des ambassadeurs vénitiens sur les affaires de France au XVIe siècle*, 2 vols. (Paris, 1838), II, 23.

60. BN, Fonds français, 17658; Fonds Dupuy, 47.

61. Carrière, *Etudes*, III, 402; C. Michaux, "Les aliénations du temporel ecclésiastique dans la seconde moité du XVIe siècle," RHEF, 67 (1981), 61–82.

62. Ladurie, *Peasants of Languedoc*, pp. 174ff; Moran, "Catholic Church," pp. 128ff. Both have detailed accounts of the sale of Church

property in Languedoc.

63. Ivan Cloulas, "Les aliénations du temporalité ecclésiastique sous Charles IX et Henri III, 1563–87," RHEF, 44 (1958), 5–56.

64. Moran, "Catholic Church," p. 125. There was a second provincial assembly in December for the same purpose.

65. Ibid., pp. 130–33; and Ladurie, *Peasants of Languedoc*, pp. 178–79. The tax for the bishop of Montpellier should have been a third of the sale price of his barony. It is a good example of the overselling in which the overly zealous royal commissioners often engaged. For the diocese of Limoges the assessment was 60,000 l, but the commissioners sold 158,912 l or 260 percent of the required amount. Cloulas, "Les ventes de biens ecclésiastiques effectivées sur l'ordres de Charles IX et Henri III dans les diocèses de Limoges et Bourges," *Bulletin de la Société historique du Limousin*, LXXXVII (1959), 150.

66. ADM, G, 11; ADC, G, 22; V. T. Holmes, ed., *Du Bartas: The Works* (Chapel Hill: University of North Carolina Press, 1935–40), I, 7.

67. Richard, *D'Epinac*, p. 69; ADHA, G, 1437; AN, G8*, 1319.

68. Abbé Richard, *De publicatis tempore motuum civilium XVI saeculi ecclesiae gallicanae bonis immobilibus (1563–1588)* (Paris: Picard, 1901), p. 433. Jonathan Dewald, *The Formation of a Provincial Nobility: The Magistrates of the Parlement of Rouen 1499–1600* (Princeton: Princeton University Press, 1980), p. 345.

69. Moran, "Catholic Church," pp. 140–41.

70. Carrière, *Etudes*, III, 404. In some sees bishops made a fairly large proportion of the sales. At Nîmes the bishop accounted for eight of the forty sales in the diocese and 19,200 l of the 60,602 l total (AN, G8*, 1336). Of the fifty bishoprics for which I have some information, only those of Rouen and Chartres appear not to have alienated any property in 1563. At Poitiers the bishop made two small sales out of the total of 271 for the diocese (AN, G8* 1319).

71. Viguier, *Décimes*, pp. 112–14.

72. Carrière, *Etudes*, III, 406–7.

73. Moran, "Catholic Church," pp. 148–49; ADHA, G, 1138.

74. Carrière, *Etudes*, III, 411–15; Michaux, "Les aliénations," pp. 62–63. The écu was pegged at 53 sols (2.65 livres) in 1569.

75. Ibid., p. 416.

76. Haton, *Mémoires*, II.

77. ADHA, G, 36, fol. 39; Moran, "Catholic Church," pp. 94–151. See Moran for a detailed discussion of the problems that the lower clergy

of Languedoc had in paying the décimes.

78. Michaux, "Les aliénations," pp. 65–81.

79. Richard, *D'Epinac*, p. 93.

80. ANG, VIII, 94, 148.

81. BN, Fonds français, 15746, fol. 22. Another source put the total at 62,441,000 l. Carrière, *Etudes*, III, 284n. On royal revenues see J. Clamageran, *Histoire de l'impôt en France*, 3 vols. (Paris, 1867–76), II, 197–98. I suspect, however, that his estimate is low.

82. ANG, II, 95–108 and passim. In 1580 Philippe Du Bec of Nantes excommunicated the officials who tried to collect the extraordinary décime of that year. Martin, *Le gallicanisme*, p. 176.

83. ANG, II, 107–8.

84. Cloulas, "Les alienations," p. 46; Ladurie, *Peasants of Languedoc*, p. 190; Archives de la Seine-Maritime, G, 936, 1096.

85. Moran, "Catholic Church," p. 144.

86. Carrière, *Etudes*, III, 176; Doucet, *Institutions*, II, 844.

87. Cloulas, "Les aliénations," p. 59; Carrière, *Etudes*, III, 285.

88. Degert, *Histoire des évêques de Dax*, p. 207.

CHAPTER V

1. ADHV, G, 12, fol. 176ff.

2. Philip Hoffman, *Church and Community in the Diocese of Lyon, 1500–1789* (New Haven: Yale University Press, 1984), p. 20.

3. Especially true of the small dioceses created in the Midi in 1317 to counter Catharism.

4. Sicard, *L'ancien clergé*, pp. 67–68; Ravitch, *Sword and Mitre*, p. 56.

5. Sicard, *L'ancien clergé*, pp. 70–75. In the Middle Ages the bishop of Paris's litter was carried by, among others, the counts of Alençon, Nevers, Montmorency, the duke of Brittany, and the king of France because of fiefs they held from the bishop. Sicard believes that this practice did not last into the sixteenth century, p. 69n.

6. François, *Tournon*, p. 234n. The cause of the quarrel was the fact that the tableware that the archbishop used and gave to the baron afterwards was not made of gold.

7. Hoffman, *Church and Community*, p. 20.

8. Sicard, *L'ancien clergé*, p. 69.

9. Ibid., p. 42. After the see of Paris was raised to an archdiocese in 1626, its archbishop became a duke-peer. In 1575, because Louis de

Guise was not yet consecrated archbishop of Reims, the bishop of Soissons claimed the privilege of consecrating Henri III as the dean of Reims's suffragan bishops, but Louis de Lorraine of Metz did the honor for his nephew.

10. C. De Vic et al., *Histoire générale de Languedoc*, 15 vols. (Toulouse: Demouily, 1872–92), IV, 303.

11. ADHA, G, 1207.

12. Richard, *D'Epinac*, p. 69; Hoffman, *Church and Community*, pp. 16–17.

13. Abbé Delettre, *Histoire du diocèse de Beauvais*, 3 vols. (Beauvais: Desjardins, 1843), III, 255.

14. Mousnier, *Les institutions*, I, 371–412; Doucet, *Les institutions*, II, 457–89. For a description of the lands and the range of seigneurial justice under the bishop of Paris, see Mousnier, pp. 401–2.

15. Paul Viollet, *Histoire des institutions politiques et administratives de France*, 4 vols. (Paris: Sirey, 1898), II, 308–9; J. H. Shennen, *The Parlement of Paris* (Ithaca, N.Y.: Cornell University Press, 1968), pp. 81–82.

16. Isambert, *Recueil des lois*, XII, 600–640, especially articles I, II, and IV. G. Picot, *Histoire des Etats généraux*, II, 440n. According to Charles Loyseau, *Traité des seigneuries* (Paris, 1609), p. 95, before the edict the bishop's court of the archdiocese of Sens had more than thirty procurers to five or six for the secular court; after the edict the numbers were reversed.

17. E. Dessalles, *Les évêques italiens de l'ancien diocèse de Béziers 1547–1669* (Toulouse: Privat, 1901), pp. 45–46.

18. See Walter Ullman's introduction to H. C. Lea, *The Inquisition of the Middle Ages* (New York: Harper and Row, 1969), pp. 30–31.

19. J. de Moreau et al., *La crise religieuse du XVIe siècle* (n.p.: Bloud and Gay, 1950), p. 273.

20. H. Baird, *History of the Rise of the Huguenots*, 2 vols. (New York: Scribners, 1879), I, 52. See also Donald Kelly, *The Beginning of Ideology of Consciousness and Society in the French Reformation* (Cambridge: Cambridge University Press, 1981), p. 171; and Baumgartner, "Heterodoxy and Humanism in the French Episcopacy Under Francis I," *Proceedings of the Western Society for French History*, VIII (1982), 57–58; and below, chapter VII.

21. Isambert, *Recueil des lois*, XII, 676–81; N. M. Sutherland, *The Huguenot Struggle for Recognition* (New Haven: Yale University Press, 1980), pp. 32–39, 337–38; Knecht, *Francis I*, pp. 397–99. Charles V, faced

with much the same problem in the Lowlands of confusion over jurisdiction and lax enforcement of heresy laws by the hierarchy, tried to solve it by imposing a zealous layman as inquisitor general. Complaints from the clergy and the Council of the Lowlands forced him to reverse his decision. W. H. Rule, *History of the Inquisition*, 2 vols. (New York: Scribners, 1874), II, 2–5.

22. N. Weiss, *La chambre ardente* (Reprint, Geneva: Slatkine, 1970), p. lvii and note.

23. See ibid., pp. 418–21, for the document creating it.

24. In this respect Henri was following the example of his father who had created a similar chamber in the Parlement of Rouen in 1545. Ibid., p. xxxiv. The first use of the term *chambre ardente* is unknown; but it appears in *Histoire ecclésiastique*, I, 87: "qu'on appeloit chambre ardente."

25. For the text of the edict, see Isambert, *Recueil des lois*, XIII, 189–208. For discussions of it, see Sutherland, *Huguenot Struggle*, pp. 44–46; Baird, *Rise of the Huguenots*, I, 279–82.

26. In response sixty-eight persons held in prison in Paris were turned over to their bishops for trial. Weiss, *Chambre ardente*, pp. 376–79.

27. Isambert, *Recueil des lois*, XIV, 31–33. Romier, *Origines politiques*, I, 244, argues that the three cardinals were chosen because they usually resided at the French court, not because Henri was trying to compromise Châtillon who was already sympathetic to Protestantism.

28. Picot, *Etats généraux*, II, 101–3.

29. Ibid., pp. 440–41.

30. Ibid., III, 164–65.

31. The bishop of Apt, Jean de Rambaud de Simiane, was involved in a bitter dispute with the commune of Apt over whether he had to pay taxes on properties he had acquired in the early 1560's. The resolution was to exempt him from the taxes but no future bishop. Bozé, *Histoire de l'église d'Apt*, p. 291. The bishop of Apt held three seigneuries that required him to provide two men of war for the feudal levy and had revenues of 570 écus.

32. BN, Fonds français, 23101, fol. 117r.

33. R. Mousnier, *Les institutions de la France* (Paris: Presses universitaires, 1974), I, 371, states that every bishop had an honorific right to sit in the royal council and many did when they came to Paris. I have seen no evidence of this practice in the sixteenth century.

34. Harding, *Anatomy of a Power Elite*, pp. 221–27.

35. Picot, *Etats généraux*, III, 90; J. Russell Major, *The Deputies to the*

Estates General in Renaissance France (Madison: University of Wisconsin Press, 1960), pp. 115, 163. Major notes that in 1560 the Cardinal de Lorraine declined to serve as speaker of the First Estate because the Second refused to accept him as speaker for the combined Estates.

36. Dessalles, *Les évêques italiens*, p. 92.

37. A benefice has been defined as "an ecclesiastical office to which is joined a certain revenue from which it cannot be separated." Abbé Fillery, *Instituts du droit ecclésiastique*, 2 vols. (Paris, 1767), I, 299. For a discussion of the types of benefices and their collation, see Marion, *Les institutions*, pp. 42–48; and Auguste Sicard, *La nomination aux bénéfices ecclésiastiques avant 1789* (Paris, 1896).

38. Marion, *Les institutions*, p. 48. He notes the case of a priory that five different collators claimed the right to fill, all based on a legitimate right.

39. Imbart de la Tour, *Origines*, II, 188; Abel Poitrineau et al., *Le diocèse de Clermont* (Paris: Editions Beauchesne, 1979), p. 98.

40. David Knowles, *The Monastic Order in England* (Cambridge: Cambridge University Press, 1963), pp. 129–34.

41. Brian Tierney, *Foundations of the Conciliar Theory* (Cambridge: Cambridge University Press, 1955), pp. 106–31; A. H. Thompson, *The English Clergy and Their Organization in the Later Middle Ages* (Oxford: Clarendon Press, 1966), pp. 73–74.

42. Katherine Edwards, *The English Secular Cathedrals in the Middle Ages* (New York: Barnes and Noble, 1967), p. 100. In many of the larger and wealthier sees the canons of the chapter came from throughout the kingdom, not only the local region. See Elaine Deronne, "Les origines des chanoines de Nôtre-Dame de Paris, 1450–1550," *Revue d'histoire moderne et contemporaire*, XVIII (1971), 1–28.

43. Amiet, *Essai sur l'organization du chapitre cathedrale de Chartres du XIe au XVIIIe siècle* (Chartres: Lainé, 1922); Doucet, *Les institutions*, II, 743.

44. Bozé, *Histoire d'Apt*, p. 287.

45. M. Tresvaux, *Histoire du diocèse d'Angers* (Paris: Picard, 1858), p. 341.

46. DBF, IV, 48.

47. Edouard de Barthelémy, *Diocèse ancien de Châlons-sur-Marne*, 2 vols. (Paris: A. Auby, 1856), II.

48. Joseph Roserot de Melin, *Antonio Caracciolo évêque de Troyes* (Paris: Letouzey et Ané, 1923), p. 224; Paul Pialin, *Histoire de l'église du Mans*,

6 vols. (Paris: Lanies, 1858–63), V, 421; Huppert, *Bourgeois gentilshommes*, p. 53.

49. Catta, "Les évêques de Nantes," I, 62.

50. ANG, II, 229.

51. ADHA, G, 1264.

52. Delettre, *Histoire du diocèse de Beauvais*, II, 495.

53. DBF, I, 167; Knowlès, *Monastic Order*, pp. 318–30, 619–22.

CHAPTER VI

1. Session XXIII, Chapter 4; H. J. Schroeder, *Canons and Decrees of the Council of Trent* (St. Louis: Herder, 1941), p. 162. All citations to the Tridentine decrees are to this work.

2. For a general discussion of the vicar general and the coadjutor, see A. H. Thompson, *The English Clergy*, pp. 48–50.

3. Bowker, *The Secular Clergy in the Diocese of Lincoln 1495–1520* (Cambridge: Cambridge University Press, 1968), p. 23; Fisquet, *La France pontificale*, article Auxerre. One must note that, unlike Bowker's English bishops, many French prelates of the era did not offer greater wisdom and experience than their vicars. Bowker leaves the impression that absenteeism was not as great a problem in the English Church.

4. M. Piton, "L'idéal épiscopal selon les prédicateurs français de la fin du XVe siècle," *Revue d'histoire ecclésiastique*, 61 (1966), 77–118, 393–423.

5. ANG, VI, 457; Evennett, *Cardinal of Lorraine*, pp. 26–33; Venard, "Une réforme Gallicane," p. 207.

6. Bishop Charles de Marillac to Henri in 1551, cited by ibid., p. 27.

7. CSPF, Spain, X, 54 and passim; CSPF, Edward, pp. 170–72; ANG, VI, 475ff; Venard, "Une réforme Gallicane," pp. 201–4; Romier, "La crise Gallicane, de 1551," *Revue historique*, 108 (1911), 225–50; 109 (1912), 27–55. For a French view that recalling the council to Trent made Julius III a "slave" of the emperor, see M. François, *Correspondance*, p. 259.

8. G. Ribier, *Lettres et mémoires d'estat sous les règnes de François I, Henri II, et François II*, 2 vols. (Paris, 1666), pp. 344–45.

9. Antoine Varillas, *Histoire de François premier* (Paris, 1685), VII, 45.

10. Isambert, *Recueil général des lois*, XIII, 484–85. A major reason for the edict was to prevent French bishops from residing in Rome and dying there, permitting the pope to fill their sees.

11. BN, Fonds François, 23101, fol. 34v.

12. Ibid., 23102, fol. 41r; ADTG, G, 193.

13. Ibid., 23102, fol. 92v.

14. Haton, *Mémoires 1553–1582*, ed. Felix Bourguelot (Paris: Imprimèrie Impériale, 1857), I, 89.

15. In De Vic, *Histoire générale de Languedoc*, XII, Preuve No. 327.

16. Fourquevaux probably revealed something of his own political position in praising the bishop of Comminges since Saint-Gelais had a reputation as a very militant anti-Protestant.

17. BN, Acquisitions françaises nouvelles, 3560, fol. 46r.

18. These statistics on absenteeism are based on the following criteria: service to the monarchy as ambassadors and royal councillors and officials which clearly kept bishops away from their sees, service to the papacy in Rome and occasionally elsewhere, service as administrators in the sees of more prominent prelates, and explicit statements in contemporary sources or such histories as the *Gallia Christiana* that a bishop was not in residence. Jean Meyer, *Histoire religieuse de la Bretagne* (Chambray: CLD, 1980), p. 134, notes that about 40 percent (no exact figures cited) of the bishops of the nine Breton dioceses in the sixteenth century were absentee prelates, a figure slightly lower than my own calculations for these diocese. But there is no question that these sees had a better record than any other region of France, perhaps because 37 percent (28 of 76) of the bishops seated in Brittany were Bretons. Meyer, p. 200.

19. Dolan, *Entre Tours*, pp. 193–96.

20. Pastor, *History of the Popes*, XI, 510.

21. Romier, *Origines politiques*, I, 202–5. The monarchy backed by the Parlement and the University of Paris objected to the decrees on the grounds that they interfered with the Gallican liberties.

22. François, *Cardinal de Tournon*, pp. 442–43.

23. Jean Du Bellay refused to give up Paris and Bordeaux, having conceded Saint-Brieuc and Bayonne. Evennett, *Cardinal of Lorraine*, p. 37n.

24. BN, Acquisitions françaises nouvelles 3560, fol. 332. I can identify only one bishop unconsecrated for any length of time in 1579—Charles de Vendôme-Bourbon of Lectoure, named in 1569.

25. Galpern, *The Religions of Champagne*, p. 120; *Histoire ecclésiastique*, I, 79–80. On Caracciolo's heterodoxy, see below, chapter VII.

26. Galpern, *The Religions of Champagne*, p. 149.

27. H. Jedin et al., *Reformation and Counter Reformation* (New York: Seabury Press, 1980), p. 530.

28. J. Michael Hayden, *France and the Estates General of 1614*

(Cambridge: Cambridge University Press, 1974), p. 92n. Pastor, *History of the Popes*, XVII, 215, in his discussion of synods during the reign of Pius V mentions only the provincial synods of Reims and Lyon. Hayden's statistics are based on A. Artonne, *Répertoire des status synodaux des diocèses de l'ancienne France du XIIIe à la fin du XVIIIe siècle* (Paris: CNRS, 1963). According to Artonne, who lists only the synods that published statutes, Lorenzo Strozzi held four diocesan synods at Aix between 1568 and 1570.

29. BN, Fonds françois, 23102, fol. 22r. See the discussion of the Synod of Narbonne in Venard, "Une réforme Gallicane," pp. 221–25.

30. Philip Benedict, "The Catholic Response to Protestantism: Church Activity and Popular Piety in Rouen, 1560–1600," in *Religion and the People 800–1700*, ed. James Obelkevich (Chapel Hill: University of North Carolina Press, 1979), p. 174.

31. Paul Broutin, *La réforme pastorale en France au XVIIe siècle* (Tournai: Desdée et cie, 1959), II, 17–31.

32. DBF, VI, 1485; Galpern, *Religions of Champagne*, p. 194. The successor to de Bourges (or Bourgeois as Galpern renders the Latin Burgensis) was called before the Parlement to compel him to provide funds for six students as de Bourges's will called for.

33. Isambert, *Recueil des lois*, XIV, 55; ADLG, G, cl bis; ADHA, G, 779; Venard, "Une réforme Gallicane," pp. 210–15; Dolan, *Entre Tours*, pp. 209–18. Dolan notes that the records she used indicate that at least four partial visitations took place in Aix for which there are no formal records. She suggests that there were likely as many undocumented visitations as documented ones.

34. The following discussion of visitations is based largely on the following sources: ADLG, G, C l bis, the visitation of the diocese of Agen made by Giovanni Valerio, bishop of Grasse, vicar general of Agen, 1 April to 16 September 1551, 266 religious establishments visited; ADLA, G, 42–46, visitations made of the various deaneries of the see of Nantes by Bishop Antoine de Crequi from 1554 to 1573; ADHV, G, 683, visitation of the part of the see of Limoges, 170 religious establishments, November 1, 1600–January 22, 1601; ADHA, G, 779, 1538–40, visitations of the see of Gap made by Bishops Gabriel de Clermont and Pierre de Paparin, 1551, 1599; Dolan, *Entre Tours*, pp. 209–18, visitations of the see of Aix-en-Provence, 1535, 1558, 1582; and Venard, "Une réforme Gallicane," pp. 215–21.

35. ADM, G, 308. At Montauban in 1628 the bishop sent out a

questionnaire to his curés asking about the state of religion in the parishes. In answer to one question whether there were any parishioners who read dangerous books without permission, one priest answered that there were no parishioners who could read. ADTG, G, 194, fol. 45.

36. Delumeau, *Catholicism between Luther and Voltaire*, pp. 17–31.

37. H. Fouqueray, *Histoire de la Compagnie de Jésus en France*, 4 vols. (Paris: A. Picard, 1910–13), I, passim. Evennett, *Cardinal of Lorraine*, p. 57–62.

38. ANG, XIII, 791n; Godefrey de Paris, *Les frères mineurs capucins en France*, 2 vols. (Paris, 1950), I, passim.

39. *Histoire ecclésiastique*, I, 45; ANG, II, 610, 623. The pope accepted d'Auraisin's contrition and did nothing in the case.

40. L'Estoile, *Mémoires*, I, 375.

41. Brantôme, *Les dames*, pp. 299–300.

42. L'Estoile, I, 238. Haton, *Mémoires*, I, 45.

43. Romier, *Origines politiques*, I, 47–48.

44. DBF, VIII, 733; Fisquet, *La France pontificale*, XII, article Arles.

45. Knecht, *Francis I*, pp. 199–202.

46. DBF, XI, 385.

47. Ibid., I, 1322.

48. See Ronsard's "Response . . . aux injures et calumnies," line 141 ff.

> Mais que diroit S. Paul, s'il revenoit icy,
> De Nos ieunes Prelats qui n'ont point de soucy
> De leur pauvre troupeau, dont ils prennent la laine,
> Et quelquefois le cuir: qui tous vivent sans peine,
> Sans prescher, sans prier, sans bon example d'eux,
> Parfumez, decoupex, courtisans, amoureux,
> Veneurs et fauconniers, et avec la paillarde
> Perdent les biens de Dieu, dont ils n'ont que la garde.

Only Jean de Monluc of Valence gained Ronsard's approval: "Presques un seul, Montluc, esloigne d'avarice/Accomplit aujourd'huy sainement son office." Cited by F. Yates, *French Academies of the Sixteenth Century* (London: Wartburg Institute, 1947), pp. 188, 203.

49. Fisquet, article Auxerre. What Lenoncourt's vices were is not made clear.

50. DBF, II, 227–30.

CHAPTER VII

1. A. C. Cochrane, ed., *Reformed Confessions of the Sixteenth Century* (Philadelphia: Westminster, 1961), pp. 120–58. *Histoire ecclésiastique des églises réformées au royaume de France*, ed. G. Baum and E. Cunitz (Paris: Fischbacher, 1883), I, 181–82.

2. Evennett, *Cardinal of Lorraine*, pp. 13–14; François, *Tournon*, pp. 505–6. The difficulty of distinguishing among the various shadings of passive indifference, toleration, and outright advocacy is compounded for the mid-sixteenth century by a problem of vocabulary. As William Huseman, "The Expression of the Idea of Toleration in French during the Sixteenth Century," *Sixteenth Century Journal*, XV (1984), 293–310, has shown, the term *tolerer* had a rather negative connotation of a higher authority suffering to allow the existence of a heterodox opinion or activity.

3. Evennett, *Cardinal of Lorraine*, p. 242n.

4. V. L. Bourrilly and N. Weiss, *Jean du Bellay, Les protestants et la Sorbonne* (Paris: Agence général de la Société, 1904), p. 18; A. Prévost, *Le Diocèse de Troyes* (Troyes: G. Fremont, 1908), p. 98.

5. Beza, *Correspondance*, ed. H. Aubert et al. (Geneva: Droz, 1963–78), I, 45–46.

6. Bourrilly, *Jean Du Bellay*, pp. 18–59; *Histoire ecclésiastique*, I, 15; A. L. Herminjard, *Correspondance des réformateurs dan les pays de langue français*, 10 vols. (Geneva: H. George, 1866–69), III, 130.

7. *Gallia Christiana*, I, 277–78. Herminjard, *Correspondance*, VI, 209; Raemond, *L'histoire de la naissance, progrez et decadence de l'hérésie de ce siècle* (Paris, 1605), book VII, 154. Raemond called Roussel a Luthero-Zwinglian and a teacher of Calvin. See also Charles Schmidt, *Gérard Roussel prédicateur de la reine Marguerite de Navarre* (Strasbourg, 1845).

8. The most thorough discussion of Briçonnet's religious views is S. Berger, "Le procès de Guillaume Briçonnet au Parlement de Paris en 1525," BSHPF, XLIV (1895), 1–39. The most recent work is that of Henry Heller, in particular his "The Briçonnet case reconsidered," *Journal of Medieval and Renaissance Studies*, II (1972), 223–58.

9. Herminjard, *Correspondance*, III, 399–401; Henri Hauser, *Etudes sur la réforme française* (Paris: A. Picard, 1909), p. 41.

10. Louise Guirard, *Le procès de Guillaume Pellicier* (Paris: Picard fils, 1907). She sees the charges against him as largely a conspiracy of canons who had opposed his appointment in 1527.

11. R. Doucet, "Pierre Du Chastel, Grand Aumônier de France," *Revue historique*, CXXIII (1920), 212–57, CXXIV, 1–57; *Mémoires de Condé*, 6 vols. (London, 1743), I, 593–94.

12. *Histoire ecclésiastique*, I, 62; E. and E. Haag, *La France protestante*, 10 vols. (reprint Geneva: Slatkine, 1966), VIII, 47.

13. G. Courrage, *Lombèz évêché rural 1317–1809* (Lombès: Prudhomme, 1973), p. 197.

14. *La France protestante*, IV, 521–23; *Histoire ecclésiastique*, I, 606.

15. "Acta consistorialia," BN, Fonds latin, 12558, fol. 33r; Beza, *Histoire ecclésiastique*, I, 48–49, 852; Antoine Varillas, *Histoire de Henri second* (Paris, 1768), p. 227.

16. Beza, *Histoire ecclésiastique*, I, 852; Haag, *La France protestante*, I, 70–72; Marguerite de Valois, *Mémoires*, ed. L. Lalanne, (Paris: Imprimerie Royale, 1842), p. 6.

17. Baird, *Rise of the Huguenots*, I, 418n.

18. I used the version found in the *Histoire ecclésiastique*, I, 278–86. According to D'Aubigné, *Histoire universelle*, ed. A. de Ruble, 10 vols. (Paris: Librairie Renouard, 1886–1909), I, 325–29, Marillac was largely responsible for a letter from Catherine de Medici to the pope calling for communion under both species and the use of French in the liturgy. Noël Valois, "Les essais de conciliation religieuse au debut de Règne de Charles IX," RHEF, XXXI (1945), 237–86, argues that the letter likely never was sent because no other source mentions it.

19. CSPF, III, 289; J.–A. De Thou, *Histoire universelle*, 10 vols. (Basel, 1742), II, 825.

20. Weiss, *Chambre ardente*, pp. lxxxvii–viii, and no. 258; Ribier, *Lettres*, II, 811–13.

21. *Gallia Christiana*, I, 354–55; DBF, VII, 1490; R. Busquet et al., *Histoire de la Provence* (Monaco: Imprimerie Nationale, 1966), pp. 203–4. Although Clermont clearly apostatized, he had not gained sufficient notoriety to warrant being cited by the Roman Inquisition in 1563. See above, chapter IV, for the dispute over his pension.

22. Leon Marlet, *Le Cardinal de Châtillon, 1517–1571* (Paris: Henri Meir, 1883), pp. 1–30. In 1551 Châtillon received an indult from the papacy to receive the revenues of the see of Tulle for a year and in 1553 a similar grant for Rennes. ANG, IX, 190. His Church income at that time was estimated at 120,000 livres a year.

23. ANG, XIV, passim; letter of the nuncio de Santa Croce in L. Cimber and F. Danjou, eds., *Archives Curieuses de l'histoire de France* (Paris:

Beauvais, 1834–50), VI, 70.

24. Pastor, *History of the Popes*, pp. 189–93. Marlet, *Le cardinal*, p. 6, stated that Châtillon had married secretly in 1561 with the bishop of Limoges, Sebastien de L'Aubespine, officiating. Châtillon's wife was said to have referred to herself as "Madame la Cardinale." *Mémoires de Condé*, II, 11. On Châtillon's attempt to regain his benefices, see A. Lynn Martin, "Fabio Mirto Frangipani and Papal Policy in France," *Archivum historicae pontificale*, 17 (1979), 214, and BN, Fonds Dupuy, 677, fol. 64.

25. For details of Spifame's life and trial, see André Delmas, "Le procès et la mort de Jacques Spifame," BHR, V (1944), 105–37. Also Fisquet, *La France pontificale*, XIII, article Nevers; and ANG, XIV, 182–83. "Acta Consistorialia," BN, Fonds latin, 12559, fol. 23, notes Spifame as being deprived of his benefices for heresy on April 24, 1559. Curiously Henri II refused to accept Spifame's resignation in favor of his nephew and tried to get a court preacher seated. The effort failed when Henri's choice was himself accused of heresy. Ribier, *Lettres*, II, 798, 811.

26. Camille Daux, *Histoire de l'église de Montauban*, (Montauban: Forutie, 1881), I, part 2, p. 31; Dessalles, *Les évêques italiens*, p. 46. Haag, *La France protestante*, VIII, 50–51. De Lettes, a native of Béziers, had a son who was active as a Huguenot captain after 1575.

27. DBF, V, 216; J. de Lahandis, *Annales de Pamiers*, I, 461–62.

28. DBF, XI, 109; ANG, IX, 82.

29. ANG, XIV, 344.

30. The cases of these eight accused bishops have been examined in detail in Antoine Degert, "Procès de huit évêques," XXVI, 60–108. They are discussed in "Acta Consistorialia," BN, Fonds latin, 12560.

31. For Caracciolo, see especially Roserot de Melin, *Antonio Caracciolo*. Also Galpern, *The Religions of Champagne*, pp. 118–19, and passim.

32. Caracciolo, *Le mirouer de vraye religion* (Paris, 1544).

33. "Acta Consistorialia," BN, Fonds latin, 12560, fol. 80v; CSPF Italy, VI-2, 979. Caracciolo had gone to Rome in 1555 in hopes that Caraffa, now Paul IV, would give him the red hat. Degert, "Procès de huit évêques," p. 67, suggests that his disappointment led to his profession to Calvinism. He visited Calvin on his way back to France.

34. *Histoire ecclésiastique*, I, 615, 849–50. Peter Martyr Vermigli apparently had told Caracciolo that he would be accepted as a true bishop by the Calvinists. Beza's letter and Calvin's reply are in Beza, *Correspondance*, III, 213–17. Calvin then considered the problem at greater length in his

"Pour des évesques et curez de la Papaulté," *Opera quae supersunt omnia* (Brunswick: Schwetschke, 1871), X, 184–87. See also Roserot de Melin, "L'illusion de Antonio Caracciolo," RHEF, IX (1923), 347–68.

35. Degert, "Procès de huit évêques," p. 69; CSPF, V, 522. Hector Regnaud, *Jean de Monluc évêque de Valence et Die* (Paris: Thorer et fils, 1893), plays down the heterodoxy of Monluc's views. According to Haag, *La France protestante*, VII, 484–91, Rome had condemned Monluc as a heretic in 1560 after the dean of his cathedral chapter complained about him, but the Parlement of Paris refused to register the bull of deprivation. Also in 1560 the Cardinals Lorraine and Tournon had sought a process against him (ANG, XIV, 275).

36. De Vic, *Histoire de Languedoc*, IX, 454.

37. According to Degert, "Procès de huit évêques," p. 71, Louis de Guillart was also a Protestant sympathizer. While there is some evidence to support that view, the contrary view seems clinched by a piece of doggerel given in S. Mayer, *Clément Marot* (Paris, 1972), p. 111, which attacked him as an "évesque papistique" and a Guisard.

38. "Acta Consistorialia," BN, Fonds latins, 12560, fol. 75r; Beza, *Correspondance*, I, 758; ibid., VI, 214–18; Evennett, *Cardinal of Lorraine*, pp. 382–83.

39. "Acta Consistorialia," BN, Fonds latins, 12560, fol. 72v; De Thou, *Histoire universelle*, III, 411.

40. The above is largely from Degert, "Procès de huit évêques," pp. 77–104.

41. Beza, *Correspondance*, V, 24–25.

42. BN, Fonds italiens, 1724, fol. 86v. Jules Loriot, "Histoire ecclésiastique de France," BN, Fonds français, 23101, fol. 283v. See also Catherine de Medici's letter to Rome denouncing the citations as contrary to the authority of the king in *Lettres*, ed. Comte de Baguehault de Puchésse (Paris, 1899), II, 119.

43. ANG, XIII, p. 164. The pope named three replacements for Saint–Gelais; none was accepted by the monarchy.

44. ANG, XII, 398. The nuncio reported in January, 1573, that he was still bishop and noted his death in the following month.

45. Abbé Bozé, *Histoire de l'église d'Apt*, pp. 291–99.

46. Fisquet, *La France pontificale*, VIII, article Riez, states that d'Auraisin later abjured Protestantism and gave up his pension as well. I have found no corroborating evidence.

47. For de Foix, see the works by Noël Didier, "Paul de Foix à la

mercuriale de 1559," *Mélanges d'archéologie et d'histoire d'école française de Rome*, LVI (1939), 396–435; and *Paul de Foix et Grégoire XIII*. Although de Foix was the last individual whose orthodoxy was suspect to become a bishop in the sixteenth century, several others were nominated in the period from 1570 to 1600 whose bulls of office Rome refused because of their reputed beliefs.

48. Beza, *Histoire ecclésiastique*, I, 255; Haag, *La France protestante*, IV, 125. CSPF, VIII, 455. Didier, "De Foix à la mercuriale," p. 434, states that his religion "apparait singulierement vacillante."

49. ANG, XII and XIII, passim; and the letter of Catherine de Medici to Gregory XIII, asserting that the charges against de Foix were "l'accusation calomnieuse." *Lettres*, VII, 257. As early as 1565 it was reported that de Foix would receive a bishopric, namely, Bourges. CSPF, VII, 330.

50. *Histoire ecclésiastique*, I, 849; Hauser, "De l'humanisme et de la Réforme," pp. 258–97.

51. Geisendorf, *Théodore de Bèze* (Geneva: Jullien, 1967), p. 175.

52. The nuncio's report to Rome, ANG, XIV, 182–83, on Spifame's flight to Geneva emphasizes the importance of the political positions that he had held rather than the impact of his apostasy on the Church.

CHAPTER VIII

1. M. Félebien, *Histoire de la ville de Paris*, 5 vols. (Paris, 1725), II, 984–85.

2. Cited in Galpern, *Religions of Champagne*, p. 111.

3. Isambert, *Recueil des lois*, XII, 292–301.

4. Baird, *Rise of the Huguenots*, I, 139–40. See the decrees of the synod of Bourges in ADC, G, 6.

5. *Gallia Christiana*, I, 408. De Thou, *Histoire universelle*, I, 541: *Histoire ecclésiastique*, I, 23–28. For a less negative view of Tournon, see François, *Tournon*.

6. See Henry Baird's comment cited above, chapter 5, note 4. See also the Cardinal of Lorraine's reprimand of the President of the Tournelle of the Parlement for returning accused heretics to the bishops. Kelley, *The Beginning of Ideology*, p. 171.

7. For a discussion of the active but ineffective opposition to the Protestants by the vicar general of the see of Rouen and the lack of interest of its archbishops, see David Nicholls, "Inertia and Reform in

the Pre-Tridentine French Church: The Response to Protestantism in the Diocese of Rouen 1520–1562," *The Journal of Ecclesiastical History*, XXXII (1981), 185–97.

8. *Histoire ecclésiastique*, I, 79–80, 852; *Mémoires de Condé*, I, 593–94.

9. Dessales, *Les évêques italiens*, pp. 39–42.

10. *Histoire ecclésiastique*, I, 48.

11. Catta, "Les évêques de Nantes," pp. 47–48; Fisquet, *La France pontificale*, XVI, article Bayeux.

12. On the Colloquy of Poissy, see Donald Nugent, *Ecumenism in the Age of Reformation: The Colloque of Poissy* (Cambridge, Mass.: Harvard University Press, 1974); Haton, *Mémoires*, I, 155–76; Evennett, *Cardinal of Lorraine*, pp. 283–93.

13. Dessales, *Les évêques italiens*, p. 49. For a discussion of the legal position on clerics taking up arms and the medieval precedents, see Carrière, *Etudes*, III, 452–61.

14. Blaise de Monluc, *Commentaires*, ed. Paul Courteault (Paris: Editions Gallimard, 1964), p. 495; Carrière, *Etudes*, III, 461–62.

15. Bouges, *Histoire de Carcassone*, p. 317; *Histoire ecclésiastique*, I, 383.

16. DBF, VI, 1485; CSPF, V, 188; Guise, *Mémoires*, pp. 478–79.

17. *Histoire ecclésiastique*, I, 938–39.

18. Carrière, *Etudes*, III, 465; De Vic, *Histoire de Languedoc*, XI, 391.

19. *Histoire ecclésiastique*, I, 783; Fisquet, *La France pontificale*, VIII, article Luçon. Henry IV restored Du Lude to the episcopacy in 1594 because he had become an ardent supporter of the Huguenot prince.

20. *Histoire ecclésiastique*, III, 60–66; Monluc, *Commentaires*, 576–79; Thompson, *Wars of Religion*, pp. 214–18. Several similar Catholic leagues appear elsewhere in the Midi, but only the one in Angers, organized in 1566, involved a bishop, Gabriel Bouvry. P. Miquet, *Les guerres de religion* (Paris: Fayard, 1980), p. 258.

21. Carrière, *Etudes*, III, 482; DBF, VI, 283, XII, 1382; DHGE, XIII, 980.

22. Fisquet, *La France pontificale*, XVI, article Bayeux.

23. Louis de La Roque, *Les évêques de Maguelone et Montpellier* (Montpellier: Imprimerie Calas, 1893), p. 119; Moran, "Catholic Church," p. 237. Moran has extensive information on the destruction or seizure of clerical property in Languedoc. He gives special attention to the cathedral chapters because their records are more complete.

24. *Mémoires de Haton*, I, 449; De Vic, *Histoire de Languedoc*, XI, 509;

J. J. Escande, *Histoire de Sarlat* (Sarlat: Imprimerie Lafary, 1903), p. 147.

25. Carrière, *Etudes*, III, 482; Monluc, *Commentaires*, p. 554 and note.

26. Baird, *Rise of the Huguenots*, II, 508.

27. Picot, *Les italiens*, p. 40n; Charles Labitte, *De la démocratie chez les prédicateurs de la ligue* (Reprint, Geneva: Slatkine, 1971), pp. 7–9; Labitte also discusses the activities of the Italian bishop of Asti, Panigarola, who was studying theology at Paris at the time.

28. On the Cardinal de Lorraine's part in the massacre, see A. Lynn Martin, "Papal Policy and the European Conflict," *Sixteenth Century Journal*, XI (1980), 35–48. The English ambassador reported the attempt on Lorraine's life at Reims that killed a member of his entourage (CSPF, VIII, 413, February 9, 1568).

29. This report has stirred up considerable controversy with several modern authors strongly denying its veracity. See especially M. C. Osmont de Courtisigny, "Jean le Henneyer et les Huguenots de Lisieux en 1573," BSHPF, XXVI (1877), 145. Miquet, *Guerres de religion*, p. 286, accepts it as true. Fisquet, *La France pontificale*, XVI, article Lisieux, makes the point that Le Henneyer likely was not in residence at the time.

30. ADHA, G, 1244; André, *Inventaire*, Series G, pp. 15, 137.

31. Fisquet, *La France pontificale*, XVI, article Bayeux.

32. G. Alzieu, *Un diocèse languedocien Lodève* (Lodève: Jean Mercadies, 1975), p. 40. Martin, *Histoire de Lodève*, II, 44. Martin includes the text of the *arrêt* of the Parlement of Toulouse ratifying the transfer to L'Estang.

33. ADHA, G, 1216 ff. The attack on the bishop was the subject of a long process before the Parlement of Grenoble that lasted until 1598. It was never resolved to the satisfaction of the bishop.

34. Gérard Lavergne, *Histoire de Périgueux* (Périgueux: Editions Fontas, 1945), p. 92.

35. Abbé Marcellin, *Histoire de Montauban*, 2 vols. (Montauban: Rethoré, 1841), II, 75–77. The others were Roussel, Jean de La Haye of Vannes, who was poisoned in 1578 by an apothecary's apprentice, and the Cardinal de Guise executed in 1588. In the first fifteen years of the next century, however, three bishops were assassinated in Provence alone. According to the English ambassador, the bishop of Castries (sic) was executed in 1568 in retaliation for the beheading of a Huguenot gentleman (CSPF, VIII, 404). I have found no corroborating evidence.

36. DBF, XI, 1043.

37. Hugh Trevor-Roper, "James I and His Bishops," *Men and Events* (New York: Octagon Books, 1976), p. 130.

CHAPTER IX

1. Pierre Victor Palma Cayet, *Chronologie novennaire*, vols. 38–43 of C.-B. Petitot, ed., *Collection complète des mémoires relatifs à l'histoire de France*, 130 vols. (Paris: Foucault, 1818–29), XXXVIII, 256.

2. P. de L'Estoile, *Mémoires-journaux*, 12 vols. (Paris: Lemerre, 1888), I, 238.

3. Haton, *Mémoires*, II, appendix IX.

4. L'Estoile, *Mémoires-journaux*, II, 361; BN, Fonds Dupuy, 678, fol. 69.

5. For a description of their activities at Rome, see A. Lynn Martin, *Henry III and the Jesuit Politicians* (Geneva: Droz, 1975), pp. 140–41.

6. Richard, *D'Epinac*, part III; Serbet, *Assemblées du clergé*, p. 108; DBF, XI, 1350–52. On the battle of pamphlets, see Baumgartner, *Radical Reactionaries*, pp. 87–88.

7. D. Taillander, *Histoire de Bretagne* (Paris, 1759), II, 366.

8. L'Estoile, *Mémoires-journaux*, II, 106–7. Rose did ask the king's forgiveness for his harsh words.

9. E. Henry, *La Réforme et la ligue en Champagne et à Reims* (Reims: Trenel, 1867), p. 85.

10. L'Estoile, *Mémoires-journaux*, III, 107.

11. Baumgartner, *Radical Reactionaries*, pp. 62–72; Eugène Saulnier, *Le rôle politique du Cardinal de Bourbon* (Paris: Honoré Champion, 1911); DBF, V, 1394.

12. See Baumgartner, "Renaud de Beaune, Politique Prelate," *Sixteenth Century Journal*, IX (1978), 99–109.

13. P. de Vaissière, *Messieurs de Joyeuse 1560–1615* (Paris: Albin Michel, 1926), pp. 278–87; Martin, *Jesuit Politicians*, pp. 140–44.

14. Sources for the above paragraph are *Mémoires de Condé*, III, 184; *Remonstrances aux Catholiques de tous les estats pour entrés en l'association de la ligue* (n.p., n.d.); *Conseil salutaire d'un bon Français aux Parisiens*, (n.p., 1589), p. 51; Eva Kushner, "Pontus de Tyard devant le pouvoir royal," *Culture et pouvoir aux temps de l'humanisme et renaissance* (Paris: Honoré Champion, 1978), p. 352; De Vic, *Histoire de Languedoc*, XI, 767.

15. J. Russell Major, *The Estates of 1560* (Princeton: Princeton University Press, 1951), appendix A, gives twenty-five bishops as present,

but he does not include the Cardinal de Bourbon who had no see in 1588. In "Episcopacy in Crisis," p. 282, I note one bishop as being of uncertain party, but since then I have found evidence that the bishop, Pontac of Bazas, was an ardent Leaguer.

16. Baumgartner, *Radical Reactionaries*, pp. 96–99.

17. *Collection des Procès-verbaux des assemblées-générales du Clergé de France*, (Paris, 1767), I, pièces justificatives, no. 1, p. 102.

18. Ibid., p. 142.

19. H. de L'Epinois, *La ligue et les papes* (Paris: Librairie Catholique, 1886), p. 354; DBF, II, 1091; *Lettre missive de l'évesque du Mans* (Paris, 1589); It was written in reply to a pamphlet by Jean Boucher.

20. "Relation de Jehan Patte," *Bulletin de la Société de l'histoire de France*, I (1851), 79.

21. L'Estoile, *Mémoires-journaux*, III, 203. According to l'Estoile, the Cardinal de Guise was executed despite the appeal of the First Estate to release him, which was carried by d'Angennes to the king.

22. *Registres des délibérations du Bureau de la ville de Paris*, ed. Paul Guerin et al., 19 vols. (Paris: Imprimerie nationale, 1879–1952), IX, 296.

23. *Gallia Christiana*, IX, 612.

24. Barthelémy Pocquet, *Histoire de Bretagne*, 6 vols. (Rennes: Philhon, 1913), V, 126.

25. Ibid., p. 187; De Vic, *Histoire de Languedoc*, XII, 191.

26. L'Epinois, *La ligue et les papes*, p. 301.

27. DBF, II, 175–59; Robert Aulotte, "Jacques Amyot et les rois, ses maîtres," *Culture et pouvoir*, pp. 319–30.

28. The information on the governors is largely from Harding, *Anatomy of a Power Elite*, appendix one.

29. B. Pocquet, *Histoire de Bretagne*, 6 vols. (Rennes: Philon, 1913), pp. 126, 149.

30. *Archives curieuses*, XII, 327–29.

31. Catta, "Les évêques de Nantes," pp. 49–51.

32. "Recueil de ce qui s'est passé en la conference des Sieurs Cardinal de Gondi et archévesque de Lion avec le Roy," *Mémoires de la ligue*, IV, 340–47. P. Ascoli, ed., *Dialogue d'entre le maheustre et le manant* (Geneva: Droz, 1977), 149, 152–53. *Registres de la ville de Paris*, IX, 127.

33. Clausse is often considered a Politique because De Thou, *Histoire universelle*, XI, 95–97, placed him among the Politiques at a meeting of 1591, but in fact he had been expelled from Châlons in 1589 for being

too zealous a Leaguer. G. Hérelle, *La Réforme et la ligue en Champagne*, 2 vols. (Reims: Charpier, n.d.), I, 183. For an interesting account of the seizure of the library of the Politique bishop of Cahors, Antoine Ebrard de Saint-Sulpice, see Nicole Marzac, *The Library of a French Bishop in the late Sixteenth Century* (Paris: CNRS, 1974). It occurred in 1589 after Ebrard had announced his support for Henri III in March.

34. DBF, XIV, 1439–40.

35. BN, Fonds Français, 23276, fol. 216–22.

36. Ibid.; Jules Lair, *Histoire de Parlement de Normandie pendant son séjour à Caen* (Caen: Hardel, 1866), I, 149–54.

37. Louis Guibert, *La ligue à Limoges* (Limoges: Imprimerie Du Coeurtreux, 1884).

38. Gustave Lambart, *Histoire des guerres de religion en Provence*, 2 vols. (Toulon: J. Laurent, 1870), II, 41.

39. B. Bligny et al., *Le diocèse de Grenoble* (Paris: Beauchesne, 1979), p. 106.

40. Vaissière, *Messeurs de Joyeuse*, pp. 285–87; Edouard de La Faille, *Annales de la ville de Toulouse depuis la réunion de la comté de Toulouse à la couronne*, 2 vols. (Toulouse, 1701), II, 438.

41. Pocquet, *Histoire de Bretagne*, V, 149; DBF, XIII, 10.

42. Etienne de Cruseau, *Chroniques*, 2 vols. (Bordeaux: Société des Bibliophiles de Guyenne, 1879), I, 16–28. Prévost served for a year as a member of the Leaguer council for Bordeaux.

43. See for example, *Le vray Catholique romain contre le ligueur covert* (n.p., 1591), p. 27; *La cause du roy de France, contre les pernicieuses maximes conclusions des ligueurs rebelles* (Tours, 1594).

44. Abel Desjardins, *Négociations diplomatiques de la France avec la Toscane*, 6 vols. (Paris: Imprimerie Nationale, 1859–66), V, 69 (October 30, 1589). The Leaguers had put considerable pressure on the cardinals to recognize the Cardinal de Bourbon as king. See the letters in the Vatican Archives, Nunziatura de Francia, MS. 23, fol. 741ff.

45. F. Caring, "La ligue et Sixte Quint," *Revue de monde Catholique* (April, 1867), pp. 72–74. See also the letters of d'Espinac of Lyon and Rose of Senlis to the cardinals, in the Vatican Archives, Nunziatura de Francia, MS. 23, fol. 741, 769, 787.

46. The royalist Parlements of Paris and Rouen (sitting at Tours and Caen) condemned the bull as an intolerable infringement on the French crown at the Gallican Church and declared it null and void. De Saintes of Evreux responded shortly before his death in his *Bref advertisement de M.*

l'évesque d'Evreux contre un pretendu arrest donné à Caen . . . establisant en France du schism, hérésie et tyrannie d'Angleterre (Paris, 1591).

47. *Collection des Procès-verbaux*, I, 512. De Thou, *Histoire universelle*, XI, 495–97; "Histoire de la ligue," BN, Fonds français 23296, fol. 444; ADEL, G, 418.

48. Kushner, "Pontus de Tyard," pp. 355–56.

49. Robert Descimon and Eli Barnavi, *La Sainte ligue le juge et la potence* (Paris: Hachette, 1985), p. 188; Catta, "Les évêques de Nantes," pp. 49–50; Delettre, *Diocèse de Beauvais*, III, 259; L'Epinois, *La ligue et les papes*, I, 496–97.

50. L'Epinois, *La ligue et les papes*, I, 573.

51. Auguste Bernard, *Procès-verbaux des Etats généraux de 1593* (Paris: Imprimerie Royale, 1842), pp. 211–14.

52. Cayet, *Chronologie novennaire*, XLI, 321–70; L'Estoile, *Mémoires-journaux*, VI, 70–76.

53. L'Estoile, *Mémoires-journaux*, VI, 69–70; *Procès verbal de ce qui s'est passé à Saint-Denis* (Tours, 1593).

54. Cayet, *Chronologie novennaire*, XLII, 139.

55. De Vic, *Histoire de Languedoc*, XII, 191; Pocquet, *Histoire de Bretagne*, V, 187.

56. De Thou, *Histoire universelle*, XII, 128.

57. Pocquet, *Histoire de Bretagne*, V, 187.

58. Génébrard, *De Sacerum Electionum jure et necessitate* (Paris, 1593). The Leaguer Estates of 1593 expressed the same opinion.

59. Thomas, *Histoire du Concordat*, III, 322.

60. One can argue that this contrast in social backgrounds is typical of prerevolutionary situations in which the elites have a major role in forming a rebellious movement that leads to radical revolution. In the League, however, the elites remained very much a part until after its demise was ensured by Henry's conversion. It is true that in Paris there was an attempt by the radicals, the Sixteen, to eliminate the elites and moderates—the murder of the three moderate Leaguers of the Parlement in 1591. The League in Paris came considerably closer to showing the dynamics of a revolutionary movement than it did in France as a whole. For a discussion on whether the Paris Sixteen can be considered revolutionary, see J. H. M. Salmon, "The Paris Sixteen, 1584–1594: The Social Analysis of a Revolutionary Movement," *The Journal of Modern History*, XLIV (1972), 540–76; Ascoli, *Dialogue d'entre le maheustre et le manant*, pp. 35–40; Baumgartner, *Radical Reactionaries*, pp. 236–39;

Descimon and Barnavi, *La Sainte ligue.*

61. John McManners, *The French Revolution and the Church* (New York: Harper and Row, 1969), pp. 48–49.

62. Francesco Panigarola, bishop of Asti, in 1590; cited by François Perrins, *L'église et l'état en France sous le règne de Henri IV,* 2 vols. (Paris: Durand 1872), I, 155.

CHAPTER X

1. ADHA, G, 779. Guibert, *La ligue,* p. 48; M. Boucasseret, *Histoire du siège épiscopal de Maguelone et Montpellier* (Montpellier: Imprimerie de Jean Martel, 1876), p. 237. See also Moran, "Catholic Church," pp. 229–68. In 1612 Bishop Charles Du Serre found little improvement in the diocese of Gap.

2. Louis de La Roque, *Les évêques du Maguelone et Montpellier* (Montpellier: Calas, 1893), p. 126. The dispute there went to the Parlement of Toulouse, which ordered the bishop to provide 2,000 l for the interior of the cathedral. On a similar situation at Nîmes, see R. Sauzet, *Contre-Réforme et Réforme Catholique en Bas-Languedoc: Le diocèse de Nîmes au XVIIe siècle* (Louvain: Mauwelgerts, 1979), pp. 65–66.

3. Abbé Marcellin, *Histoire de Montauban,* II, 95.

4. Sauzet, *Contre-Réforme,* pp. 54–55.

5. G. Doublet, "Guillaume du Blanc," *Annales de Midi,* XIII (1901), 176–89. Rome had agreed to let Du Blanc, already bishop of Vence and a Leaguer, to combine it with Grasse, but Henri IV supported the candidacy of the Politique, Georges de Poissieux. In 1599 Etienne Le Meingre de Boucicault was nominated and confirmed.

6. Baumgartner, "Crisis in the French Episcopacy," p. 283; Peronnet, *Les évêques,* I, 501–2; L. Ravenez, *Histoire du Cardinal de Sourdis* (Bordeaux, 1807), p. 8.

7. For a more extensive discussion of this affair, see Baumgartner, "Renaud de Beaune," pp. 111–12.

8. DBF, VII, 975. Peronnet, *Les évêques,* I, 477, argues that the story about Camelin and the see of Fréjus cannot be true because his bulls were issued in 1594. None of Henri IV's nominees received papal bulls before 1596, and Eubel, *Hierarchia,* III, article Fréjus, following the "Acta Consistorialia," dates Camelin's bulls to 1599. Contrary to Peronnet, the fact that Camelin was a canon of Fréjus by no means eliminates the possibility of this simoniac arrangement.

9. DBF, IV, 1527; E. Price, *Cardinal de Richelieu* (London: McBride, 1912), p. 16.

10. Peronnet, *Les évêques*, II, 1440, table 59, attributes 126 bishops to the period of 1589 to 1610 while Hayden, "Social Origins," p. 32, gives the figure as ninety-eight from 1594 to 1610. The difference between my figure of 109 bishops seated under Henri IV and Peronnet's 126 can be explained partly in that he likely included three nominations made in 1589 by Henri III and the six bishops successfully seated by the League between 1589 and 1594. On his part Hayden apparently did not include the five bishops named by Henri IV before 1594 who were eventually confirmed. Furthermore it also appears that Hayden likely classified as commoners those bishops for whom he did not have evidence of a higher social status since my categories of commoners and unknowns virtually match his thirty-five commoners.

11. A Guise, Cardinal Louis III, returned to the see of Reims in 1605. On the ecclesiastical careers of the Guises after 1588, see Bergin, "The Guises and Their Benefices," 434–58.

12. "Social Origins," pp. 32, 40.

13. Prunel, *La Renaissance Catholique en France au XVIIe siècle* (Paris: Auguste Picard, 1921), p. 20.

14. *Les évêques*, I, 509–13.

15. Baumgartner, "Party Alignment in the Parlement of Paris, 1589–1594," *Proceedings of the Western Society for French History*, VI (1978), 34–45. See also the *brevet* of resignation by Cardinal d'Ossat for Bayeux in 1603 to Jacques d'Angennes, son of a man whom, the *brevet* makes clear, Henri IV wanted to reward (BN, Fonds français, 23, 239, fol. 8). Professor J. A. Bergin called this reference to my attention.

16. The third, Jean de Chevagnoc, may have cost himself a promotion by actively opposing the Edict of Nantes.

17. DBF, VI, 157; G. Grente, *Jean Bertaut* (Paris: Lecoffre, 1903), pp. 42–44; E. de La Faille, *Annales de la ville de Toulouse*, 2 vols. (Toulouse, 1701), II, 518. Henri ordered Rattes's condemnation expunged from the records.

18. Fisquet, VIII, article Luçon. Daillon had been appointed bishop of Luçon in 1553 but had resigned without ever being consecrated.

19. Peronnet, *Les évêques*, I, 507.

20. The most celebrated case of an underage bishop from Henri IV's reign was the choice of his four-year-old bastard son, Henri de Verneuil, as bishop of Metz in 1607. See, for example, Lavisse, *Histoire de France*,

VI, Part 2, 92. Metz was not yet under the Concordat, but the chapter elected Verneuil under pressure from Henri. He eventually was confirmed in 1612. Lavisse cites another such case, that of the four-year-old Charles de Levis, nominated to Lodève in 1604. He became the family heir eight years later and was laicized.

21. Hayden, "Social Origins," p. 33, states: "When Henry IV acted like other kings his bishops were more or less the same as bishops of other kings but when he acted differently, and that was often, the result was quite different"—namely, in the appointment of bishops who were commoners and new nobles who were far more qualified and zealous. Having not analyzed the bishops seated by Henri's four predecessors, he is unaware that the last two Valois also had a high incidence of nominations from the lower social levels. Furthermore, his own table 3 shows that the old nobles held diocesan synods at a greater rate (36 percent) than did the commoners (28 percent).

22. Perrens, L'Eglise et l'état, I, 248–50; Jedin, Reformation and Counter Reformation, p. 302.

23. Jedin, pp. 499–534; F. W. Willocx , L'introduction des decrets du Concile de Trent dans les Pays-Bas et Liège (Louvain: Librairie universitaire, 1929).

24. ADHA, G, 779; DBF, XII, 855. In 1612 Bishop Du Serre was not permitted to enter his family's château while he was on a visitation of his see because it was a Huguenot security place.

25. La Roque, Evêques de Montpellier, p. 126.

26. Poitrineau, Clermont, pp. 122–24.

27. Artonne, Répertoire des status synodaux, passim.

28. For a thorough discussion of the pastoral visitations of one of Henri IV's bishops, Valernod of Nîmes, see Sauzet, Contre-Réforme, pp. 59–64. Limited information for nearly half of the French sees is available in the two published volumes of Répertoire des visites pastorales de la France (Paris: CNRS, 1977–79). Henri IV took an active interest in the pastoral duties of the bishops and in 1600 ordered that they see that visitations were made (ADHV, G, 683, fol. 1).

29. Moran, "Catholic Church," pp. 370–87; Peattie, Immortal Village, p. 127.

30. René Pillorget, Les mouvements insurrectionels de Provence (Paris: Editions Pedone, 1975), pp. 245, 255–56.

31. Peronnet, Les évêques, II, 435–72.

CHAPTER XI

1. See appendix III, table VI.

2. Peronnet, *Les évêques*, I, 541.

3. L. Stone, *The Crisis of the Aristocracy, 1558–1641* (Oxford: Oxford University Press, 1965), p. 406.

4. Ravitch, *Sword and Mitre*, pp. 162–63, discusses changes in the clerical levies after 1700. The décime itself was reduced, but other levies reached 19,000,000 l by mid-century. Episcopal income had risen so substantially that the proportion of revenues the bishops paid to the monarchy dropped to 3 to 5 percent.

5. P. Benedict, *Rouen during the Wars of Religion* (Cambridge: Cambridge University Press, 1981), p. 192.

6. DBF, VIII, 1397; ADHA, G, 779–80.

APPENDIX I

1. See Frank Spooner, *The International Economy and Monetary Movements in France 1493–1725* (Cambridge, Mass.: Harvard University Press, 1972) pp. 101, 163; Knecht, *Francis I*, pp. 432–33.

APPENDIX II

1. Copies of the "Acta" are in the BN, Fonds latin, 12557–12563, Julius III to Clement X.

2. Conrad Eubel, *Hierarchia Catholica*.

3. Fisquet, *La France pontificale*, which covers a quarter of the ancient dioceses, draws heavily from the *Gallia Christiana*. A. Chapeau et al., "L'épiscopat françois de Clement VIII à Paul VI," fascicules 103–4 of *Dictionnaire d'histoire et géographie ecclésiastique*, (Paris: Letouzay et Ané, 1912–) is useful for the period after 1592.

4. (Paris: Schlesinger, 1863–76), 19 vols.

5. Three vols. (Basel: Brandmuller, 1760).

6. *Paris et Ile-de-France: Mémoires*, 5–6 (1953–54).

7. (Paris: A. Picard, 1914), vol. 3.

8. Eight vols. (Rouen: Edouard Frères, 1841). The term *noblesse de robe* is not satisfactory for the sixteenth century. Too many newly ennobled families received their status for reasons other than service in the law courts. Therefore I use the term *anobli*, new noble, for individuals from families with recent patents of nobility.

9. BN, Nouveau d'Hozier, Fonds français, 31416.

BIBLIOGRAPHY

MANUSCRIPT SOURCES

Bibliothèque Nationale, Paris:

Fonds français, Mss 4714–15, 10270, 10489, 15746–48, 16041–46, 17656–58, 23101–02, 23107, 23276, 23295–96, 23039, 23338, 25024–25.

Nouvelles acquisitions français, Mss 3560, 5128.

Fonds Latin, Mss 1724, 12557–63.

Fonds Baluze, Mss 179, 285.

Collection Du Puy, Mss 543, 677–78, 958.

Cabinet des titres: Les pièces originales,
Les dossiers bleus, Le cabinet d'Hozier; diverse pieces.

Archives Nationales, Paris: Minutier central des notaires parisiens, Etude LXXXII. Fonds de l'agence du clergé, Série G8*, 1–6, 241–43, 1302–56.

Archives Départementales de la Cher, Bourges: Série G, Mss 3, 6, 8, 15, 30.

Archives Départementales de l'Eure-et-Loir, Chartres: Série G, Mss 6, 126–28, 418.

Archives Départementales de les Hautes-Alpes, Gap: Série G, Mss 1, 799–80, 1138, 1142, 1147–1244, 1427.

Archives Départementales de l'Haute-Vienne, Limoges: Série G, Mss 12, 31, 183, 214, 683, 777–83.

Archives Départementales de l'Ille-et-Vilaine, Rennes: Série G, Mss 3, 13, 58, 163.

Archives Départementales de la Loire-Atlantique, Nantes: Série G, Mss 5, 36, 43–46.

Archives Départementales de la Lot-et-Garonne, Agen: Série G, Mss C 1, D 1–7, 18.

Archives Départementales du Morhiban, Vannes: Série G, Mss 10–11, 292–95.

Archives Départementales de la Seine-Maritime, Rouen: Série G, Mss 94–137, 311, 632, 936, 1096, 2605.

Archives Départementales de la Tarne-et-Garonne, Montauban: Série G, Mss 71, 193–94, 200, 209.

Vatican Archives, Rome: Nunziatura di Francia, Mss 23–25.

PRINTED PRIMARY SOURCES

Acta nuntiaturae Gallicae. Edited by Pierre Blet et al. 16 vols. to date. Rome: Université Pontificale Grégorienne, 1954–.

Ancel, R. *Nonciatures de France. Nonciatures de Paul IV.* Paris: LeCoffre, 1909.

André, Ferdinand, et al. *Inventaire sommaire des Archives Départementales de Lozère, Archives ecclésiastiques.* Mende: Privat, 1882.

Angennes, Claude d'. *Lettre missive de l'évesque du Mans.* Paris, 1589.

Artonne, A. *Répertoire de status synodaux des diocèses de l'ancienne France de XIIIe à la fin du XVIIIe siècle.* Paris: CNRS, 1963.

Aubigné, A. d'. *Histoire universelle.* Edited by A. de Ruble. 10 vols. Paris: Librairie Renouard, 1886–99.

Barbiche, Bernard. *Lettres de Henri IV concernant les relations du Saint-siège et de la France.* Vatican: Biblioteca Apostolica, 1969.

Bernard, Auguste. *Procès-verbaux des Etats-généraux de 1593.* Paris: Imprimerie Royale, 1842.

Beza, Theodore. *Correspondance.* Edited by H. Aubert, et al., 6 vols. Geneva: Droz, 1963–78.

Beza, Theodore, et al. *Histoire ecclésiastique des églises réformées au royaume de France.* Edited by G. Baum and E. Cunitz. 3 vols. Paris: Fischbacher, 1883.

Calendar of State Papers Foreign. Edited by William Turnbull, et al. 22 vols. London: Royal Stationary Office, 1861–1936.

Calvin, Jean. *Opera quae supersunt omnia.* 10 vols. Brunswick: Schwetschke, 1871.

Catalogue des Actes de François I. 10 vols. Paris: Imprimerie Nationale, 1887–1910.

Catalogue des Actes de Henri II. Paris: Imprimerie Nationale, 1980.

Cimber, L., and Danjou, F., eds. *Archives curieuses de l'histoire de France.* Paris: Beauvais, 1834–50.

Cochrane, A. C., ed. *Reformed Confessions of the Sixteenth Century.* Philadelphia: Westminster, 1861.

Collection des procès-verbaux des assemblées-générales du clergé de France depuis l'anné 1560 jusqu'à present. 3 vols. Paris, 1767.

Conseil salutaire d'un bon Français aux Parisiens. N.p. 1589.

Cruseau, Etienne de. *Chroniques.* Bordeaux: Société des Bibliophiles de Guyenne, 1879.

Desjardins, Abel. *Négociations diplomatiques de la France avec la Toscane.* 6 vols. Paris: Imprimerie Nationale, 1859–86.

Dialogue d'entre le maheustre et le manant. Edited by Peter Ascoli. Geneva: Droz, 1977.

Froumenteau, Nicolas. *Le secret des finances de France.* N.p., 1581.

Génébrard, Gilbert. *Liber jure et necessitate sacrum electorum ad ecclesiam Gallicam redintegrationem.* N.p., 1593.

Goulart, Simon. *Mémoires de la ligue.* 6 vols. Amsterdam, 1758.

Haton, Claude. *Mémoires 1553–1582.* Edited by Felix Bourguelot. 2 vols. Paris: Imprimerie Impériale, 1857.

Henri III. *Lettres.* Edited by Pierre Champion. 3 vols. Paris: Librairie C. Klincksieck, 1965.

Henri IV. *Recueil de lettres missives.* Edited by Berger de Xivrey. 9 vols. Paris: Imprimerie Royale, 1843–76.

Hérminjard, A. L. *Correspondance des réformateurs dans les pays de langue française.* 10 vols. Geneva: H. Georg, 1866–69.

Isambert, François, et al. *Recueil général des anciennes lois françaises.* Paris: Belin-Leprieur, 1828.

La Houssaie, Amelot de. *Lettres du Cardinal d'Ossat.* Amsterdam, 1708.

L'Estoile, Pierre. *Mémoires-journaux.* 12 vols. Paris: Lemerre, 1888.

Le vray Catholique romain contre le liqueur covert. N.p., 1591.

Loyseau, Charles. *Traité des seigneuries.* Paris, 1609.

Loroux, A., et al. *Inventaire sommaire des archives département de Haute-Vienne, Série G.* Limoges: Imprimerie Ducourtieux, 1908.

Medici, Catherine de. *Lettres.* Edited by Comte de Baguenault de Puchésse. 9 vols. Paris: Imprimerie Nationale, 1899.

Mémoires de Condé. 6 vols. London, 1743.

Monluc, Blaise de. *Commentaires.* Edited by Paul Couteault. Paris: Editions Gallimard, 1964.

Palma Cayet, Pierre. *Chronologie novennaire.* Vols. 38–43 of C. B. Petitot, ed. *Collection complète des mémoires relatifs à l'histoire de France*. 130 vols. Paris: Foucault, 1818–29.

Procès-verbal de ce qui s'est passé à Saint-Denis. Tours, 1593.

Raemond, Florimond de. *Histoire de la naissance, progrez et decadence de l'hérésie de ce siècle*. Paris, 1605.

Receuils des actes, titres, mémoires concernant les affaires du clergé de France. 12 vols. Paris, 1721.

Registres des délibérations du Bureau de la ville de Paris. Edited by Paul Guerin, et al. 19 vols. Paris: Imprimerie Nationale, 1879–1952.

Remonstrances aux Catholigues de tous les estats. N.p., n.d.

Répertoire des visites pastorales de la France. Paris: CNRS, 1977–79.

Saintes, Claude de. *Bref advertisement de M. l'évesque d'Evreux*. Paris, 1591.

Schroeder, H. J. *Canons and Decrees of the Council of Trent*. St. Louis: Herder, 1941.

Seyssel, Claude de. *The Monarchy of France*. Translated by J. H. Hexter. New Haven: Yale University Press, 1981.

Taix, Guillaume de. *Mémoires des affaires du clergé de France*. Paris, 1625.

Theiner, Auguste. *Annales ecclesiastici*. Rome: Typographia Tibernia, 1856.

Thou, Jacques-Auguste de. *Histoire universelle*. 10 vols. Basel, 1742.

Tommaseo, M. *Relations des ambassadeurs vénitiens sur les affaires de France au XVIe siècle*. 2 vols. Paris: Imprimerie Royale, 1838.

Valois, Marguerite de. *Mémoires*. Edited by L. Lalanne. Paris: Imprimerie Royale, 1842.

BIBLIOGRAPHICAL AND INSTITUTIONAL DICTIONARIES

Dictionnaire de biographie française. 14 vols. to date. Paris: Letouzey et Ané, 1932–.

Dictionnaire de géographie et d'histoire ecclésiastique. Paris: Meyer et van Cauwenberg, 1912–.

Doucet, R. *Les institutions de la France au XVIe siècle*. 2 vols. Paris: Picard, 1948.

Durand de Maillane, M. *Dictionnaire de droit canonique et de practique bénéficiale*. Lyon, 1770.

Eubel, Conrad, et al. *Hierarchia Catholica medii aevi*. 7 vols. Münster: Libraria Regensbergiana, 1918–36.

Farge, James K. *Biographical Register of Paris Doctors of Theology*

1500–1536. Toronto: Pontifical Institute of Medieval Studies, 1980.

Fillery, Abbé. *Instituts du droit ecclésiastique*. 2 vols. Paris, 1767.

Fisquet, Honoré. *La France pontificale*. 21 vols. Paris: E. Repos, 1864–73.

Gams, Pius. *Series episcoporum ecclesiae Catholicae*. Graz: E. Staht, 1957.

Haag, E., and E. Haag. *La France protestante*. 10 vols. Geneva: Slatkine, 1966.

La Chenoye-Desbois, François de. *Dictionnaire de la noblesse*. 19 vols. Paris: Schlesinger, 1863–76.

Marion, Marcel. *Dictionnaire des institutions de la France au XVIIe et XVIIIe siècles*. New York: Burt Franklin, 1968.

Moreri, Louis. *Le grand dictionnaire historique*. 3 vols. Basel, 1760.

Mousnier, Roland. *Les institutions de la France sous la monarchie absolue 1598–1789*. Paris: Presses universitaires de France, 1974.

Saint-Marthe, Frères. *Gallia Christiana*. 16 vols. Paris: V-Palme, 1856–99.

Viollet, Paul. *Histoire des institutions politiques et administratives de France*. 4 vols. Paris: Sirey, 1898.

Zeller, G. *Les institutions de la France au XVIe siècle*. Paris: Presses universitaires de France, 1948.

SECONDARY STUDIES

Biographies of Bishops

Baumgartner, Frederic. "Renaud de Beaune, Politique Prelate." *Sixteenth Century Journal*, IX (1978), 99–109.

Baguenault de Puchésse, G. *Jean de Morvillier évêque d'Orléans*. Paris: Didier, 1870.

Bourrilly, V. L. *Jean Du Bellay, Les Protestants et la Sorbonne*. Paris: Agence général de la Société, 1904.

Busson, Henri. *Charles d'Espinay Evêque de Dol et son oeuvre poétique*. Paris: Honoré Champion, 1923.

Cioranescu, Alexandre. *Vie de Jacques Amyot*. Paris: Droz, 1941.

Delmas, André. "Le procès et la mort de Jacques Spifame." *Bibliothèque d'humanisme et renaissance*, V (1944), 105–37.

Didier, Noël. *Paul de Foix et Grégoire XIII 1572–84*. Grenoble: Université de Grenoble, 1941.

Doublet, G. "Guillaume de Blanc." *Annales de Midi*, XIII (1901), 176–89.

Doucet, R. "Pierre Du Chastel, Grand Aumônier de France." *Revue historique*, CXXIII (1920), 212–57; CXXIV (1921), 1–57.

Evennett, H. O. *The Cardinal of Lorraine and the Council of Trent.* Cambridge: Cambridge University Press, 1930.

François, Michel. *Le Cardinal François de Tournon, Homme d'etat, diplomate, mécène et humaniste.* Paris: Boccard, 1951.

Grente, Georges. *Jean Bertaut.* Paris: Librairie Victor Le Coffre, 1903.

Guillemin, J.-J. *Le Cardinal de Lorraine son influence politique et religieuse au XVIe siècle.* Paris: Joubert, 1847.

Guiraud, Louise. *Le procès de Guillaume Pellicier évêque de Maguelone-Montpellier.* Paris: Picard fils, 1907.

Harrie, Jean. "François Foix de Candale and the Hermetic Tradition in Sixteenth-Century France." Ph.D. diss., University of California–Riverside, 1975.

Kushner, Eva. "Pontus de Tyard devant le pouvoir royal." *Culture et pouvoir aux temps de l'humanisme et renaissance.* Paris: Honoré Champion, 1978.

Lerosey, Auguste. *La légende à la place de l'histoire: Arthur de Cossé-Brissac.* Evreux: Imprimerie de l'Eure, 1916.

Marlet, Leon. *Le Cardinal de Châtillon, 1517–1571.* Paris: Henri Meir, 1883.

Niel, Louis. "Jean de Genouilhac Trentième évêque de Tulle." *Bulletin de la Société scientifique et historique de la Corèze,* XIII (1891), 306–52.

Richard, Pierre. *La papauté et la ligue française: Pierre d'Epinac, archévêque de Lyon (1573–1599).* Paris: Picard, 1902.

Roserot de Melin, Joseph. *Antonio Caracciolo évêque de Troyes.* Paris: Letouzey et Ané, 1923.

Renaud, Hector. *Jean de Monluc évêque de Valence et de Die.* Paris: Thorer et fils, 1893.

Saulnier, Eugène. *Le rôle politique de Cardinal du Bourbon.* Paris: Honoré Champion, 1911.

Tamizey de Larroque, Philippe. *Arnaud de Pontac: Evêque de Bazas.* Bordeaux: Paul Challet, 1883.

Vaissière, Pierre de. *Charles de Marillac ambassadeur et homme politique.* Paris: Wetter, 1896.

Local, Regional, and Diocesean Histories

Alzieu, G., et al. *Un diocèse languedocien Lodève.* Lodève: Jean Mercadies, 1975.

Amiet, L. *Essai sur l'organization du chapitre cathedrale de Chartres du XIe au XVIIIe siècle.* Chartres: Lainé, 1922.

Barthelémy, Edouard de. *Diocèse ancien de Châlons-sur-Marne.* 2 vols. Paris: Auby, 1856.

Bellaud-Dessalles, E. *Les évêques italiens de l'ancien diocèse de Béziers 1547–1669.* Toulouse: Edouard Privat, 1901.

Benedict, Philip. *Rouen during the Wars of Religion.* Cambridge: Cambridge University Press, 1981.

Bligny, B., et al. *Le diocèse de Grenoble.* Paris: Beauchesne, 1979.

Bouges, Thomas-Augustin. *Histoire ecclésiastique et civile de la ville et diocèse de Carcassone.* Marseille: Laffitte Reprints, 1978.

Bozé, Abbé. *Histoire de l'église d'Apt.* Apt: Tremallois, 1820.

Brimont, Le Vicomte de. *Le XVIe siècle et les guerres de la réforme en Berry.* 2 vols. Paris: Pericard, 1905.

Busquet, R., et al. *Histoire de la Provence.* Monaco: Imprimerie Nationale, 1954.

Catta, E. "Les évêques de Nantes, 1500–1617." *Revue d'histoire de l'église de France,* LI (1965), 23–70.

Challe, A. *Histoire des guerres du calvinisme et la ligue dan l'Auxerrais.* 2 vols. Auxerre: Perriquet et Rouille, 1863.

Choley, Gérard, et al. *Le diocèse de Montpellier.* Paris: Beauchesne, 1976.

Collombet, F. Z. *Histoire de la Sainte église de Vienne.* 3 vols. Lyon: A. Mathone, 1847.

Courrage, Georges. *Lombèz évêché rural 1317–1809.* Lombès: Prodhomme, 1973.

Daux, Camille. *Histoire de l'église de Montauban.* 2 vols. Montauban: Forutie, 1881.

Degert, Antoine. *Histoire des évêques de Dax.* Paris: Librairie Delhomme et Briquist, 1903.

Delettre, Abbé. *Histoire du diocèse de Beauvais.* 3 vols. Beauvais: Imprimerie Desjardins, 1843.

Delumeau, Jean, et al. *Le diocèse de Rennes.* Paris: Beauchesne, 1979.

Deronne, Elaine. "Les Origines des chanoines de Nôtre-Dame de Paris, 1450–1550." *Revue d'histoire moderne et contemporaine,* XVIII (1971) 1–28.

De Vic, Claude, and Vaissette, Joseph. *Histoire générale de Languedoc.* 15 vols. Toulouse: Demouily et fils, 1872–92.

Dewald, Jonathon. *The Formation of a Provincial Nobility, the Magistrates of the Parlement of Rouen 1499–1600.* Princeton: Princeton University

Press, 1980.

Dolan, Claire. *Entre Tours et Clochers*. Sherbrooke, Québec: Editions de l'Université de Sherbrooke, 1981.

Drouot, Henri. *Mayenne et la Bourgogne, Etude sur la ligue en Bourgogne 1587–1596*. 2 vols. Paris: Auguste Picard, 1937.

Du Tressay, Abbé. *Histoire des moines et des évêques de Luçon*. 2 vols. Paris: LeCoffre et fils, 1869.

Galpern, A. W. *The Religions of the People in Sixteenth-Century Champagne*. Cambridge, Mass.: Harvard University Press, 1976.

Guibert, Louis. *La ligue à Limoges*. Limoges: Imprimerie Du Coeurtreux, 1884.

Hénelle, G. *La Réforme et la ligue en Champagne*. 2 vols. Reims: Charpien, n.d.

Henry, E. *La Réforme et la ligue en Champagne et à Reims*. Reims: Imprimerie de Progrès Trenel, 1867.

Héron, A. *Histoire ecclésiastique du diocèse de Coutances*. Paris: Méterie, 1881.

Hoffman, P. *Church and Community in the Diocese of Lyon, 1500–1789*. New Haven: Yale University Press, 1984.

Imberdis, André. *Histoire des guerres de religion en Auvergne*. Moulins: Desrosiers, 1840.

Jordan, J. B. *Histoire de la ville d'Agde*. Marseille: Laffitte, 1975.

Kalas, R. J. "Wealth, Place, and Power in Sixteenth-Century France: The Rise of the Selve and Noailles Families." Ph.D. diss., New York University, 1982.

La Faille, E. de. *Annales de la ville de Toulouse*. 2 vols. Toulouse, 1701.

Laffon, J. B., ed. *Le diocèse de Tarbes et Lourdes*. Paris, n.d.

Lahandis, J. de. *Annales de Pamiers*. Toulouse: Le Henneyer et fils, 1882.

Lambart, Gustave. *Histoire des guerres de religion en Provence*. 2 vols. Toulon: Laurent, 1870.

La Pijardière, M. de. *Histoire de la ville de Montpellier*. 4 vols. Montpellier: Caulet, 1930.

La Rochette, Charles de. *Histoire des évêques de Mâcon*. 3 vols. Mâcon: Protal, 1867.

La Roque, Louis de. *Les évêques de Maguelone et Montpellier*. Montpellier: Imprimerie Calas, 1893.

Laverne, Gérard. *Histoire de Périgueux*. Périgueux: Editions Fontas, 1945.

Lodge, E. C. *The Estates of the Archbishop and Chapter of Saint-André of Bordeaux under English Rule*. New York: Octagon Books, 1974.

Long, J. D. *La Réforme et les guerres de religion en Dauphiné.* Paris: Didot frères, 1856.

Marcellin, Abbé. *Histoire de Montauban.* 2 vols. Montauban: Rethore, 1841.

Martin, Ernest. *Histoire de la ville de Lodève.* 2 vols. Montpellier: Imprimerie Serre, 1900.

Mesnard, M. *Histoire civile, ecclésiastique et littéraire de la ville de Nîmes.* Paris, 1754.

Monlezun, J. J. *Histoire de la Gascogne.* 6 vols. Auch: Portes, 1846–50.

Moran, G. "The Catholic Church and the Protestant Party in Languedoc during the Wars of religion, 1559–1588." Ph.D. diss., Cornell University, 1978.

Osmont, M. C. "Jean le Henneyer et les Huguenots de Lisieux en 1573." *Bulletin de la Société d'histoire du Protestantisme français,* XXVI (1877).

Pialin, Paul. *Histoire de l'église du Mans.* 6 vols. Paris: Lanies, 1858–63.

Pillorget, René. *Les mouvements insurrectionels de Provence.* Paris: Pedone, 1975.

Pocquet, Barthelémy. *Histoire de Bretagne.* 6 vols. Rennes: Philon, 1913.

Poitrineau, Abel, et al. *Le diocèse de Clermont.* Paris: Beauchesne, 1979.

Prévost, Antoine. *Le diocèse de Troyes.* Troyes: G. Fremont, 1908.

Ricard, Antoine. *Les évêques de Marseille.* Marseille: Imprimerie Chaufford, 1972.

Sauzet, Robert. *Contre-Réforme et Réforme Catholique en Bas-Languedoc: Le diocèse de Nîmes au XVIIe siècle.* Louvain: Mauwelaerts, 1979.

Taillandier, Charles. *Histoire ecclésiastique et civile de Bretagne.* 3 vols. Paris, 1756.

Tresvaux, M. *Histoire de l'église et du diocèse d'Angers.* Paris, 1858.

Tuloup, François. *Saint-Malo histoire religieuse.* Paris: Editions Klincksieck, 1975.

Other Books

Baird, Henry. *History of the Rise of the Huguenots of France.* 2 vols. New York: Scribners, 1879.

Baumgartner, Frederic. *Radical Reactionaries: The Political Thought of the French Catholic League.* Geneva: Droz, 1976.

Blet, Pierre. *Le Clergé de France et la monarchie.* Rome: Librairie de l'Université Grégorienne, 1959.

Bowker, M. *The Secular Clergy in the Diocese of Lincoln 1495–1520.*

Cambridge: Cambridge University Press, 1968.

Broutin, Paul. *La Réforme pastorale en France au XVIIIe siècle*. Tournai: Desdée, 1959.

Cans, A. *L'organization financière du clergé de France à l'époque de Louis XIV*. Paris: Picard et fils, 1918.

Carrière, V., et al. *Introduction aux études d'histoire ecclésiastique locale*. 3 vols. Paris: Letouzey et Ané, 1936.

Christie, Richard C. *Etienne Dolet, the Martyr of the Renaissance*. London: Macmillan, 1899.

Clergeac, Adrien. *La curie et les bénéficiers consistoriaux*. Paris: Picard, 1911.

Dainville, François de. *Cartes anciens de l'église de France*. Paris: J. Vrin, 1956.

Delumeau, Jean. *Catholicism between Luther and Voltaire*. London: Burns and Oates, 1977.

Duggan, L. G. *Bishop and Chapter: The Governance of the Bishopric of Speyer to 1552*. New Brunswick, N.J.: Rutgers University Press, 1978.

Du Tems, Jean. *Le clergé de France*. Paris, 1774.

Edelstein, Marilyn. "The Recruitment of the Episcopacy under the Concordat of Bologna in the Reign of Francis I." Ph.D. diss., Columbia University, 1972.

Edwards, K. *The English Secular Cathedrals in the Middle Ages*. New York: Barnes and Noble, 1967.

Fleury, Claude. *Histoire ecclésiastique*. 36 vols. Brussels, 1723–39.

Floquet, A. *Histoire du Parlement de Normandie*. 8 vols. Rouen: Edouard Frères, 1841.

Geisendorf, Paul. *Théodore de Bèze*. Geneva: Jullien, 1967.

Harding, Robert. *Anatomy of a Power Elite: The Provincial Governors of Early Modern France*. New Haven: Yale University Press, 1978.

Hauser, Henri. *Etudes sur la réforme française*. Paris: Picard, 1909.

Hay, Denys. *The Church in Italy in the Fifteenth Century*. Cambridge: Cambridge University Press, 1977.

Hayden, J. M. *France and the Estates General of 1614*. Cambridge: Cambridge University Press, 1974.

Head, Felicity. *Of Prelates and Princes*. Cambridge: Cambridge University Press, 1981.

Huppert, George. *Les bourgeois gentilshommes*. Chicago: University of Chicago Press, 1977.

Imbart de La Tour, Pierre. *Les origines de la Réforme*. 4 vols. Paris: Hachette,

1905–35.

Jedin, Hubert, et al. *Reformation and Counter Reformation*. New York: Seabury Press, 1980.

Kagan, R. L. *Students and Society in Early Modern Spain*. Baltimore: The Johns Hopkins University Press, 1974.

Knecht, R. J. *Francis I*. Cambridge: Cambridge University Press, 1981.

Knowles, David. *The Monastic Order in England*. Cambridge: Cambridge University Press, 1963.

Labatut, P.-P. *Les ducs et pairs de France au XVIIe siècle*. Paris: PUF, 1972.

Labitte, Charles. *De la démocratie chez les prédicateurs de la ligue*. Geneva: Slatkine, 1971.

Lair, Jules. *Histoire de Parlement de Normandie pendant son sejour à Caen*. Caen: Hardel, 1866.

Lavisse, E., ed. *Histoire de France*. Vol. 6 by Jean Mariéjol. *La réforme et la ligue*. Paris: Hachette, 1911.

L'Epinois, Henri de. *La ligue et les papes*. Paris: Librairie Catholique, 1886.

LeRoy Ladurie, E. *The Peasants of Languedoc*. Champaign: University of Illinois Press, 1974.

Lunt, William. *Papal Revenues in the Middle Ages*. 2 vols. New York: Octagon Books, 1965.

Major, J. Russell. *The Estates of 1560*. Princeton: Princeton University Press, 1951.

Martin, A. Lynn. *Henry III and the Jesuit Politicians*. Geneva: Droz, 1975.

Martin, Victor. *Le Gallicanisme et la Réforme Catholique*. Geneva: Slatkine, 1975.

———. *Les origines du Gallicanisme*. 2 vols. Paris: Bloud and Gay, 1939.

Marzac, Nichole. *The Library of a French Bishop in the Late XVIth Century*. Paris: CNRS, 1974.

Maugis, Edouard. *Histoire du Parlement de Paris*. 3 vols. Paris: Picard, 1914.

Miller, Michael. "The Bavarian Episcopacy in the Fourteenth century." Ph.D. diss., The Ohio State University, 1980.

Miquet, Pierre. *Les guerres de religion*. Paris: Fayard, 1980.

Oroux, Abbé. *Histoire ecclésiastique de la Cour de France*. 2 vols. Paris, 1776.

Pastor, L. von. *The History of the Popes from the Close of the Middle Ages*. 36 vols. St. Louis: Herder, 1952.

Peronnet, Michel. *Les évêques de l'ancien France*. 2 vols. Paris: Honoré Champion, 1978.

Perrins, François. *L'église et l'état en France sous le règne de Henri IV et la régency de Marie de Médicis*. 2 vols. Paris: Durand, 1872.

Picot, Emile. *Les italiens en France au XVIe siècle*. Bordeaux: Gounouilhan, 1918.

Picot, Georges. *Histoire des Etats Généraux de 1355 à 1614*. 4 vols. Geneva: Megriotis Reprints, 1979.

Poirson, A. *Histoire du règne de Henri IV*. 3 vols. Paris: Didier, 1862–67.

Prunel, Louis. *La renaissance Catholique en France au XVIIe siècle*. Paris: Picard, 1921.

Ravitch, Norman. *Sword and Mitre*. The Hague: Mouton, 1966.

Richard, Abbé. *De publicatis tempore motuum civilium XVI saeculi ecclesiae gallicanae bonis immobilibus (1563–1588)*. Paris: Picard, 1901.

Romier, Lucien. *Les origines politiques des guerres de religion*. 2 vols. Paris: Perrin, 1914.

———. *Le Royaume de Catherine de Médicis*. 2 vols. Paris: Perrin, 1925.

Salmon, J. H. M. *Society in Crisis: France in the Sixteenth Century*. New York: St. Martin's Press, 1975.

Serbet, Louis. *Les assemblées du clergé de France 1561–1615*. Paris: Honoré Champion, 1906.

Shennen, J. H. *The Parlement of Paris*. Ithaca, N.Y.: Cornell University Press, 1968.

Sicard, Auguste. *L'ancien clergé de France*. 3 vols. Paris: LeCoffre, 1893–1903.

———. *La nomination aux bénéfices ecclésiastiques avant 1789*. Paris: LeCoffre, 1896.

Southern R. W. *Western Society and the Church in the Middle Ages*. Baltimore: Penguin Books, 1980.

Spooner, Frank. *The International Economy and Monetary Movements in France 1493–1725*. Cambridge, Mass.: Harvard University Press, 1972.

Stone, Lawrence. *The Crisis of the Aristocracy, 1558–1641*. Oxford: Oxford University Press, 1965.

Sutherland, N. M. *The Huguenot Struggle for Recognition*. New Haven: Yale University Press, 1980.

Tattegrain, Robert. *Du temporel des bénéfices ecclésiastiques sous d'ancien régime*. Paris: Larose et Tenin, 1909.

Thomas, Jules. *Le Concordat de 1516, ses origines, son histoire au XVIe siècle*. 3 vols. Paris: Picard, 1910.

Thompson, A. H. *The English Clergy and their Organization in the Later Middle Ages*. Oxford: Clarendon Press, 1947.

Tierney, Brian. *Foundations of the Conciliar Theory*. Cambridge: Cambridge University Press, 1955.

Tilley, Arthur. *Studies in the French Renaissance*. Cambridge: Cambridge University Press, 1922.

Vaissière, P. de. *Messieurs de Joyeuse 1560–1615*. Paris: Albin Michel, 1926.

Varillas, Antoine. *Histoire de Henry second*. Paris, 1768.

Viard, Paul. *Histoire de la dîme ecclésiastique en France au XVIe siècle*. Lille: Giard, 1914.

Viguier, J. *Les contracts et la consolidation des décimes à la fin du XVIe siècle*. Paris: Imprimerie de H. Jouve, 1906.

Weiss, N. *La chambre ardente*. Reprint, Geneva: Slatkine, 1970.

Willaert, Léopold. *Après le Concile de Trente la restauration Catholique 1563–1648*. Tournai: Bloud and Gay, 1960.

Willocx, F. W. *L'introduction des decrets du Concile de Trente dans les Pays-Bas et Liège*. Louvain: Librairie Universitaire, 1929.

Wolf, Martin. *The Fiscal System of Renaissance France*. New Haven: Yale University Press, 1972.

Yates, Frances. *French Academies of the Sixteenth Century*. London: Wartburg Institute, 1947.

Articles

Baumgartner, Frederic. "Crisis in the French Episcopacy: The Bishops and the Succession of Henry IV." *Archiv für Reformationsgeschichte*, LXX (1979), 278–301.

———. "Henry II's Italian Bishops: A Study in the Use and Abuse of the Concordat of Bologna." *Sixteenth Century Journal*, XI (1980) 49–58.

———. "Party Alignment in the Parlement of Paris, 1589–1594." *Proceedings of the Western Society for French History*, VI (1978), 32–45.

Berger, S. "Le procès de Guillaume Briçonnet au Parlement de Paris en 1525." *Bulletin de la Société d'histoire du Protestantisme français*, XLIV (1895), 1–39.

Bergin, Joseph. "The Decline and Fall of the House of Guise as an Ecclesiastical Dynasty." *Historical Journal*, XXV (1982), 781–803.

———. "The Guises and Their Benefices." *The English Historical Review*, XCIX (1984), 434–58.

Blet, Pierre. "Le concordat de Bologne et la réforme tridentine." *Gregorianum*, XLV (1964), 241–79.

Bluche, François. "L'origine des magistrats du Parlement de Paris au XVIIIe siècle." *Paris et Ile-de-France: Mémoires*, 5–6 (1953–54).

Boulet, M. "Les élections épiscopales en France au lendemain de Concordat de Bologna." *Mélanges d'archéologie et d'histoire d'école française de Rome*, LVII (1940), 190–234.

Caring, F. "La ligue et Sixte Quint." *Revue de monde Catholique*. (April, 1967), 72–74.

Cloulas, Ivan. "Les aliénations du temporalité ecclésiastique sous Charles IX et Henri III, 1563–87." *Revue d'histoire de l'église de France*, XLIV (1958), 5–56.

————. "Les rapports de Jérôme Ragazzoni, évêque de Bergome, avec les ecclésiastiques pendant sa nonciature en France." *Bulletin de l'école français de Rome*, LXXIII (1960), 518–50.

————. "Les ventes de biens ecclésiastiques effectivées sur l'ordres de Charles IX et Henri III dans les diocèses de Limoges et Bourges." *Bulletin de la société historique du Limousin*, LXXXVII (1959), 141–69.

Degert, Antoine. "Procès de huit évêques Français." *Revue des questions historiques*, XXVI (1904), 60–108.

Didier, Noël. "Paul de Foix à la mercuriale au 1559." *Mélanges d'archéologie et d'histoire d'école française de Rome*, LVI (1939), 399–435.

Edelstein, Marilyn. "Les origines sociales de l'épiscopat sous Louis XII et François Ier." *Revue d'histoire moderne et contemporaine*, XX (1978), 239–47.

————. "The Social Origins of the Episcopacy in the Reign of Francis I." *French Historical Studies*, VIII (1974), 377–92.

Evennett, H. O. "Pie IV et les bénéfices de Jean Du Bellay: Etude sur les bénéfices français vacants en curie après le concordat de 1516." *Revue d'histoire de l'église de France*, XXII (1936).

Gagnol, P. "Les décimes et les dons gratuits." *Revue d'histoire de l'église de France*, II (1922), 465–81.

Hayden, J. Michael. "The Social Origins of the French Episcopacy at the Beginning of the Seventeenth Century." *French Historical Studies*, X (1977), 27–38.

Heller, Henry. "The Briçonnet case reconsidered." *Journal of Medieval and Renaissance Studies*, II (1972), 223–58.

Huseman, William. "The Expression of the Idea of Toleration in French During the Sixteenth Century." *Sixteenth Century Journal*, XIV (1984),

293–310.

Jadin, Louis. "Procès d'informations pour la nomination des évêques et abbés des Pays-Bas." *Bulletin de l'Institut historique belge de Rome*, VIII (1928), 5–25.

Knecht, R. J. "The Concordat of 1516: A Reassessment," *Government in Reformation Europe 1520–1560*. Edited by Henry J. Cohn. London: Macmillan, 1971, pp. 91–112.

Laplatte, C. "L'administration des évêchés vacants et la régie des économats," *Revue d'histoire de l'église de France*, XXIII (1937), 161–225.

Lestocquoy, J. "Les évêques français au XVIe siècle." *Revue d'histoire de l'église de France*, XLV (1959), 25–40.

Long, E. J. "Utrum iurista vel theologus plus proficiat ad regimen ecclesia." *Medieval Studies*, 30 (1968), 134–63.

Madelin, Louis. "Les premiers applications de Concordat de 1516." *Mélanges d'archéologie et d'histoire de l'école française de Rome*, XIV (1897), 323–85.

Martin, A. Lynn. "Fabio Mirto Frangipani and Papal Policy in France." *Archivum Historicae Pontificale*, XVII (1979), 197–240.

———. "Papal Policy and the European Conflict." *Sixteenth Century Journal*, XI–2 (1980), 35–48.

Michaux, C. "Les aliénations du temporel ecclréstiastique dans la seconde moité du XVIe siècle." *Revue d'histoire de l'église de France*, LXVII (1981), 61–82.

Nicholls, David. "Inertia and Reform in the Pre-Tridentine French Church: The Response to Protestantism in the Diocese of Rouen 1520–1562." *Journal of Ecclesiastical History*, XXXII (1981), 185–97.

Piton, M. "L'idéal episcopal selon les prédicateurs français de la fin du XVe siècle." *Revue d'histoire ecclésiastique*, LXI (1966), 77–118, 393–423.

Romier, L. "La crise gallicane de 1551." *Revue historique*, CVIII (1911), 225–50, CIX (1912), 27–55.

Salmon, J. H. M. "The Paris Sixteen, 1584–1594: The Social Analysis of a Revolutionary Movement." *The Journal of Modern History*, XLIV (1972), 540–76.

Trevor-Roper, Hugh. "James I and His Bishops." *Men and Events*. New York: Octagon Books, 1976.

Valois, Nöel. "Les éssais de conciliation religieuse au debut du règne de Charles IX." *Revue d'histoire de l'église de France*, XXXI (1945), 237–86.

Venard, Marc. "Une réforme Gallicane? Le projet de concile national de 1551." *Revue d'histoire de l'église de France*, LXVII (1981) 201–25.

INDEX

Frederic J. Baumgartner is Associate Professor of History, Virginia Polytechnic Institute and State University, Blacksburg, Virginia.

DATE DUE
